The Fastest Billion

The Fastest Billion

The Story Behind Africa's Economic Revolution

CHARLES ROBERTSON

with Yvonne Mhango, Michael Moran, Arnold Meyer,
Nothando Ndebele, John Arron, Johan Snyman,
Jim Taylor, Dragan Trajkov, Sven Richter,
Bradley Way

Foreword by
Dr. Ngozi Okonjo-Iweala, Coordinating Minister for the
Economy and Minister of Finance, Federal Republic of Nigeria

Renaissance
Capital

Charles Robertson is Global Chief Economist, Head of Macro-strategy, Renaissance Capital

© Renaissance Capital Securities Limited

Printed in the UK by:
Servicepoint UK Ltd (CFI Division)
Tower Bridge Business Complex
Unit N01 The Biscuit Factory
100 Clements Road
London
SE16 4DG

ISBN-13: 978-0957420304

Paper details:
Edixion Offset
GSM 90

This paper is FSC approved.

MIX
Paper from responsible sources
FSC
www.fsc.org   FSC® C004869

Contents

Acknowledgements

This in-depth, on-the-ground look at Africa's economic revolution resulted from a decision by Renaissance Group in 2005 to grow beyond its home markets of Russia and the CIS, to Africa. In seven years, the Firm has established seven offices across Africa and invested over $1bn of its own capital in the continent. The centrepiece of our investment has been the people – over 180 on the ground in Africa – who work for the Group and its businesses. This book would not have been possible without the groundwork they have laid and knowledge base they have created in order to support the team of economists, analysts and other Renaissance experts who contributed to this book.

As this is Renaissance Group's first book, there is no shortage of people to thank for their inspiration, wisdom and guidance as we created a narrative from the 2,500 research reports we prepared on Africa since 2005.

Stephen Jennings, the founder and CEO of Renaissance Group, took that fateful decision seven years ago to hitch up our business to Africa's coming growth and gamble that the long-term strength of the Firm lay in diversity, and in Africa. He was right.

Paul Collier, author of *The Bottom Billion: Why the Poorest Countries are Failing and What Can Be Done About It*, pioneered recent research into Africa and gave us inspiration for our title.

The Renaissance Capital Research team and its editors Michiko Fox, Mark Porter and Abigail Mauldin run a 24/7 operation across several continents, perfecting the impressive output of dozens of the best emerging-markets analysts.

We are grateful to Preston Mendenhall, Alexandra Waldman, Sergey Turov, Daria Khilenkova, Sabir Aliev, Natalia Pchelintseva, Ivan Aleshin, Svetlana Mitina, Lyudmila Bibina and Olesya Latyshko for engineering the project. Brunswick Group has provided strategic advice to Renaissance Group for many years. Sally Tickner supplied invaluable publishing-industry insight. Richard Walker and Duncan Robertson lent their editing prowess to our work.

We are indebted to Her Excellency Ngozi Okonjo Iweala, Coordinating Minister for the Economy and Minister of Finance, Federal Republic of Nigeria, for contributing the foreword to *The Fastest Billion*.

The entire Renaissance Group team is thankful to their families for their tolerance of frequent absences, during the compilation of this book and as part of our work for one of the most hard-charging and innovative emerging-markets firms in the world.

Accra, Harare, Johannesburg, Lagos, Lubumbashi, Lusaka, Nairobi and London
October 2012

Foreword

Africa Unbound

By Ngozi Okonjo-Iweala

Imagine a continent torn by multiple wars, beset by ethnic and religious warfare, malnutrition, disease and illiteracy – all of it complicated by poorly drawn borders, a still potent post-colonial stigma and the incessant meddling of outside powers.

With a single exception, per capita income hovers at $400, primary school education reaches only a fraction of the region's vast population, and its authoritarian rulers ensure any revenue generated by the region's rich natural resources is spent on personal, rather than national priorities. Prospects for pulling the multitudes who live at, or just above, subsistence levels seem remote, at best.

Too many readers will by now have concluded that the continent referred to above is my own, Africa. In fact, while Sub-Saharan Africa has suffered the same problems in recent decades, the region described above is Developing Asia in the mid-1970s: an area of the world that had endured 200 years of decline, imperial domination and economic stagnation before beginning on the path that would transform it into the most economically vibrant zone on Earth.

Just as SSA has suffered through its despots and destitution, so the seedlings of transformation have pushed through the African soil. As an increasing number of economists, investors and financial policymakers have realised, SSA has emerged from its own malaise, into a dawn that promises growth to rival, if not surpass, that recorded by Asia's 'Tigers' over the past two decades.

Indeed, as Charles Robertson and his Renaissance Capital colleagues point out in *The Fastest Billion: The Story Behind Africa's Economic Revolution*, the macroeconomic, demographic and geopolitical picture below the Sahel today bears a strong resemblance to the start of East Asia's climb in the early 1980s, when emerging-market powerhouses like India, South Korea, Malaysia and Indonesia were still regarded as basket cases by many in the so-called First World: more likely to be targets for development aid and pedantic lectures than long-term investment. Yet what portfolio manager today would not love to be able to say, 'And, of course, we were overweight Asia back when the Tigers were mere cubs.'

It is the argument of this book that the best-performing nations of SSA today are poised for their own historic period of growth, driven not just by the continent's rich and still largely untapped natural resources, but also its growing domestic strengths, its agricultural potential and its unique internal dynamism. With over a billion people, national economies of increasing sophistication and openness, vaulting improvements in governance, health and education, and the distinction of being the fastest-growing region on the planet, Africa will indeed claim its due, and global capital markets will play a vital role.

Much has been made in the West of the enormous sums China has invested in African economies over the past decade. In some cases, this natural desire by Beijing and other emerging powers to find new markets for their products while buying raw materials for their booming economies has been cast in conspiratorial, even Cold War terms. This is vastly overdone, to my mind.

In fact, emerging markets and developing countries are contributing more to global growth than they ever did – 60 percent or more – and their seemingly disproportionate activities in Africa are part of this trend. In many developing countries, the biggest investors are now other developing countries, and not just China, but India, Singapore, Russia, Brazil and others. China, in particular, often includes massive infrastructure improvements in its commercial dealings with SSA, leaving behind railways, roads and port facilities that make trade easier for all nations.

"I think in private there is very little US concern about what China is doing in Africa," commented Todd Moss[1], a senior fellow at the Center for Global Development who served as a deputy assistant secretary of state in the Africa division from 2007 to 2008, during US Secretary of State Hillary Clinton's 2012 visit to Africa. "The US is not going to build highways and bridges and airports, and that is something Africa needs, so we should be grateful that the Chinese are doing this."

Sadly, too many accounts of economic and political developments in Africa remain couched in language that suggests the scope of the changes under way on

1 Lydia Polgreen, "US, Too, Wants to Bolster Investment in a Continent's Economic Progress," *The New York Times*, 8 August 2012.

the continent simply has not penetrated Western consciousness. References to Africa still contain outdated, throwaway allusions to an allegedly hopeless zone of war, pandemics, ignorance and destitution. This is not to say that Africa does not have its problems. Challenges abound, from infrastructure deficits to poor human development indicators, weak institutions and weak governance. The point is, Africa is not alone in confronting such challenges.

Asia still struggles with Maoist insurgencies in India and Nepal, civil conflict in Pakistan and Myanmar, tensions in the South China Sea and abject poverty in selected parts of almost all its nations. But it would be absurd today to describe Africa as a place of "little joy and less hope," as CBS's *60 Minutes* did in a report this year from the DRC. Leaving the economic and political trends aside, writing off a billion people as without joy or hope is not a far cry from writing off their dreams, their dignity, and indeed their very lives.

For those better informed, those who have seen the transformation of Nairobi or Lagos or Kampala over the past decade, the pages that follow will add vital detail to an already familiar narrative. For those still capable of being startled by the thought of Africa as a golden opportunity for investors, the book will be a revelation.

After decades of genuine struggle, Africa's time has arrived, and its people are crying out to be recognised. Africa, as this book's title rightly projects, will be quickest to succeed. The question for global investors and international policymakers is whether they want to share in the profits.

Dr. Ngozi Okonjo-Iweala
Coordinating Minister for the Economy and Minister of Finance, Federal Republic of Nigeria
Author, Reforming the Unreformable: Lessons from Nigeria
Abuja, October 2012

Introduction

The Fastest Billion and $29 Trillion

By Charles Robertson

The rise of the fastest billion will be the last phase of a global economic transformation that began a little over 200 years ago. This transformation saw countries move from agrarian to industrial states, from tyranny to pluralistic middle-class societies and increasingly into economies driven by the information age. These stages of growth have become the benchmark by which we recognise a nation's economic progress and its population's steady journey from subsistence towards the unprecedented prosperity and political pluralism now enjoyed by the world's most-developed countries. The process will not be complete by 2050, but Africa is set to be the final beneficiary of this revolution. Furthermore, the most remarkable progress will occur in the next two generations. We expect the billion Africans who in the past decade have already experienced the fastest growth the continent has ever seen to become the fastest two billion, and Africa's GDP to increase from $2 trillion today to $29 trillion in today's money by 2050. By 2050 Africa will produce more GDP than the US and eurozone combined do today, and its basic social, demographic and political realities will also be transformed.

The necessary elements that have propelled countries from late medieval commerce with authoritarian government through to industrialised nations with comprehensive and far-reaching social and legal institutions are well known. To note but a few: educated populations, a means to generate energy and power, trade and sophisticated financial instruments and, above all, improved government. Growth has been spurred by competition in the market as well as in conflict. The demands of the modern industrial states have seen their influence spread, through trade and colonies, to encompass the world. As they have grown, so other countries in turn have followed – not necessarily the same staged progress, but taking advantage of the lessons learnt by the pioneers, and managing to climb onto the trajectory of growth more quickly by telescoping the time to adapt and learn.

Africa, a continent rich in natural resources – mineral, agricultural and in energy – is also rich in the youth of its population and the intensity of the desire of its peoples to succeed in growing their economies to match the living standards of the pioneer industrialised nations. The whole world is expanding links with Africa, so they can be part of the success of this last continent to join the world's largest economies.

Renaissance wants to take you on a journey to show you what is happening. You will see a continent that is thriving, that is demonstrating rates of growth which will surpass that of all other continents, whose populations are becoming wealthier more rapidly than at any time in Africa's history, and whose peoples have seen that they can achieve and succeed in this modern competitive world. Africa will be the fastest continent to reach the fourth economic age. It is and will continue to generate huge financial benefit for its peoples and for those who invest in its future. Renaissance is unequivocal in its enthusiasm. We are there now – we believe you should be, too. Follow us through this exploration of what is making Africa the most exciting continent to do business in and see why we believe that Africa will be the most exciting and rewarding continent for the next 30 years.

Africa has firmly shifted into the high-growth camp after the stagnation of 1980–2000, in line with the transition so many have made from the undemocratic post-feudal poverty that was the global norm in the 18th century to the high-income, low-corruption and generally democratic norms of most OECD countries in the 21st century. It is a combination of the demonstration effect of other emerging-market success stories and the higher aspirations from Africa's youth to its leaders that perhaps form the most important catalyst. Others include Africa's success in attracting foreign capital seeking higher returns. We believe that should inevitably benefit Africa today when returns in more-expensive developed markets threaten to be so low for years to come. A further catalyst is that productivity gains are made ever easier by technological transfers. The pace of technological innovation globally is now so rapid, and technology is so easy to transfer – as evidenced by the boom in mobile phone technology and the roll-out of broadband across the continent – that Africa is not just the recipient of technology, but via M-PESA banking is becoming an exporter of it.

The process of accelerating growth never happens overnight, but it is accelerating. What took the UK centuries can now be a matter of decades, or even years. The US and Germany "borrowed" and then improved on UK technology in the 19th century, Japan did the same more quickly in the 20th century and China accelerated the process still further over the past 30 years. Today Africa has the greatest room to boom on the back of two centuries of global progress.

The take-off in Africa began around the turn of the century, 40 years after independence. Why not earlier? Because human capital was extremely constrained by a lack of primary and secondary education, while global capital could find better opportunities in countries such as China. Political leaders in the 1960s and 1970s were inexperienced, often self-serving and were offered contradictory advice on how best to develop a country. There were no strong Asian role models to emulate. International involvement in Africa was too often geared towards Cold War geopolitics, feeding civil wars and strife, rather than trade and investment.

What has changed? Many governments have learnt from their mistakes and seen the positive reform examples not just in Asia, but more importantly in Africa itself, from Mauritius to Botswana and Cape Verde, and now Ghana to Rwanda. In most countries there has been no single reform miracle, such as Deng Xiaoping's first embrace of market capitalism in 1978 or India's shift in 1991. Yet by gradually reducing the obstacles to business, the private sector has been able to thrive and aspirations have grown. Governments have supported this by using foreign debt forgiveness programmes to put public finances on a sound footing, and have been able to deliver the essentials of strong primary education and wider access to secondary school education. This in turn has provided higher-quality public administration and better workforces for the private sector. Higher growth has resulted, reinforcing government finances and providing funds for infrastructure investment. Stronger growth and good public finances – Africa's numbers are far better than those of Europe, the US or Japan – has helped draw in record levels of foreign private-sector capital. The success of companies such as MTN has encouraged new foreign investors to seek out the opportunities in the continent. Productivity has improved as foreign investment has seen mobile telephony sweep the continent, making business and indeed government easier for all those now able to use a phone. That IT revolution is now fostering a banking revolution, with Kenya's Equity Bank a leading example. At a time when excessive debt threatens to sink peripheral Europe, Africa has begun a banking revolution that should help the continent thrive.

The additional kicker of higher commodity prices after the 1980–2000 bear market has undoubtedly helped. Oil revenues that averaged approximately $34 billion per year in SSA in the 1990s more than trebled to $124 billion by 2005 and have since doubled again. Higher metal prices have seen new foreign direct investment in mines and infrastructure that has dramatically accelerated growth from Sierra Leone to Zambia. The stronger balance of payments has helped most in the continent move away from the growth-destroying uncertainty of bouts of currency weakness and very high inflation, towards a confidence-inducing environment of low inflation and higher investment. Yet commodities cannot take sole credit. Even those without mineral wealth are achieving great gains. Oil does not explain the doubling of GDP in Ethiopia, Rwanda, Tanzania and Uganda in the past decade. In these countries as well as the energy producers, the benefits of better governance, stronger public finances (aided by large-scale debt relief) and growth in the private sector have made Africa's fastest billion people.

Why is the world slow to recognise Africa's story? Partly the problem is that too many compare Africa today with Western countries or even established emerging markets today – rather than with OECD countries when they were at similar income levels. Among existing eurozone member states, there has been no military coup within the memory of most working-age adults (the last was Portugal's in 1974), but we've seen two in West Africa in 2012. The corrupt politics and autocracy in many African countries is condemned without any reference to the fact that these were once common across Europe. Too many come to the facile conclusion that Africans are not suited to democracy, or don't care about corruption, and this makes the continent un-investable. Such thinking was wrong in Asia in the 1970s, and wrong in Europe prior to that. France, after all, is still governed by a system born out of the coup that put General Charles de Gaulle in power in 1958.

Moreover, there is too little knowledge of what is changing in Africa because few outsiders ever knew what the *Economist* once dubbed "the hopeless continent." To be fair, the obvious improvement in Africa is only a little over a decade old. Global attention has been focused on China's dramatic rise from the seventh-largest economy in 1999 to the second-largest in 2010, and the global financial crisis since 2007. It takes time for us to update our views – where once Hong Kong produced our cheap plastic toys and could not match the manufacturing skills of Western Europe, now China manufactures the iPad with which you may be reading this book. While Ethiopia in 1983–85 captured global attention when autocratic government, drought and war produced a famine that impacted horribly on 18 million children, no one now reports when it consistently succeeds in providing far more calories to 34 million children. Even the progress Africa does make sometimes receives negative attention, from the problems of China financing infrastructure improvements, to the "carbon cost" as Africa exports vegetables to London and Moscow. A "negative halo effect," as described in Daniel Kahneman's book *Thinking, Fast and Slow,*[1] engulfs Africa and could take decades to shift. We believe that focusing on what is changing, and showing the growth trajectory Africa is on, might help accelerate this.

We consider the impact of urbanisation, which is a widely documented trend in China, but few realise its 50% urbanisation rate is also shared with Nigeria. UN-Habitat estimates that 11 African cities will see population growth of over 50% from 2010–25, including Lagos and Nairobi. Academic research is increasingly focusing on how urbanisation helps increase efficiency and productivity, an additional factor propelling Africa's boom. Rendeavour, a development arm of Renaissance Capital, is now building the kind of modern cities required by this expansion, from Tatu City in Kenya to King City and Appolonia in Ghana. Africa's surging population needs houses – but jobs, too. We expect manufacturing and service jobs to arrive in Africa, providing opportunities to the multi-decade 15–20% rise in the 15–24-year-old African cohort, at a time when East Asia tries to manage a 20-30% decline in that same demographic.

These are just two components in a SSA growth acceleration to 7–8% annually for the next four decades, with 9% for the lowest-income countries in the 2020s, and double-digit growth over 2030–50. Africa today has already recorded a decade of growth double what it achieved in the late 20th century, and like India in 1990 after it experienced the very same, it is on course to deliver an outperformance that will rival the best we have seen in Asia. Of course the African growth story will not be uniform. In Asia, Singapore's growth has so outpaced Myanmar's that its per capita GDP is 58 times higher today. In Africa, too, some countries will lag. But the most successful will not only be far richer, but will be rapidly outpacing the slowing performance out of Asia and developed markets.

There will be a dramatic social impact. We expect SSA healthcare spending to rise 16-fold by 2050, from $123 billion to $1,944 billion in today's money, helped by public healthcare expenditure rising from 2.8% of GDP to 4.1% of GDP. The number of nurses will rise from less than 1 million to 11 million, and physicians from a World Bank estimate of 0.2 million to 4.4 million. The trend of falling HIV infection rates and malaria cases across Africa – both already down over a quarter from their peak – should accelerate and child mortality rates will plunge.

Public spending on pan-African education will expand from $93 billion to $1,384 billion by 2050, with the greatest impact on secondary schools. Primary-school enrolment was already 96% in 2005. Surging demographics will mean primary-school teacher numbers should rise from 4 million to 10 million. Secondary-school enrolment should top 50% by 2020, and be close to 100% by 2050.[2] The two billion of 2050 will be the best-educated and best-medically supported people the continent has ever seen. Already by 2020, Renaissance expects a 72% real increase in healthcare and 69% rise in education expenditure from today's levels.

Those of a nervous disposition may be reassured that security will have improved, too. Already the riskiest countries are clustered in Latin America, the Caribbean and the Middle East – not Africa, where conflict has decreased significantly since the Cold War era. Pan-African defence spending was only around $34 billion in 2011,[3] not quite enough to buy four US aircraft carriers. By 2050 the figure would be $471 billion, if defence spending is maintained at the current SSA share of 1.6% of GDP. But we would not be surprised if the figure is lower. The vast majority of countries will be democratic, and as democracies do not need to go to war with each other, governments should be able to spend more on much-needed infrastructure improvements.

Today we count around 30 democracies across the continent, some strong and immortal, but many fragile and still vulnerable. Renaissance expects 50 democracies by 2050, with just a few autocratic, energy-rich exporters left that are wealthy enough to buy off their middle class. As soon as 2013, South Africa will join a few others such as Botswana and Mauritius above the key $10,000 per capita GDP level above which no democracy has ever died. Most of Africa will have crossed the same threshold to join them well before 2050. Democratisation is an inevitable march, one which may not be as loud as the boots of soldiers interrupting this trend, but will nonetheless show steady progress. Morocco and Swaziland are likely to be the next to democratise within 10 years.

Corruption will not have disappeared by 2050. Neither democracy nor high per capita income are sufficient for all countries to achieve the near-perfect scores that Finland or New Zealand regularly record in Transparency International surveys. Yet already Africa surprises by having 14 countries that are less corrupt than per capita GDP implies they should be, and only seven that are more corrupt than is normal at these income levels. Renaissance does expect an across-the-board 24% improvement in the corruption score by the mid-2020s, with a further 10% improvement the decade after. Those countries that outperform on this index will do best in attracting foreign equity interest, including South Africa, Ghana and Rwanda. Those that underperform will still attract debt investors. Locals and foreign investors will feel the benefits of lower corruption, and governments can accelerate the process via ease of doing business reforms, which pioneers such as Rwanda have enacted in recent years.

Africa's Place in the World Economy Will Shift

TODAY the continent is using the benefits of high commodity prices and exports to China to begin the process of infrastructure investment that accelerates growth. Renaissance sees huge room for this to expand. As the renowned economist Paul Collier has shown, in the year 2000, Africa had 20% of the discovered sub-soil resources per square mile that OECD countries have. The missing 80% is now being discovered. New iron ore projects in western and central Africa could add nearly 600 million tonnes of output by 2022. Mozambique is on course to be one of the largest coking coal exporters by 2020. Commodity export growth, in minerals and agriculture, will be key themes in coming decades. They should help jump-start growth like the 21% GDP rise in 2012 that Sierra Leone assumes on the back of new mining production.

Each year, in the oil sector alone, a major new discovery is heralded, from Ghana to Uganda and most recently Kenya, pushing Africa's share of world oil reserves to 10%. African oil production growth has already been the fastest in the world over the past 10 years, all of it in SSA. From 316,000 barrels per day in 1965, bringing in $1 billion of revenue (in 2011 dollars), SSA now produces 5.8 million barrels per day, equivalent to all of China's import needs, and delivering $235 billion of oil revenue annually or 20% of 2011 GDP.[4] Renaissance expects volume increases to ensure this tops $300 billion even with no change in oil prices by 2019. Nearly a trillion dollars of oil revenue every three years means unprecedented inflows of foreign exchange to fund imports of investment and consumption goods.

Rapid economic growth means growing African demand for resources. Do not be surprised if Nigerian steel consumption rises from 1.6 million tonnes annually today to 115 million tonnes annually by 2050. African motor vehicle sales of 8 million by 2020 may reach 14 million by 2030, higher than the US today. The next Geely or Tata may well be found in Nigeria, Kenya or Ethiopia. Road and rail transportation demand will treble, while the number of passenger flights will more than double every decade from around 100 million today and 1.7 billion by 2050. Instead of just exporting commodities, Africa will be consuming them, too.

An Enviable Macro-Economic Backdrop

THE macro-economic backdrop is probably the best it's ever been in Africa, and supportive for stronger growth. SSA inflation dropped into the single digits in 2003, while government finances have vastly improved since a generation ago. While the West was on its debt-fuelled binge in the run-up to the global financial crisis, SSA was slashing its public debt ratio from 70% of GDP in 2000 to 32% of by 2009. As consumers in the UK, Spain and the US pushed personal debt levels towards 100% of GDP, household debt in Africa has remained at levels closer to 0–10% of GDP across much of the continent. And while Western banks promoted increasingly complex instruments that neither they nor their customers fully understood, Kenya's Safaricom pioneered a new way of moving money via mobile phones that has provided access to financial services for millions. The increasingly well-known M-PESA system offers a template for the entire continent and much of the emerging world to copy from Africa.

Increased macro stability has helped deliver credit ratings across Africa that support the growing global appetite for African assets. Local-currency debt markets, which in emerging markets were short-term and volatile in the 1990s, already extend out to 30 years in Kenya. Local pension funds – with assets of nearly $260 billion in SSA – are significant players in local debt and equity markets, and we cautiously assume they will grow to $7 trillion in SSA and $10 trillion across Africa by 2050. Many African countries have already done more to encourage private pension provision than most Asian and many European countries, and will be in a strong position to provide a secure future for the fastest billion.

It's possible that the Renaissance vision of a democratic, richer, healthier, increasingly educated Africa will be seen as optimistic. Or deluded, or self-serving. But we think that what we outline below will convince you otherwise.

Our base case is that Africa continues the trajectory it began a decade ago, taking up the baton of "fastest growth" from Developing Asia and India, as it follows the path they have already trodden, with added fuel provided by ever-larger global markets and new technology. The continent is already more democratic, safer and better run than it has ever been. The macro framework is dramatically improved, thanks to better governance – recent negative examples such as Zimbabwe's recent hyper-inflationary episode have only served to underline the benefits of good governance. We focus on Equity Bank in Kenya for the good reason that it highlights how technology and innovation are fusing in ways that mean Africa is leap-frogging into the future.

The development of new cities, the expansion of new mines and the exploration of the continent's oil potential are all reasons why foreign direct investment is pouring into the continent. The Internet and broadband access help to reduce the "land-locked" constraint on exports. Governments are increasingly aware of the benefits of improving the ease of doing business, as Rwanda shows as it emulates Singapore's success of the 20th century.

Over-optimistic? We would prefer to have you finish this book asking why Renaissance Capital is so cautious in its outlook on Africa. And then we'd like to see you consider investing there yourself – just as we are.

Notes

1. Daniel Kahneman, *Thinking, Fast and Slow* (New York: Farrar, Straus and Giroux, 2011).
2. Unless otherwise cited, projections throughout this book are attributed to Renaissance Capital Research.
3. Stockholm International Peace Research Institute, *SIPRI Yearbook 2012: Armaments, Disarmament and International Security* (Oxford: Oxford University Press, 2012).
4. US Energy Information Administration, International Energy Statistics database, http://www.eia.gov/cfapps/ipdbproject/IEDIndex3.cfm.

PART I

From Last to Fast

A Historical Reason for Optimism

By Charles Robertson

No one can claim to trace the precise reasons why trends in economic growth and power suddenly undergo a major shift. Economists have yet to agree (do we ever?) on why India and China's once-dominant percentage of global GDP waned after 1700, and why East Asia after 1980 suddenly experienced a resurgence. The metrics clearly fall short of empirical evidence. Nonetheless, it's worth undertaking a quick review of the past couple millennia to help illuminate the erroneous assumptions that have littered world economic history.

There is of course still no consensus on why the UK became the first country to experience an industrial revolution and a relative growth explosion. From 0-1,000 CE, UK GDP was roughly stable at $400 per capita – roughly 15% below Chinese and Indian wealth levels. By 1500, the UK had superseded both these great Asian powers, but with per capita GDP of $714, it did not quite match France and clearly lagged the financial giant that was Medici Italy, with per capita GDP of $1,100. Even 200 years later, after an impressive 0.3% annual growth rate, UK per capita GDP was $1,250 and double that of China or India, but only just over half that of the new financial powerhouse that was the Netherlands, on $2,130. The great leap forward only kicked in from 1820 to 1850, when per capita GDP began rising by 1.0% annually, after which UK per capita income was the highest in the world.

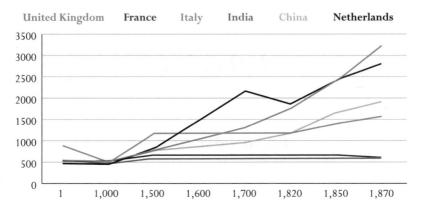

Figure 0.1: Per capita GDP, 0–1870 CE, $

Source: Madison

Naturally the Victorian British had many explanations for this, many of which assumed an innate English superiority over other peoples (and most satisfyingly over their age-old enemies, the French). But rather alarmingly, other Europeans began to catch up with the UK. Americans and Germans proved adept at copying and then improving on UK iron and steel manufacturing techniques. The Germans became more efficient in steel making than the English themselves – and most distressing of all, beat us in the football arena, too. Through the 19th century, Germany, the US, France and Australia and New Zealand began to grow more quickly than the UK, by importing foreign capital (often British) and modern industrial equipment, and by improving British manufacturing techniques – much as Kenya is doing with telephone and agency banking today.

Figure 0.2: Growth spreads outside NW Europe – per capita GDP, 1870–1910, $

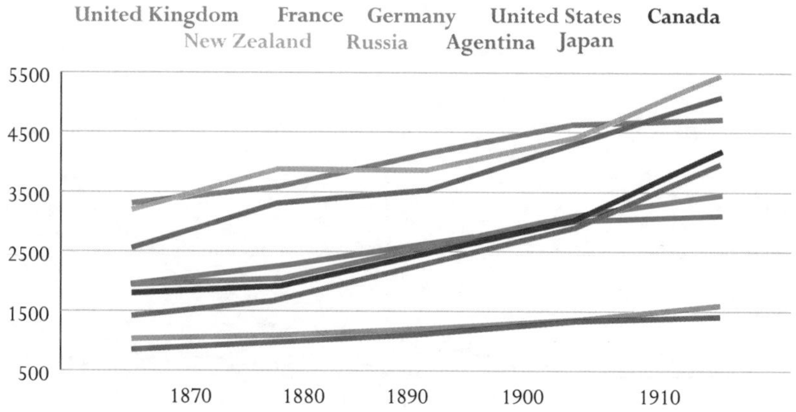
United Kingdom
France
Germany
United States
Canada
New Zealand
Russia
Agentina
Japan
5500
4500
3500
2500
1500
500
1870
1880
1890
1900
1910

Source: Madison

By the late 19th century, while the British could no longer feel quite so superior, it still seemed that at least north-west Europeans and their colonists in the US and Oceania had some natural advantage over others, whether this was rooted in political, religious or social norms. Yet seemingly out of nowhere, imperial Orthodox Russia, Catholic Argentina and Japan began the same catch-up process others had experienced. In Russia and Argentina this was primarily financed from abroad (France and the UK, respectively), while the Japanese used domestic savings. Russia boomed on oil and grain, and Argentina on meat and grain, while Japan shifted from silkworms to textiles and other light manufacturing.

By 1960, the gap between what was now termed the West (including Japan) and the rest of the world was wider than ever. It was not clear who, if anyone, could repeat what the West had achieved. Of all the continents, few would have chosen Asia as the likely success story of the second half of the 20th century. Communism was holding back, or even reversing, growth in China, North Korea and North Vietnam. War and political instability threatened South Korea, Southeast Asia, India and Pakistan. Per capita GDP in Singapore and South Korea was around $400. The English-speaking Philippines, protected by the US, would have seemed to many the most likely success story.

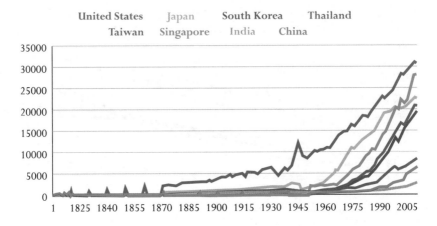

Figure 0.3: The growth story crosses the Pacific – per capita GDP , $

Source: Renaissance Capital estimates

Instead it was the resource-poor Dragons of Taiwan, Hong Kong, Singapore and South Korea which soared despite the commodity boom of the 1970s. By the 1980s and 1990s, they had been joined by the Tigers of Thailand, Malaysia and Indonesia. China finally arrived at the growth party in the 1980s, and India, too. While it is only just beginning to be recognised, Africa joined the boom over a decade ago. The oil-rich economies of Angola and Equatorial Guinea were the fastest-growing African economies, but a number of East African countries, including Ethiopia and Rwanda, have achieved record growth rates, too. Africa saw 10 countries grow at an average of 7% or more over 2000–11, the rate sufficient to double GDP every decade.

The speed of growth has also accelerated. The improvement in Nigerian per capita GDP in constant prices over the six years of 2002–08 took India eight years to achieve in the late 20th century, took Korea 11 years to achieve in the mid-20th century and took France 27 years to manage in the 19th century.

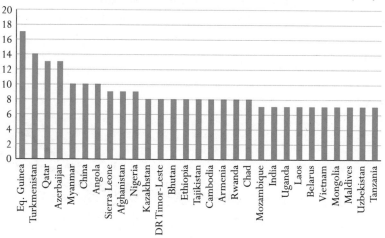

Figure 0.4: Over 2000-11, 10 African countries achieved at least a 7% annual average GDP growth rate, sufficient to double an economy's size every 10 years

Source: IMF

Clearly the growth trajectory does not respect ethnic, religious or geographic boundaries. It is not Victorian English values, Chinese Confucianism/communism or East African entrepreneurship that offers the only model to follow. Growth and high living standards have been created in resource-rich Canada and resource-less South Korea, in the tropical swamps of Singapore and the cold winters of Sweden. There is no reason to assume it will not encompass us all, even if there are interruptions along the way, as we've seen from Germany's bid for hyper-inflationary fame to North Korea's sad devotion to a discredited ideology.

Figure 0.5: Catching up is a global phenomenon – per capita GDP since 1820

United Kingdom   France   **Germany**   **Italy**   **Spain**   United States
Canada   Czechoslovakia   **Argentina**   Brazil   **Chile**   Japan
South Korea   **Thailand**   Taiwan   Singapore   India

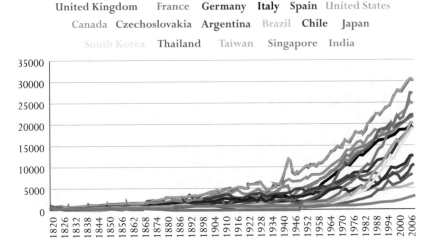

Source: Madison

The only potential long-term barrier we see is the risk that the earth itself cannot cope with the consumption levels demanded by an ever-richer human race. This assumes that our ingenuity is unable to respond to the challenge. History is, however, encouraging. The agricultural revolution saved us from Malthusian starvation. In the 1830s, Europe was running short of wood and panic buying was driving up lumber prices and cutting down the forests of the Austrian empire. Coal saved our forests and provided the energy needed to fuel the industrial revolution. Oil saved the whales and gave us the transport revolution. It may yet be African solar power that saves us from global warming if technology solves the problem of electricity transmission over distance. Yet these are subjects for a different book. The focus here is on how Africa has joined the growth revolution, and specifically what the growth trajectory implies for the next two generations.

Chapter 1

Getting Macro Right

By Yvonne Mhango and Charles Robertson

Critical to the region's recent success has been the steady progress and economic resilience of the region's 26 low-income and fragile economies... [T]otal output has grown by more than 5% in every year since 2004. Furthermore, the share of investment in this output has risen steadily – from 18% in 2004 to 23% now. I would ascribe key importance to sound policy choices by African governments – both in terms of pursuing appropriate macroeconomic policies and pressing ahead with important reform measures.

—Antoinette Sayeh, former Liberian finance minister, director of the IMF's Africa Department[1]

MORE wealth has been created in Africa in the past 10 years than at any point in the continent's history. It is a transformation that is both bottom up – new businesses and even whole sectors have sprung up and engulfed the continent – and top down. Governments have got policy spectacularly right and created the low-debt, low-inflation, much-improved macro conditions that have enabled growth to take off. Africa's private sector is thriving, supported by better governance, with new resource discoveries and production helping trigger growth, but services contributing the greater gains. The consequences have been a quintupling of exports, record inflows of foreign direct investment and a doubling of per capita GDP.

To take one key example, public debt in Africa is now among the lowest of any continent. The fundamentals are not just good: they are exceptional. Africa has benefited from the work of the IMF and the World Bank starting in 1996 to such an extent that today most African nations enjoy the benefits of key euro convergence criteria – improved currency stability, low public debt/GDP and low budget deficits. Taken together they have enabled governments to increase the maturity of their domestic debt and access the global pool of capital more easily than ever before. This happy situation has come from following demanding fiscal policies, in marked contrast to the period up to the 1990s.

Africa is getting richer faster than ever before, and faster than most of the rest of the world, and it is achieving this against a background of stability and sustainability that is often unmatched anywhere in the world. Debt forgiveness was one catalyst, but this only came thanks to the responsible fiscal policies of African leaders and officials, who had previously endured far-greater problems than peripheral Europe is struggling with today. Renaissance believes these factors have been key in turning around Africa's trajectory from stagnation to ever-faster growth.

The contrast with the West is vast. If developed-market finance ministers were offered three wishes today, many would ask for Africa's public debt ratios, Africa's budget balances and Africa's growth rates. Germany, Japan and the US would in recent years have been rejected had they applied to join the euro-zone (happily so, in the circumstances), as they would have failed to meet the prudent ratios enshrined in the Maastricht criteria required for euro adoption. The vast majority of African countries we focus on would meet the Maastricht public finance requirements with ease. The macro mess in developed countries means some investors fear European debt deflation will lead to default, or that US money printing will lead to high inflation, or that currency devaluation (via euro exit) will lead to both. Such an environment discourages investment, hurts growth and produces a vicious circle that only intensifies the problems. Many Africans learnt this lesson the hard way in the 20th century. The consequence of what followed is that today, Africa has vastly improved macro ratios and good policy management, which has helped fuel the strong recovery in the 21st century.

African public finances were not always perfect. Rather too often they were a pot to be raided by politicians and officials, either for personal use or to be spent on grandiose white elephant projects. Even when intentions were better, and government taxes were spent on policies aimed at securing high growth, the post-colonial policies themselves (sometimes promoted by the West) were often flawed. Attempts to kick-start industrialisation despite an unskilled and un-educated workforce were understandable but not fated to succeed. Poor policy choices and increased borrowing did not matter too much in the first years after the independence wave began in 1960, as debt levels were low and commodity prices were high. Sub-Saharan African growth excluding South Africa rose from 3.3% in the 1960s to 4.3% in the 1970s, with the peak years of 1969–70 seeing growth reach 10%.[2] But by the time the 20-year commodity bear market began in 1980, debt levels were already high and became unbearably so.

The 1980s and 1990s saw a host of African nations struggle with, or default on, their debt. It became common to note how many governments spent more on servicing debt than on investment and education. The outflow of capital to meet external debt requirements ensured the balance of payments was under strain, often leading to hefty currency devaluations, high inflation and an unpredictable macro-environment that hurt investment by the private sector. Foreign investors avoided the continent, while many locals chose to take their capital offshore.

In response, the IMF and World Bank developed a new set of initials mainly for Africa. The Highly Indebted Poor Countries (HIPC) initiative of 1996 aimed "to ensure no poor country would face a debt burden it cannot manage," and was initially open to 36 countries, all but five from Africa. It required countries to show "a track record of reform and sound policies through IMF- and World Bank-supported programmes" and work towards achieving Millennium Development Goals such as "education for all." Since then, 24 African countries have completed HIPC deals, with another six soon to follow, reducing debt ratios by 38–80% of GDP. The total cost of all HIPC deals is estimated at $74 billion, somewhat less expensive than Greece's recent default, and benefiting far more people.[3]

With debt forgiveness, better governance, the emergence of new sectors such as telecoms, improved education, and a recovery in commodity prices, the vicious cycle has become a virtuous cycle. Rising exports, combined with less debt to repay, have improved the balance of payments. Currencies have become easier to manage, less susceptible to sudden forced devaluations, and the management of currency policy has matured to the point where significant volatility is increasingly accepted by central banks from Kenya to Ghana. Currency controls have been loosened, which encourages domestic capital to remain at home, and encourages foreign capital to flow in. Central banks have been able to focus on delivering lower inflation, often via higher real interest rates, which has incentivised local savings. Loan-to-deposit ratios of around 70% in SSA are common and would be the envy of a Spanish banker.

Falling inflation and stable public finances have allowed countries to developed long-dated yield curves. Lengthening the government yield curve to 10 years in local currency bonds was a great achievement for Russia, Mexico, Turkey and Brazil in the past 12 years – in Kenya, the government regularly issues 20-year or even 30-year bonds. Such issuance has encouraged government infrastructure spending and long-term investments by the private sector. Mobile phone companies have tapped local currency debt markets to fund growth. Higher government investment aims to address infrastructure bottlenecks that contribute to inflation and deter FDI.

Government commitment to sustainable public finances should not surprise us. We learn from painful experiences. Sweden, Canada and Australia learnt lessons from banking crises in the late 20th century that meant they avoided the worst of the Western financial crisis since 2007. Asian countries since the 1997–99 Asian crisis tend to stockpile foreign exchange reserves. African countries have been impressive in sticking to commitments to the IMF in the past decade or more. In some cases, the commitment started long before the 1990s. In Ghana, for example, in 1981 a coup brought Flight Lieutenant Jerry Rawlings to power. To the surprise of everyone, the Rawlings government recognized the failures of the 1970s and began working with the IMF, introducing rational economic policies designed to foster business, which most recently helped Ghana win classification as a middle-income country. African ministers and officials are all too well aware of the 1980–2000 experience and are loath to repeat it. We might hope that politicians in peripheral Europe learn the same lesson from their post-crisis experiences.

Debt Is at a Historic Low

The graphs below highlight some of these improvements. SSA's government debt dropped to 32% of GDP in 2009, from 70% in 2000 (see figure 1.2). The significant reduction, particularly of external debt, considerably improved sovereign risk and therefore access to external long-term credit. This helped the affected countries raise much-needed long-term financing, especially for infrastructure projects. Approximately 23 African countries now have credit ratings from the largest three agencies, with Botswana rated A and Mauritius, Namibia, Morocco, South Africa and Tunisia all having investment-grade ratings from at least one agency.

In September 2012, the tradeable dollar debt of Ghana, Nigeria and Namibia was offering yields of 4–5% and South Africa sub-3% out to 2021. Such low interest rates reflect international investor trust in the credit-worthiness of these governments. It is a huge shift in just one decade.

The SSA budget balance turned positive in 2004 and showed a surplus for five years. Thereafter the global crisis hit and the budget balance reverted to a sizeable deficit in 2009 (5–6% of GDP), when SSA economies put in place expansionary fiscal policy to counter the dampening effect of the slowdown in global growth (see figure 1.1). The budget deficit has narrowed since 2009, owing both to economic recovery and fiscal consolidation programmes. Getting finances back on track is very encouraging and suggests the lessons of the 1980s and 1990s have sunk in.

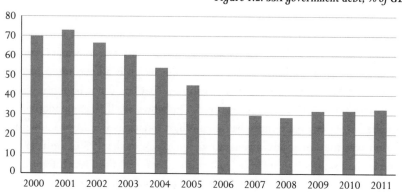

Figure 1.1: SSA budget balance, % of GDP

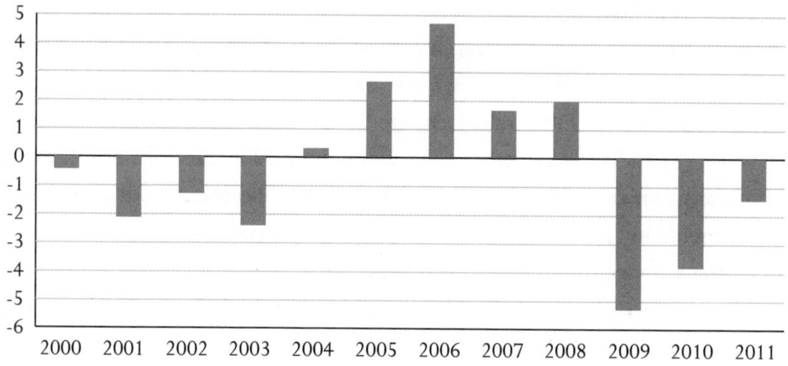

Source: IMF

Figure 1.2: SSA government debt, % of GDP

Source: IMF

'You Can't Eat Inflation' – The Achievement of Macro Stability

FOLLOWING sound macro policies does not always win a government an election. But when Zambia's Movement for Multiparty Democracy (MMD) party was campaigning for re-election in 2011, it laboured the point that it achieved low and stable inflation during its two decades in office. The Patriotic Front (PF), which was in opposition at the time, tried to undermine this achievement by responding that "you can't eat inflation." The PF was attempting to demonstrate that it is more familiar than the MMD with the needs of Zambia's largely poor electorate. Yet the experience of neighbouring Zimbabwe shows that the poor suffer most from high inflation.

Ruvimbo Kuzviwanza, a research analyst in Zimbabwe, shared her experience of living through the challenges of hyperinflation. Rapid price increases meant her Zimbabwe dollar salary changed every time she got paid – basically more zeros got added to her salary. She would be paid in Zimbabwe dollars and fuel coupons, which were tradeable for cash. Ruvimbo spent a lot of her time queuing, including at ATMs. Even after queuing for up to four hours, she would find that the withdrawal limit had been cut.

At the height of hyperinflation, she could only withdraw enough money to get to work, but not enough to get back to home. This is when several Zimbabweans, including Ruvimbo's father, fled to other countries including South Africa and the UK. Farmers left for better-run Zambia and Nigeria. The diaspora would then remit money back to Zimbabwe, which helped keep families afloat. Even when one had cash, the goods one wanted could not be found, as shop shelves were empty. Households looking for cash would sell anything, even groceries, to purchase what was needed. You may not be able to eat inflation, but Ruvimbo's experience shows that it can certainly affect what, how and if you eat.

Zimbabwe is an extreme example, and one which is all too often taken as indicative of African macro-economic realities. That could not be more wrong. Along with most African countries, even Zimbabwe itself, having adopted the US dollar as its currency, now has single-digit inflation. But high-double-digit inflation was the norm just a generation ago. Back in the 1980s, only 18 SSA countries had single-digit inflation, of which 12 were in the French franc zone, and thus effectively importing monetary policy from abroad. Just six countries could claim to be running macro policy well enough to deliver single-digit inflation. By the 2000s, there were 30 countries with low inflation, with overall SSA inflation dropping to 9.9% as early as 2003. Inflation has since been stable in the single digits, with the exception of 2008, when commodity prices spiked ahead of the global economic crisis.

Figure 1.3: Inflation, % YoY, average

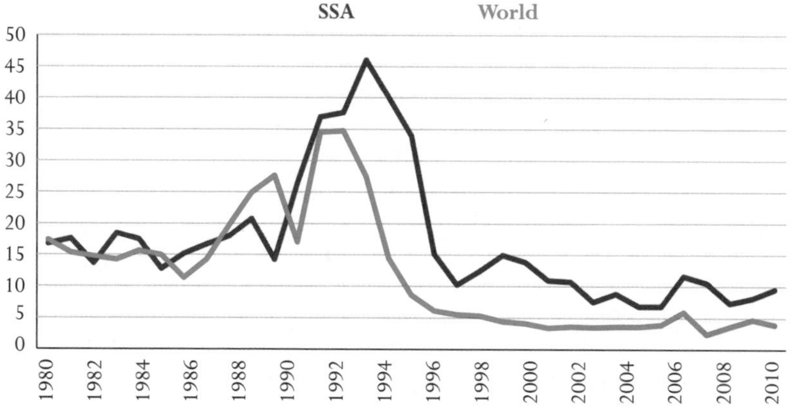

Source: IMF

Figure 1.4: SSA countries with double- and single-digit inflation

Countries	1980s	2000s
Single-digit inflation	Republic of Congo, Benin, Seychelles, Niger, Rwanda, Togo, Burkina Faso, Chad, Ethiopia, Comoros, Cote d'Ivoire, Mali, Central African Republic, Angola, Gabon, Senegal, Burundi and Cameroon (18 countries)	Guinea-Bissau, Gabon, Cape Verde, Mali, Cameroon, Cote d'Ivoire, Niger, Togo, Republic of Congo, Benin, Central African Republic, Chad, Comoros, Equatorial Guinea, Mauritius, Tanzania, South Africa, Uganda, The Gambia, Lesotho, Swaziland, Namibia, Sierra Leone, Rwanda, Kenya, Botswana, Seychelles and Liberia (30 countries)

Figure 1.4 continued

Countries	1980s	2000s
Double-digit inflation	Uganda, Sierra Leone, Guinea-Bissau, Democratic Republic of Congo, Ghana, Mozambique, Zambia, Guinea, Tanzania, Equatorial Guinea, Nigeria, Madagascar, The Gambia, Malawi, Swaziland, Sao Tome & Principe, South Africa, Lesotho, Mauritius, Cape Verde, Kenya and Botswana (22 countries)	Democratic Republic of Congo, Angola, Eritrea, Ghana, Zambia, Sao Tome & Principe, Guinea, Malawi, Nigeria, Ethiopia, Burundi, Mozambique and Madagascar (13 countries)

Source: IMF

Lower and stable inflation has encouraged higher rates of investment and so improved productivity. It helps sustain price competitiveness for exporters and controls costs for importers. And it inspires higher levels of consumer and business confidence, which increases activity and demand.

But there is more to stability than just low inflation. The euro convergence criteria, for example, define macroeconomic stability with four other variables, in addition to low and stable inflation. Firstly, currency stability, as that enables importers and exporters to develop long-term growth strategies, and lowers investors' exchange rate risk. Secondly, low public debt/GDP, which implies that the government has the fiscal space to use its tax revenue to address domestic needs instead of servicing foreign debt. Thirdly, low budget deficits, as they temper growth in public debt. Lastly, low long-term interest rates, as they reflect stable future inflation expectations. (SSA's long-term debt market is small, however, so this last variable is of lower importance in assessing the region's macro stability.)

Currencies Are Key

CURRENCY stability is important for keeping inflation stable. Many countries still import food and African countries import most of their capital equipment and machinery too. Most of the region's economies (including the oil exporters) are fuel importers, which implies that their inflation rates are significantly exposed to international oil prices. So lower inflation has come in part because

SSA's most liquid currencies (including the Nigerian naira, Kenyan shilling, Ghanaian cedi and Zambian dollar) have become significantly less volatile since mid-1994 (see figure 1.5). Since then, Nigeria's naira has been one of the least volatile currencies.

Figure 1.5: Currency volatility – percentage annual change in the exchange rate against the US dollar

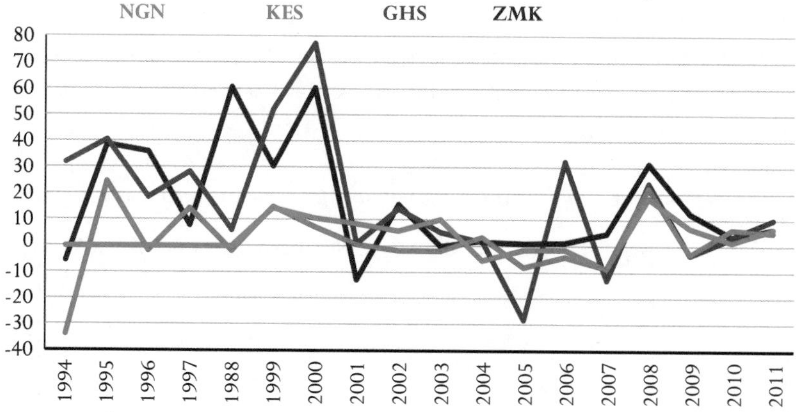

Source: Bloomberg, Renaissance Capital estimates

The decline in exchange rate risk, coupled with broader macro stability and fewer capital controls, has encouraged a boom in FDI over the past two decades (see figure 1.6).

Even though we know how dire Africa's economic performance was in the late 20th century, it is still surprising to see just how unattractive it was for FDI. From 1971–92, annual FDI never exceeded 1.1% of GDP. No foreign capital meant no transfer of skills or training – exacerbating the human capital problem referred to in the introduction – and no export-orientated export boost. This began to change with inflows to Nigeria in the 1990s, and then in the late 1990s it was the turn of Middle Africa: Angola, Equatorial Guinea and the Republic of Congo. Since 2001, and despite tech bubbles bursting in the West and the global financial crisis, FDI flows to Africa have never fallen below 2.0% of GDP. Indeed, FDI into West and East Africa has never been as high as over the average of the past three years. This success in attracting FDI beats what any of Asia's regions achieved in the 1970s and 1980s.

The greatest FDI impact has often come from energy- and mining-related investment. Annual FDI net inflows were worth an extraordinary 86% of Liberian GDP in 2003 and 90% of Equatorial Guinean GDP in 1996. But oil or mining is not the only explanation, as the following shows. Since 2000, African countries which have seen FDI exceed 10% of GDP for at least two years include Angola, Cape Verde, Chad, the Republic of the Congo, the DRC, Equatorial Guinea, The Gambia, Guinea, Liberia, Madagascar, Mozambique, Niger, Seychelles and Zambia. To put this into perspective, UNCTAD data show that China has never received FDI worth more than 6% of GDP, Pakistan's best achievement was two years of FDI at 4% of GDP annually, India's peak was 3% of GDP and Bangladesh has never seen FDI above 1% of GDP.

Figure 1.6: Foreign direct investment into Africa and its regions, as a % of GDP

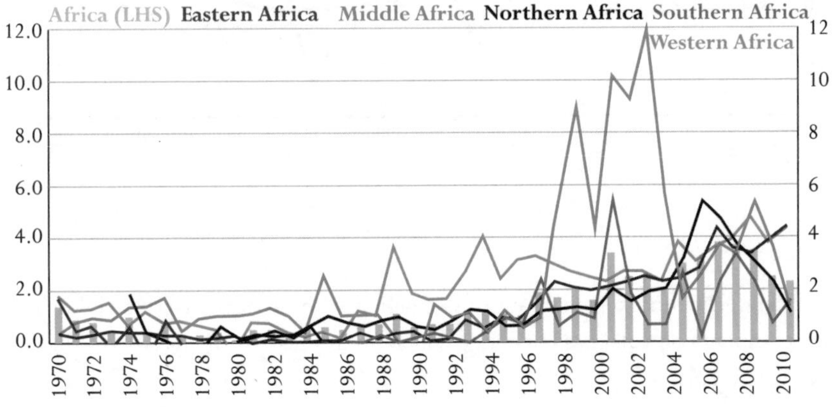

Source: UNCTAD

Africa in 2011 accounted for its largest share ever of global FDI, according to the 2012 Africa attractiveness survey by Ernst & Young: inflows rose 27% in 2011 to $80 billion and are expected to reach $150 billion by 2015. Over 2003–11, Ernst & Young estimates that 30% of capital invested in Africa was in manufacturing, 38% in infrastructure, 28% in extraction and 4% in services. The consultancy notes a "stark contrast" between the upbeat views of those that already invest in Africa and other investors: "for those respondents with no business presence in Africa, the continent is viewed as by far the least attractive investment destination in the world." When all were asked what would improve perceptions, 87% said changes in political stability would have a high impact on them, 82% cited curbs on corruption, and 67% cited ease of doing business, while less than 50% said a high impact would come from local access to finance, one-stop border posts and harmonized taxation.[4] It is our expectation that the changes we outline below will encourage ever more FDI into the continent.

Something happens when countries begin to attract FDI, and usually that something is a lift to exports. In Africa's case, it has been more of a rocket. Over 1996–99, Africa's exports averaged $150 billion annually. The annual total rose above $200 billion in 2003, $400 billion in 2006 and $700 billion in 2011. One year of exports now brings in more revenue than five years of exports in the 1990s. Africa's share of global exports has risen by half, from 2.0% in 1998 to 3.3% in 2011. This is very largely commodity driven, but it is not just a price effect. Volumes have picked up sharply, supported by the FDI noted above – investments that have rewarded the better governance in the continent. What we outline in the following chapters is that new FDI planned in mining and energy should continue to deliver further volume gains, so even if commodity prices do not continue to rise, the value of African exports will still expand.

Figure 1.7: Exports ($ million) out of Africa

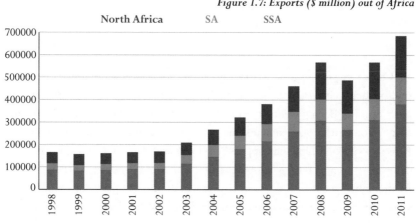

Source: UNCTAD

Booming exports allow a consequent boom in imports of investment and consumption goods. Annual imports of $160 billion in the late 1990s which Africa used to struggle to finance have now reached nearly $700 billion. Africa now runs a trade surplus with the world, whereas it used to run a trade deficit.

This even extends to China, which is most perturbed by this unusual imbalance. Chinese imports from Africa have risen from $2 billion in 1999 to $107 billion (in the year to June 2012). Despite strenuous efforts to balance that with exports of Chinese goods – from telecoms equipment to the cheap (and apparently not very reliable) diesel generators sitting on the shop counters in downtown Harare – China is now running a $27 billion trade deficit with Africa.

Figure 1.8: China's trade with Africa, rolling 12-month data, in $ million

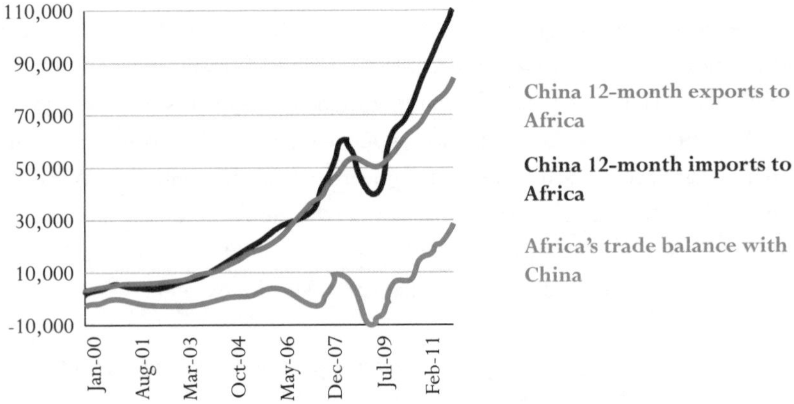

China 12-month exports to Africa

China 12-month imports to Africa

Africa's trade balance with China

Source: Bloomberg

China's engagement with Africa is a direct reflection of the import boom and trade deficit. First, China is determined to secure long-term commodity supplies. Second, Beijing wants to lever its dependence in a positive way, by lending money to African governments that is secured against Chinese payments for Africa's exports. China then hopes these loans are spent on Chinese construction companies, using Chinese equipment, and sometimes Chinese workers, to build African infrastructure. It does not always work quite like that, but China has won some service contracts to offset its trade deficit. What Africa gets in return is a large consumer of its raw materials, and a trade partner prepared to lend money at low rates over long periods, more flexibly than traditional lending partners such as the World Bank, which then delivers infrastructure improvements. It does not always work out quite as well as some African governments hope either, but in general we are seeing infrastructure being built in Africa more quickly and more cheaply than would normally be the case.[5]

A key risk to Africa's export boom is of course a global depression, akin to 2008 but lasting much longer. Yet a short one-to-two-year collapse in developed -market GDP – due to a euro break-up, for example – probably won't do it. What 2008–9 showed is that in fact such a crisis can drive up commodity prices over the medium term, as global investments in commodity supply do stop on a temporary basis, meaning that when the world gets back on its feet, underlying shortages become even more apparent. Those shortages exist because the growth trajectory implies Developing Asia should still achieve 7% growth for another decade, and India beyond that. We also know that if China or India consumed oil at the same rate as Japan did when it was an emerging market in 1965, each would annually run through more than 20 million barrels per day (Mbpd), compared with actual data of 9.5 Mbpd in China, 3.3 Mbpd in India and 19 Mbpd in the US. Given that Chinese vehicle sales now exceed US sales, we might worry that one day Chinese oil con-sumption will reach US levels per capita, implying annual Chinese demand of 83 Mbpd – nearly equalling the global oil supply of over 87 Mbpd in 2010. While this is not realistic, the point we are making is that while we can easily imagine a one-to-two-year disruption to global commodity prices – something Africa has already sailed through – we do not assume another 20-year bear market in commodities, which would require a catastrophic confluence of negative global macro events.

In any case, African exports will start to diversify from commodities. Manu-facturing has played only a small role in SSA growth, though it has been significant (as it usually is) in countries with higher per capita income, such as those in North Africa, and of course in South Africa, too. We will not be surprised if some states begin to consider the advantages of gently depreciating currencies to help create jobs, as seen in much of Asia, once an export lobby is big enough to push for this. So far, many governments have prioritised currency strength, arguing that cur-rency weakness would only import inflation, when local manufacturing remains too small to service domestic demand. Current policies help pay for imports of investment and consumption goods, with tariff barriers used to maintain competi-tiveness and build up domestic companies. It is a policy that has worked to create self-sufficiency in the Nigeria cement industry for example, helped by capital in-flows. Over time, better governance, higher productivity and new infrastructure, combined with plentiful labour, should reduce the cost of doing business, and support real currency appreciation even if there is nominal depreciation.

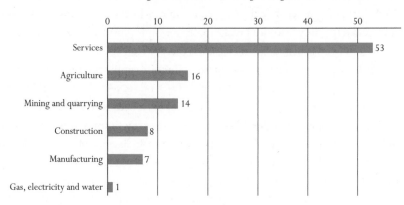

Figure 1.9: Sector share of change in real GDP, 2002-2009

Source: World Bank, IMF, Renaissance Capital estimates

But what is most interesting when looking at sectoral growth is that services, not commodities (however high-profile they are), have been the direct growth driver in Africa. Based on 11 countries, accounting for 78% of GDP, over 2002–9, we find that services represent 53% of growth, with agriculture next at 16% and mining at 14%.[6] Within services, we assume wholesale and retail trade, along with telecoms and transport account for around half of the services growth. This fits with the hefty 60% upward revision in Ghana's GDP in 2011 that reflected previously unrecorded growth areas such as telecoms – we expect a 40% rise in Nigeria.

Such data also explain the growth in Ethiopia, Rwanda and Uganda, three of Africa's fastest-growing economies. Telecoms was the fastest-growth sector in Uganda in the latter half of the last decade, with private-sector construction rising an impressive 16% from 2002–7 and with public-sector infrastructure spending (especially roads) kicking in later in the decade. Ethiopia has also seen significant public infrastructure spending, while a road trip to Rwanda's gorillas after similar road investment is a pleasurable affair.

The consequence of all we have noted above is that SSA has moved from growing more slowly than the global economy, to becoming the second-fastest-growing region in the world behind Developing Asia (see figure 1.10). The region grew on average by 2.6% and 2.2% in the 1980s and 1990s, respectively, compared with global growth of 3.2% and 3.0%.

Figure 1.10: The change in GDP around the world

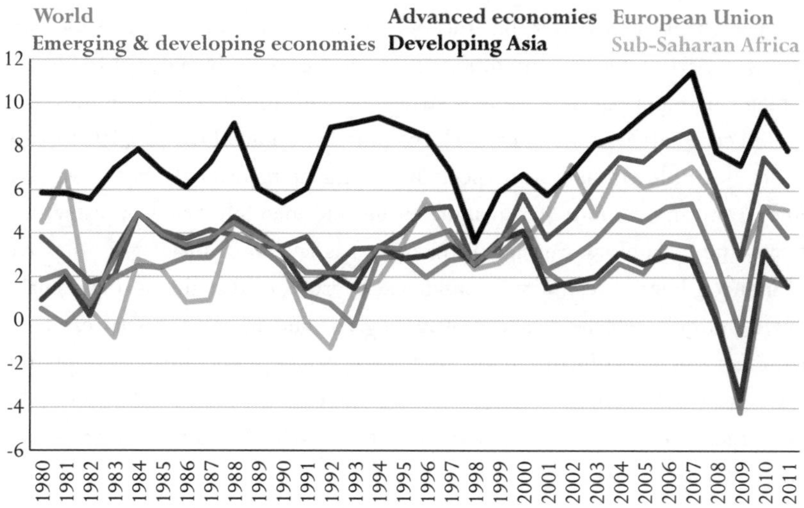

Source: IMF

However, the turn of the century saw underperformance turn into outper-formance. In the first decade of this millennium, the 2000s, SSA's economic growth of 5.7% trumped the global economy's growth of 3.6%. Some today criticise the African growth boom as meaningless because it comes from a low base. We believe this is nonsensical. Africa achieved only minimal growth with all the advantages of a low base in 1980–2000. Renaissance believes that the strengthening of real GDP growth over the past decade reflects the positive and stimulatory impact of better governance, price stability and smaller debt levels on household consumption, rates of investment and export growth.

This coincided with a moderate slowdown in population growth, implying positive per capita income growth. Population growth slowed from a year-on-year average of 2.9% in the 1980s, to 2.7% in 1990s, to 2.5% in the 2000s. The softening of population growth largely reflects improving healthcare and family planning. The combination of faster growth and slowing population growth is particularly evident in the sharp increase in per capita income (at purchasing power parity) in the 2000s – SSA per capita income increased by 62% in 2009 to $2,189, compared with $1,352 a decade earlier.

In short, Africa is getting richer faster than ever before, and faster than most of the rest of the world, and it is achieving this against a background of improved stability and sustainability that is hard to match anywhere in the world. Debt forgiveness was one catalyst, but this only came thanks to the responsible fiscal policies of African leaders and officials, who had previously endured far greater problems than peripheral Europe is struggling with today. The harsh lessons of the 20th century have been learnt. The commodity boom of the past 10–15 years has not been blown, and we expect the continent to diversify in the years to come, from services into light manufacturing and then into heavy industry, too. Already the technology transfer of telecoms has become a major growth driver and induced huge investment. Confidence is growing that this is a sustainable growth outlook, which is in turn attracting the human and financial capital to Africa that can give a further boost to growth. Sound public finances imply that the financial sector can increasingly play a constructive role in the African boom. Taking these various factors together, we can see why Africa has embarked on a new growth trajectory.

Figure 1.11: The population of Africa in 2010 (each box represents 1m people) and colours reflecting political labels

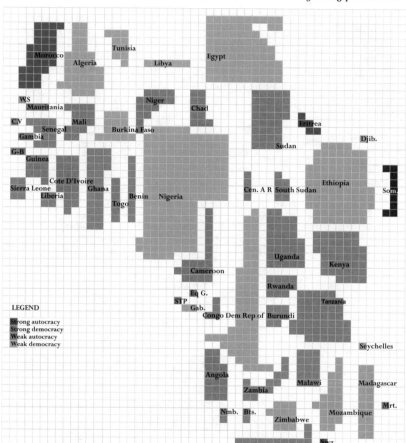

Note: IMF estimates show Nigeria's 165m population in 2010 was larger tha Russia's 142m and close to Bangladesh's 169m
DRC's 75m, Egypt's 81m and Ethiopia's 89m compare to Turkey's 75m, Iran's 77m and Germany's 82m
SA's 51m compraes to Spain's 46m and Italy's 61m
Kenya's 42m and Tanzania's 43m compares to Ukraine's 45m or Argentina's 41m
Angola's 20m and the 23m of Cote D'Ivoire or 25m in Ghana, compared to Australia's 23m, Taiwan's 23m and Sri Lanka's 21m

Source: IMF 2012 World Economic Outlook, Polity IV and Freedom House(or Renaissance Capital where 2011/12 changes are not reflected by those organisations)

Figure 1.12: GDP of AFRICA in 2012 ($bn) with each box representing $1bn of GDP and colours reflecting political labels

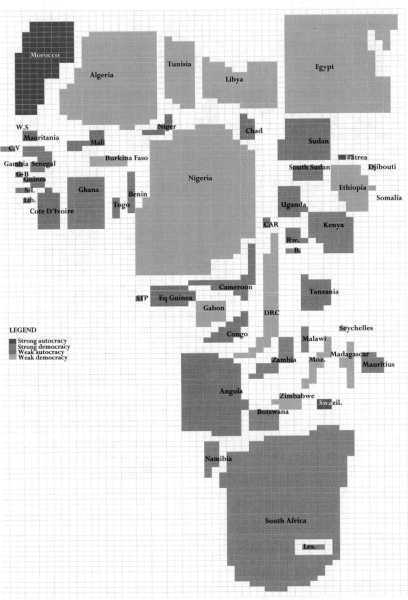

Source: IMF April 2012 World Economic Outlook except for Nigeria, Polity IV and Freedom House (or Renaissance Capital where 2011/12 changes are not reflected by those organisations)

Notes

1. Antoinette Sayeh, "Africa and the Great Recession: Changing Times," *iMFDirect* (blog), 14 May 2012, http://blog-imfdirect.imf.org/2012/05/14/africa-and-the-great-recession-changing-times/.
2. World Bank data.
3. *Heavily Indebted Poor Countries (HIPC) Initiative and Multilateral Debt Relief Initiative (MDRI)—Status of Implementation*, International Development Association and IMF, 14 September 2010, http://www.imf.org/external/np/pp/eng/2010/091410.pdf.
4. *Building bridges: Ernst & Young's 2012 attractiveness survey, Africa*, Ernst & Young, 2012, http://www.ey.com/Publication/vwLUAssets/EY–2012_Africa_attractiveness_survey/$FILE/attractiveness_2012_africa_v17.pdf.
5. For more on China's engagement with Africa, see Renaissance Capital's report *EMEA: China in Africa*, 21 April 2011.
6. The graph is of course inspired by McKinsey Global Institute's "Lions on the Move," though our countries are Algeria, Angola, Côte d'Ivoire, Egypt, Ethiopia, Ghana, Kenya, Morocco, Nigeria, South Africa and Sudan, and include an additional two years of data. Our figures, derived from current dollar figures, are unweighted. Indirect GDP benefits from commodities may well be higher.

Chapter 2

A Trajectory of Promise, 2012–2050

By Charles Robertson

The darkest thing about Africa has always been our ignorance of it.
—Africanist and geographer George H.T. Kimble, 1962

ECONOMIES of the world can be placed upon what we term the trajectory of growth. Some are at the top stage, the fourth economic age of the information economy; a few are still at the agrarian. But the trajectory is not a simple linear graph; it also portrays the growth rate through the steepness of the curves. Here we can see not only what stage of economic growth countries have reached, but also their speed of change and the rate of growth. This holds the key to understanding the opportunity for investment.

Africa is where India was in the early 1990s and Developing Asia was in the early 1980s. The surging African growth rate, so reminiscent of the pattern we have seen in India and China in the 20th century, has not been seen clearly for the precursor of great emerging wealth that it portrays. Few people saw the growth rates of India in the 1980s as the springboard for the wave of prosperity that has swept the subcontinent since then. We can see that across Africa, growth rates of 6–8% since the turn of this century have already underpinned a sharp rise in global portfolio interest in Africa, a vast increase of investment and a remarkable rise in per capita GDP. But the best is yet to come.

The growth rates we have seen to date will continue to rise in the decades to come and continue well into the 2040s. The lowest-income countries will be recording growth rates accelerating from 7% towards 13%, pushing GDP per capita over $10,000 across the continent. This heady but sustainable rise will dramatically alter the politics of Africa as well as the lives of its people – and provide the basis for long-term and safe investment.

"Feels like Mumbai 10 years ago," was the description of Lagos given by one virgin visitor attending our annual Africa conference there in 2011. It was a good comparison. The challenges in India include a lack of infrastructure, rapid urbanisation, an underfunded health system, corruption, terrorism and expensive government-funded subsidies – and all this after 20 years of strong growth.

But for much of Africa, the better comparison is India in 1990. At that time most assumed the country was condemned to the sluggish "Hindu" growth of the most of the previous 40 years, which saw the world's largest democracy rapidly outpaced by China, the world's most successful communist country. Poor governance, a lack of internal or external competition, and poverty were seen as facts of Indian life.

Even 10–20 years after reforms were first unleashed around 1991, still the India versus China debate has been framed as a democratic country failing to match its Asian one-party rival. What gets missed in this analysis is firstly that India is doing extremely well – its per capita GDP in constant prices is up more than six-fold in 30 years – and, more importantly, that China, India and now Africa are at different points of the growth trajectory. This trajectory is common to many countries and has seen growth accelerate at a rising pace for decades, before falling significantly once high per capita income levels are achieved. We saw this in Japan, which boomed at 9% growth annually until the early 1970s and then saw growth halve to around 4%. We are seeing this now in China, which will never again record sustainable growth at 10%.

The graph below shows that India's growth trajectory has been remarkably similar to Developing Asia's, once we lag the data by nearly 10 years. The Developing Asia boom of the 1990s was what India experienced in the 2000s. Even the recent slowdown echoes Asia's post-1998-crisis GDP slump.

Figure 2.1: Growth in India (lagged nearly 20 years), Developing Asia (lagged 30 years) and SSA

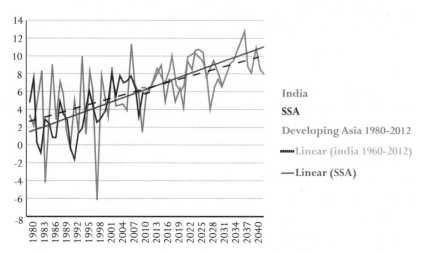

Source: Renaissance Capital estimates

India has slowed sharply in 2012, but the growth trajectory suggests the best is yet to come. It is unwise to hold a forecast hostage to developments in a single country; we cannot be certain India will follow the pattern set by all of Developing Asia. But if we are right, then by 2015–2020, we shall be reading articles about the success of India's democratic model and how the openness and transparency of the system is better suited to high growth than the sluggish hand of the Chinese Communist Party. It will echo the 1980s commentary, "why Japan is so much better than the US," or the commentary which presumably was written in 1900 about "why Germany's economy is more efficient than the UK."

What we find more interesting is the Sub-Saharan African growth trajectory since the 1980s. While Lagos may echo Mumbai 10 years ago, for SSA as a whole the similarity is to India 20 years ago. India's population in 1990 of 874 million is within 10% of UN estimates of SSA's population in 2010 at 806 million (excluding Sudan and Somalia). India's purchasing power parity GDP of $1.2 trillion was a little less than the $1.65 trillion of SSA – although PPP figures should be treated with caution. Both India from 1960–80 and SSA from 1980–2000 had two long decades of weak growth. Even when India recorded annual growth of 5.6% in the 1980s, double the 2.9% seen in the 1970s, few paid much attention.

Equally, the SSA average growth rate in the 2000s of 5.6%, more than double the 2.2% of the 1990s, has only recently begun to attract positive interest from abroad.

It was 1991 and the reforms unleashed by the new Indian government that really captured the attention of investors. Stock market capitalisation jumped from $39 billion in 1990 to $128 billion by 1994, and the number of Indian-listed companies rose from 2,435 in 1990 to nearly 6,000 by 2000. Even without a sudden reform miracle, the implication is that SSA asset prices could soar as investors focus on the change in Africa.

Unlike India in 1991, there is no obvious single event that has triggered the wave of positive reports, from McKinsey's 2010 "Lions on the Move" to the *Economist* in December 2011 recanting its infamous "hopeless continent" cover of May 2000. The way SSA sailed through the global financial crisis largely unscathed probably helped. Some began to ask why rapid Chinese GDP growth of 8–9% was being exceeded by a more than 10-fold increase in Chinese trade turnover with Africa. This rose from $11 billion in 2000 to approximately $180 billion in 2011/12, as China anxiously sought (and failed) to maintain a trade surplus with commodity-exporting Africa. Rwanda surprised the world in 2010 when it became the first SSA country to take the top spot among reformers in the World Bank's Doing Business report. The largest election in African history – the generally peaceful Nigerian presidential election of May 2011 – probably should have attracted more attention than it did, at a time when the Arab Spring was toppling dictators in North Africa. Whatever the reason, interest in Africa is on the rise.

As we outline in this book, the underlying drivers of the SSA growth acceleration are manifold, as they were in India in the 1980s, Developing Asia in the 1970s and OECD countries before that. Demographics clearly help (see chapter 8), but that was also a theme in the 1980s and 1990s. It is the development of an educated demographic surge that is a key change (see chapter 5), allowing labour to support innovation (see part III), which we already see in information and communications technology (see chapter 10), but expect, too, from the agricultural sector (see chapter 13). Improvements in governance stem from economic growth (see chapter 3), encouraging officials to be supportive of the private sector by improving the ease of doing business (see chapter 4), which helps reinforce these positive drivers. While exports of commodities can kick-start growth (see chapters 6 and 7), following decades should see foreign direct investment (see chapter 1), a growing middle class (chapter 8), credit growth (see chapter

9), urbanisation (see chapter 12) and infrastructure spending (see chapter 11) all contribute to turbo-charged growth in following years.

The template provided by India and Developing Asia means we can draw out Africa's accelerating growth trajectory until at least 2042, even as Developing Asia sees its growth slow towards 7% through this decade, with India likely to slow in the 2020s. SSA may achieve 6.7% growth in the 2010s, 7.2% in the 2020s and 8.2% in the 2030s, before slowing to around 7.4% in the 2040s. Note that we are already ignoring the trend line in the chart above suggesting that SSA will in fact grow faster than India (we want you to accuse us of being too pessimistic by the time you finish this book).

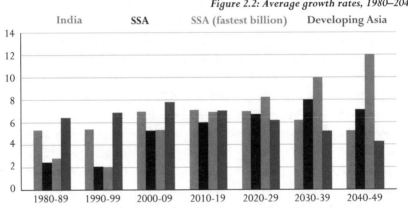

Figure 2.2: Average growth rates, 1980–2049

Source: IMF, Reserve Bank of India, Renaissance Capital

Average SSA growth rates of 7–8% annually for 40 years will conceal massive variations. It may be overly cautious, but we assume an average growth rate of just 3.5% annually for South Africa and Seychelles, despite a strong temptation to suggest both will do better as Africa booms. In addition, we assume that growth will be no higher than 5% annually for any African country after its per capita GDP has risen beyond $10,000 in 2012 dollars. Some energy-rich countries do achieve faster growth above that income level, but many others start to slow at income levels closer to $7,000-8,000; we took $10,000 as an easy compromise. Consequently, the growth rate of the remaining countries will need to trend higher with each decade that passes, as richer countries drop out of the fastest growth rate. Already in this decade some African countries are likely to exceed

India's growth rate. To maintain an average SSA growth rate equal to what India achieved on its growth trajectory, countries with per capita GDP below $10,000 should grow by 7.3% this decade, 8.6% in the 2020s, 10.5% in the 2030s and a remarkable 12.6% from 2040–49. We believe that increasing global wealth, the benefits of globalisation and the lack of alternative cheap labour elsewhere will make it ever easier for countries to achieve such high levels of growth our forecasts imply.

The fastest billion today will change their composition. In 2038 our forecasts imply roughly 300 million Nigerians will be enjoying an average per capita income of $10,000, and their GDP will have reached $3 trillion, similar to Germany today (though less than Germany in 2038, assuming Germany keeps growing). At that point we assume Nigeria's growth will slow from around 10.5% to a more sedate growth of 5%, still sufficient for Nigeria to become the size of present-day Japan before 2050. Meanwhile, 91 million Kenyans will only slow in 2047, when their GDP has reached $1 trillion. Uganda's 94 million people in 2050 will still be recording growth of around 12% by 2050, even with a GDP of $755 billion, as will 145 million Ethiopians with a GDP of $1.5 trillion.

Figure 2.3: When will Nigeria equal the 2012 GDP of others?

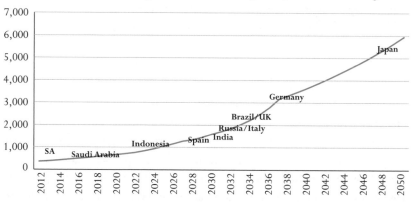

Source: Renaissance Capital estimates

Where We May Differ from Consensus

THOSE who prefer to look backwards – as many economists do – will have a different view on the African outlook. A common approach to forecasting is to consider long-term averages, such as 10-year average data, and use these to extrapolate forwards. On that basis, in the year 2000, most such economists would have forecast roughly 2.5% annual GDP as the norm for SSA. Perhaps such thinking was what prompted the *Economist's* "The hopeless continent" front page of that year.

We're not taking a cheap shot at our own profession here – we're an easy enough target as it is. Forecasts are hard to get right. Even central banking has been compared to driving a car while looking in the rear-view mirror. However, looking backwards guarantees that economists will miss significant changes, such as the global growth of the past 200 years.

Figure 2.4: SSA GDP growth and the 10-year moving average

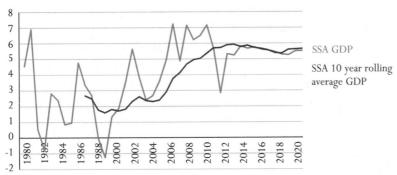

Source: IMF, Renaissance Capital

Today, such economists will be more optimistic, but they will only be assuming growth of around 5–6% this decade. Some of the more pessimistic will question even that. They will look at the performance of the 1980s and 1990s and ask whether the 2000s were in fact an aberration, perhaps caused by China's demand for commodities. They may feel more comfortable assuming long-term growth closer to 3–4% or even fear a decline to what we saw in the 1980s and 1990s.

Probably there were many who felt that way in 1990 about India. They might have attributed India's growth in the 1980s to the decline in commodity prices. As late as 2005, IMF papers were still struggling to explain the Indian growth acceleration of the 1980s that came before the rapid reforms post-1991.[1]

Compared with this reasoning, we will appear to be Africa bulls. Instead, we are merely showing that Africa is already achieving the same growth rates as Developing Asia and India attained when they entered the accelerating growth trajectory, and that later growth then does become faster growth. This means that many African countries will in fact beat that average growth rate. We hope some of the chapters below will help explain why our forecasts may in fact prove simply realistic, or even excessively cautious.

Figure 2.5: The population of African countries in 2050 (each box represents 1m people) with colours reflecting Renaissance Capital expectations of political realities

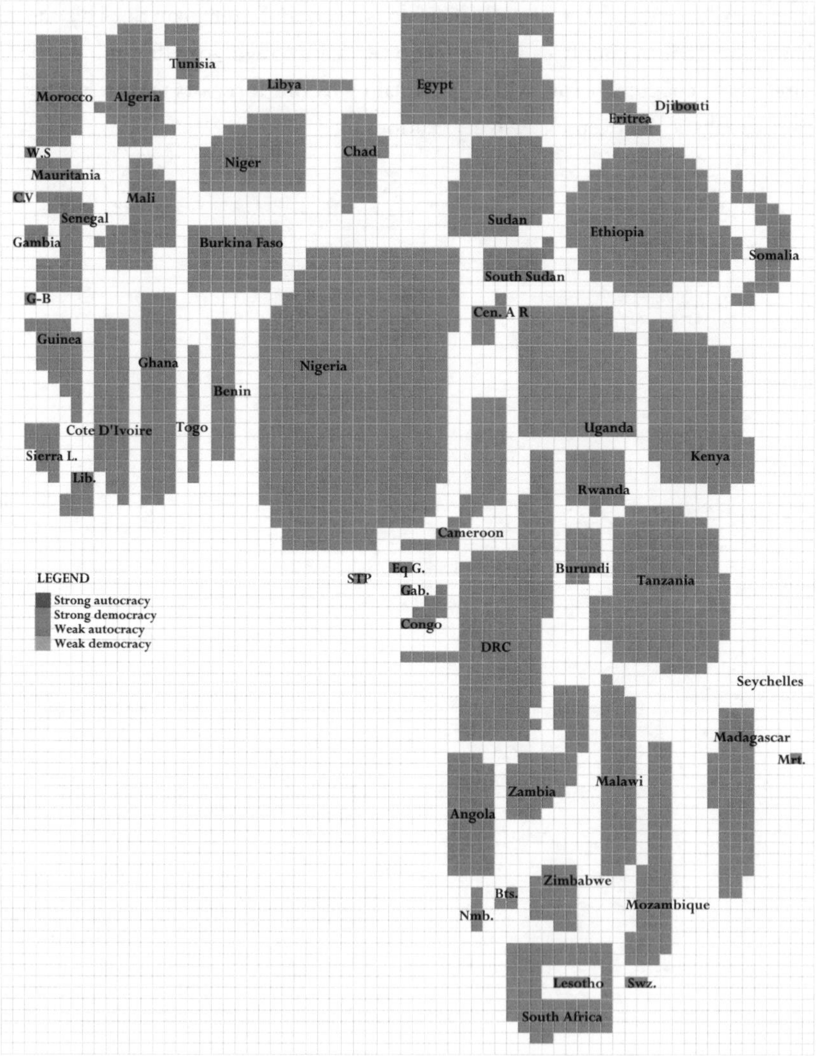

LEGEND
- Strong autocracy
- Strong democracy
- Weak autocracy
- Weak democracy

Source: UN

Figure 2.6: The GDP of Africa's countries in 2050 ($bn, in 2012 dollars) with each box representing $20bn of GDP with colours reflecting the political change

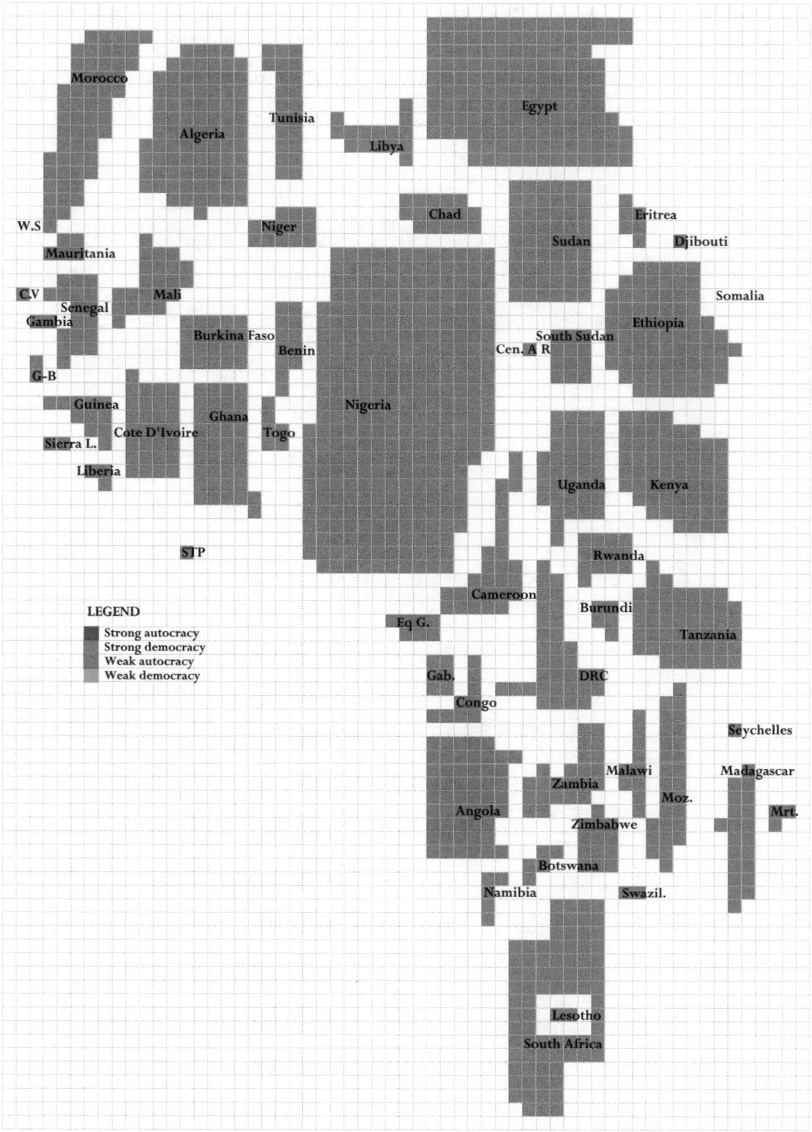

Source: Renaissance Capital estimates

Notes

1. Dani Rodrik and Arvind Subramanian, "From 'Hindu Growth' to Productivity Surge: The Mystery of the Indian Growth Transition," IMF Staff Paper 52, no. 2 (2005), International Monetary Fund, http://www.imf.org/external/pubs/ft/staffp/2005/02/pdf/rodrik1.pdf.

Chapter 3

Counting Accountability: A Maturing Democratic Culture

By Michael Moran and Charles Robertson

Zambia must not go backwards, we must all face the future and go forward as one nation. Not to do so would dishonour our history. ... Did we become grey and lacking in ideas? Did we lose momentum? Our duty now is to go away and reflect on any mistakes we may have made and learn from them. If we do not, we do not deserve to contest power again.

—Zambian President Rupiah Banda conceding defeat in a general election before handing power to the opposition, September 2011

THE 1990s saw a dramatic shift in the African political and geopolitical land-scape. This was a continent beset by internal conflicts, often fuelled by Cold War interventions, with both East and West keen to bolster rulers however undemocratic they might be. Now there are more democracies than autocracies in Africa and fewer conflicts, while violent deaths across Africa have fallen so significantly that travel to parts of the Middle East, Asia and Latin America warrants more concern. It is important to remember the 2011 warnings that the Arab Spring might spread south – when in fact we saw the most successful Nigerian election in history in 2011, an uncontroversial transition of presidential power in Ghana in 2012, and we now hear Kenyan confidence that their 2013 election will reflect the hard work put into widely supported constitutional changes.

There are renewed efforts to deepen regional integration, creating a $1 trillion free trade area among 26 countries, which is encouraging foreign and local investment that can benefit from larger markets. While we believe it would be unwise for these regions to adopt common currencies even in the long term, it is indicative of greatly improved relations within these regions, that this remains a target in west, east and southern Africa. Pessimism and rising mistrust within the eurozone contrasts with the optimism and growing cooperation within key regions of Africa.

Our own research shows that greater economic growth resulting from these improvements is becoming self-reinforcing, as higher wealth leads to democratisation and therefore more responsive government. Greater political stability in turn will address the concerns of those who don't yet invest in Africa, but will take the plunge in the future, so boosting growth as new capital is attracted to the continent, and pushing up per capita GDP. Historically, coups only occur in low-income countries, and no democracy has been overthrown when per capita GDP has been above $10,000 (2005, PPP dollars). Rising wealth is correlated with more democracy in all countries except those where energy production per capita is on par with the Gulf states. From Morocco and Swaziland within 10 years, to nearly the entire continent by 2050, we expect the growing middle class to ensure its voice is heard. The vast majority of Africans will be living in strong democracies by the 2030s.

IN the spring of 2012, when cliques of young military officers in Mali and Guinea-Bissau deposed their elected presidents, the response from Western capitals was predictable. From the foreign ministries of London, Brussels, Washington and London, as well Mali's former colonial ruler, France, and the Portuguese who once ran Guinea-Bissau, calls for an immediate restoration of the elected government rang out. "We believe that grievances should be addressed through dialogue, not through violence," said the State Department's spokeswoman, Victoria Nuland. Ban Ki-Moon, the UN's secretary-general, expressed "deep concern."

Had the reaction ended there, the coup leaders might have followed the path blazed by dozens of previous African military men who toppled their governments during the continent's post-colonial history: execute the deposed leader, exile his family, jail and torture his followers, outlaw his party and declare the army the sole guardian of the nation's soul (and treasury).

Instead, a robust regional reaction – including a trade, credit and membership embargo by the African Union (AU) and the threatened deployment of troops from the Economic Community of West African States (ECOWAS) – quickly isolated the leaders of both rebellions. What's more, the AU and ECOWAS stance emboldened outside players, prompting US and European officials to toughen their own line. Both seized assets of the coup leaders and launched reviews of vital aid programmes.

"What we're seeing is something different, something new," a senior West Africa analyst at America's Central Intelligence Agency told Renaissance Capital. "We've seen these groups send peacekeepers in the past, or seal borders. But the level of coordination here is new. Africans are now imposing a price for the disruption of constitutional order." At the time of writing, Mali's interim leader had just invited ECOWAS to send troops to restore order in the north, where Islamic militants hold sway.

Coups, internal conflicts and terrorism remain risks in parts of Sub-Saharan Africa, to be sure, just as coups in Thailand and unrest across MENA continue to make headlines. But Africa's increasing experience with democracy, bolstered by robust growth rates in many countries, a commodity-price boom, greater access to capital and a less paternalistic relationship with the West, has created a regional consensus that what happens across the border is highly relevant to any nation's destiny. China may have displaced the US as SSA's leading trade partner, but China's posture of non-interference in the affairs of other nations has not been adopted by SSA foreign ministries.

Quite the opposite. Since the end of the Cold War, an abiding lesson for Africa's leaders is that they must mobilise the collective will and resources of regional nations if they are to prevent the kinds of running conflicts that invariably spill trouble into more peaceful, sustainable societies. And, by and large, they are doing just that. With help from Europe or America fickle and often too slow to materialise, African countries increasingly are developing multinational means to meet security challenges. In spite of the high-profile establishment of America's AFRICOM military command, and the less and less frequent forays by France into its former colonial zone, Africa has risen to this challenge. From the Sahel to the Great Lakes, from the Horn to the Atlantic coast, the continent's political leaders have recognised the need to act locally and in coordination to prevent states like Liberia or the DRC or Sudan from teetering towards failure.

An Improving Trend Line

THEY have also begun to transform their own domestic politics. The year-over-year statistics indicate a general move towards geopolitical stability in most of the continent. Widely accepted measures of geopolitical stability and political freedom show the improvement clearly. With regard to constitutional legality, the index of record, the Polity IV series of the Center for Systemic Peace, shows that most of the continent has moved from pure authoritarian rule to something approaching democracy since 1990.

Figure 3.1: Sub-Saharan Africa trends toward democracy, 1990–2008

(N=50)	1990	1995	2000	2005	2008
Average	-5.38	-1.50	-0.82	+0.38	+1.34

Source: www.systemicpeace.org/polity/polity4.htm (accessed: 4 August 2010)
Note: autocracies (-10 to -6), anocracies (-5 to +5) and democracies (+6 to +10)

A very similar trend can be traced through annual Freedom House ratings of the extent of civil and individual liberties in a society. From 1990, when only four of the 53 SSA countries rated ranked as completely free, the number had jumped to nine by 2009 (and, indeed, had topped off at 11 four years earlier – reflecting short-lived post-election violence in Kenya and a coup in Madagascar).

Just as significantly, the number of countries judged as partially free – which can be assumed to be in transition to fuller freedom – grew from 18 to 24. And those lingering under repressive regimes dropped from 30 in 1990 to 20 in 2009.

Figure 3.2: Africa's progress toward freedom, 1990–2009

Year	# of Electoral Democracies	% of EDs in Sub-Saharan Africa	"Free" Democracies	"Partly Free" Democracies
1990	3	7%	3	0
1995	18	38%	8	10
2000	20	42%	8	12
2005	20	42%	11	9
2010	19	40%	9	10
2012	19	39%	9	10

Source: Freedom House[1]

While many of these changes derive from a transformed international environment – the end of the Cold War, primarily – since 1989 other factors, both native and international, have also played a role.

Indeed, coups like those described above occurred at an alarming rate during the last quarter of the 20th century – occasionally, as in Sierra Leone, tipping a previously stable society into a spasm of violence that is only now healing.

For all the improvement in governance within African countries – as well as between them in multilateral institutions – the current alphabet soup of regional economic and political groups hardly provides an efficient check on backsliding. On occasion, for instance, the AU – the continent's political umbrella – has found itself at odds with regional players able to move more quickly or resolutely, whether on economic or political grounds. This has been especially true of Nigeria-dominated ECOWAS, which has led Africa in developing the new interpretation of multilateral action, and the Southern African Development Community, which has tended to tread carefully and take a view of national sovereignty – on Zimbabwe for instance – much more in line with the Chinese model than the Western concept.

Figure 3.3: SSA's tangled multinational web

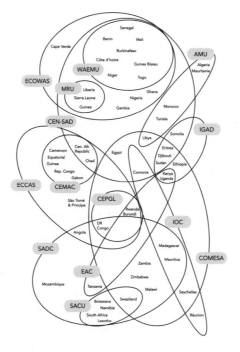

AMU – Arab Maghreb Union
AU – African Union
CEMAC, Economic Community of Central African States
CEN-SAD – Community of Sahel-Saharan States
CEPGL – Economic Community of the Great Lakes Countries
COMESA – Common Market for Eastern and Southern Africa

EAC – East African Community
ECOWAS – Economic Community of West African States
IGAD – Inter-Governmental Authority on Development
IOC – Indian Ocean Commission, **SACU** – Southern African Customs Union
SADC – Southern African Development Community

Source: Wilson Center

Nonetheless, the leaders of several blocs – the East African Community, the Common Market for Eastern and Southern Africa, and the SADC – agreed to work towards the creation of a Grand Free Trade Area that would unite 26 nations with a combined GDP of about $1 trillion and a population of 600 million. Rob Davies, South Africa's minister of trade and industry, has said that a zone including regional economic powers such as Ethiopia, Uganda, Kenya, South Africa, Zimbabwe and Angola, as well as Egypt, could eventually provide the foundation of a broader union including security and other concerns.

Additionally, the AU in 2010 adopted new guidelines requiring specific steps be taken when "unconstitutional changes of government among member states" take place. These steps, seen in action in the case of Guinea-Bissau and Mali, can include broad military action in serious cases and even invoke the controversial "doctrine to protect" in cases of genocide or other atrocities. The AU has been less successful in dealing with leaders who refuse to vacate their posts even after losing elections. But we believe the recent appointment of Nkosazana Dlamini-Zuma shows the AU sees the need to transform itself to boost its credibility on the continent and abroad.

Getting Their Act Together

STILL, to put flesh on such bones, and to create truly workable regional security mechanisms, African countries – acting individually or as groups – need to address a serious capacity problem. For the time being, few interventions on the scale of the AU's deployments in Somalia or Darfur could be sustained – or even begun – without US or European airlifts, intelligence and other logistical help.

African military forces face a number of other challenges, too. By and large, while traditional nation-to-nation wars of the kind fought by Ethiopia and Eritrea in the 1990s have waned, militaries across the region have continued to battle asymmetric threats, such as terrorism. The fallout from Libya's regime collapse – including the spread of Muammar Gaddafi's looted munitions stores across the Sahel – helped fuel a resurgent Tuareg separatist rebellion that contributed to the coup in Mali. Vast areas of the sparsely populated Sahel also serve as staging areas for Islamic extremists, including Al-Qaeda in the Islamic Maghreb, as well as messianic gangs such as Joseph Kony's Lord's Resistance Army, once the bane of northern Uganda but now largely confined to the Central African Republic and parts of the DRC.

Similarly, rebels in the Nigerian Delta and Boko Haram Islamists in the north of the country, warlords and ethnic militias in DRC and Somalia, rebels in Ethiopia's restive Ogaden region, and tensions between Sudan and the newly in-dependent state of South Sudan, all stand as challenges that will require improved capabilities by central governments and multinational institutions.

Most African states do not spend significantly on defence. According to SIPRI, the Swedish security think tank, most spend less than 2% of GDP on military forces, against 2.5% of GDP globally. With a few exceptions (Algeria, Angola and Sudan during long civil wars; Rwanda during its mid-1990s tumult; Chad, and Burundi and Uganda, as their forces became embroiled in Darfur and the DRC, respectively; and Eritrea), there has been no upsurge in defence spending in SSA when measured against the growth of regional economies.

Figure 3.4: Defence spending by region, 2011 ($ billion)

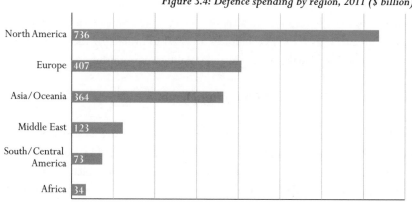

Source: SIPRI

Our own calculations suggest defence spending was 1.6% of GDP in 2012 or $35 billion, which is the equivalent of buying nearly four new US aircraft carriers for the whole continent. Based on our GDP calculations, 1.6% of GDP means defence spending will reach $58 billion in 2020 in 2012 dollars, $119 billion by

2030 and $471 billion by 2050. Renaissance expects the democratisation wave to reduce the risk of conflict, given the old (and 99% accurate) saying that democracies do not go to war with each other. So our base case is no rise in spending as a share of GDP.

The spending stemming from growth could help address the capacity problem many African military forces face. The legacy of authoritarian years, when defence resources were distributed as much for patronage as strategic reasons, has left even the larger military forces on the continent with aging, often inappropriate weapons typically transferred from Soviet or Western European militaries during the Cold War.

Now, militaries are being tailored to do what they should do: protect the nation. Besides the anti-terror training and joint operations with the US military, most of which focus on the Sahel and Maghreb, bilateral and AU efforts to police internal migration in the continent and the narcotics trade, as well as to track criminal syndicates, are all gaining momentum.

Given the West's outdated image of Africa, the idea of greater resources being devoted to local military and security forces has raised hackles in some quarters. However, to the extent that they provide professional capacity for established military forces – and assuming the democratising wave that has washed over the continent continues to soak deeper into government and military and police bureaucracies – the expenditures are vital to protecting the progress that greater economic growth, education and stability are promising.

A Changing Dynamic

INDEED, while conflicts rage in several corners, most of Africa today is at peace. Contrary to its grim reputation, the number of people killed in violent conflict – direct conflict deaths, as political scientists categorize such violence – has been diminishing for over a decade. Such deaths account for a relatively small proportion of violent deaths globally – about 10% or 55,000 per year across the world. (By far the largest proportion of violent deaths – some 396,000 per year – are intentional homicides - i.e., murder, according to the Geneva Declaration on Armed Conflict and Development.[3])

With regard to direct conflict deaths, Africa's share has been falling more quickly than other regions – particularly South and Central America and the

Middle East. In the middle of the last decade, only the DRC, Sudan and Somalia were among the top-10 most deadly countries.

Figure 3.5: Direct conflict deaths, most deadly countries, 2004–2007

Conflicts	Direct conflict deaths	% of total conflict deaths
1. Iraq	76,266	36.6%
2. Sudan	12,719	6.1%
3. Afghanistan	12.417	6.0%
4. Colombia	11,832	5.7%
5. DRC	9,346	4.5%
6. Sri Lanka	9,065	4.4%
7. India	8,433	4.0%
8. Somalia	8,424	4.0%
9. Nepal	7,286	3.5%
10. Pakistan	6,581	3.2%

Source: Global Burden of Armed Violence, Geneva Declaration on Armed Conflict and Development

Two years later, and using a broader measure of violence, Africa had fallen further down the list. Using deaths per 100,000 people, the Geneva Declaration's researchers found that by 2009, the DRC no longer ranked among the 30 most violent countries in the world. Only five of the 48 countries in SSA show up in the top 30, and in two of them – South Africa and Uganda – the cause is a high homicide rate, not civil violence. Only Somalia, Sudan and Burundi rank high because of such violence; furthermore, in all five of these SSA countries, the 2009 rates were an improvement on the 2004 figures. By comparison, such well-worn tourist destinations at the Bahamas, Jamaica and Puerto Rico rank above most of them.

Figure 3.6: Violent deaths per 100,000 population, 2004 and 2009[2]

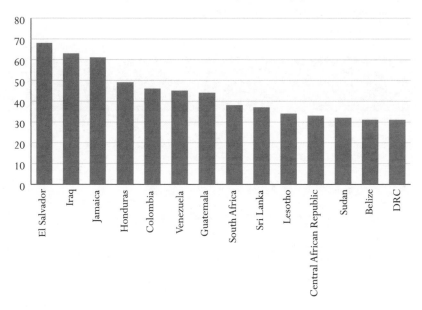

Source: UN/Global Burden of Armed Violence, 2011 database

Africa Goes Global

THE stabilization of African societies – helped along by strides in governance, progress against corruption, improved child care and metrics like access to health services and infant mortality – has also bolstered the continent's demands for a voice in the larger world. With the addition of South Africa to the BRICS, officials in Johannesburg realized a long-held dream – that Africa would gain a voice in one of the world's leading forums, rather than have to rely, as in years past, on European or non-aligned proxies. Nigeria and Egypt may resent their exclusion from the G-20 club of major economies, but can take solace in the fact that their growth rates will see them leap-frog past many European economies probably within a decade.

There is a growing clamour, meanwhile, for the addition of major new players to the world's premier international geopolitical body – the UN Security Council. Previous proposals at reform – adding, say, a champion from Latin America, Africa, the Arab world and East Asia, plus the large economies of Japan, India and Germany – have all failed due to the existence of a veto in the hands of the so-called P5, the five permanent members – the US, China, Russia, France and Britain.

That mix looks increasingly out of touch with the 21st century world, and even European diplomats have conceded as much. Agreeing on which new powers should join the "P" club – let alone on what terms – has proved impossible. The prerogatives of the P5 will not be stripped away easily, as was recently shown by the decision of the US to impose its preferred candidate as World Bank president rather than back a more qualified African, Nigerian Finance Minister Ngozi Okonjo-Iweala.

Most Security Council reform plans have fallen victim to regional rivalries. For every logical addition (Nigeria, for instance, the most populous nation in SSA) a rival emerges to challenge (South Africa, though its challenge based on GDP will not be sustainable for long).

The AU, too, has stumbled on this issue – with South Africa, Nigeria and Egypt all insisting they should represent the continent. This situation plagues other regions, as well – India versus Pakistan, Brazil versus Mexico, Indonesia versus South Korea (the latter being China's preference). For now, Africa may have to settle for the old rules at the UN even if its increasing clout and right to be heard is widely acknowledged.

What Growing GDP Implies for Democratisation

THE spread of democracy should be largely complete across Africa by 2050, less than 100 years after most countries achieved independence. Rising wealth guarantees this for all countries except energy exporters. The 30 democracies, as labelled by the Polity IV database, or Freedom House, or by us (we include Tunisia, Libya and Egypt), should be roughly 50 by 2050, based on methodology we demonstrated in *Frontier and Emerging Markets: The Revolutionary Nature of Growth*.[4]

The table below shows that just five democracies in Africa in 2012 have a per capita GDP of $10,000 (2005, PPP dollars), which is the crucial threshold above which no democracy has ever died. Weimar Germany lost democracy with an income level around half that level, while the Roman republic (if unlike us, you could consider a slave-owning society to be democratic) lost its form of democracy at $1,000. Of those above $10,000 today, Botswana and Mauritius both record such high scores from the Polity IV rating database that we classify them as strong democracies. Gabon and Seychelles can be classed as weak democracies due to their low Polity IV rating or the "partly free" label from Freedom House. We include Libya, too, after its debut June 2012 free elections. South Africa will join this group, as a strong democracy, in 2013, and based on our GDP estimates, Algeria's weak democracy will also become immortal (but quite possibly still weak) in 2016. Namibia, Cape Verde and Egypt will join them in the 2020s, followed by a larger wave including Nigeria, Ghana and Zambia in the 2030s. The only threat to immortal democracies is if their per capita GDP slips back below $10,000.

The risk to democracy is highest at very low income levels, but plunges to negligible levels of less than a 1% chance each year, once per capita income rises above $6,000. There are only five cases in history where democracy has died above this level (Greece, Argentina, Iran, Venezuela and Thailand). Very safe but not immortal African democracies include Algeria, South Africa and Namibia, which already have per capita GDP above $6,000. Based on our growth estimates for Africa as a whole, Egypt could join this very safe group in 2014 if it gets through the next two years. Cape Verde will join in 2019, followed by Nigeria and Djibouti in 2029. A large share of the African continent will have very safe democracy in the 2030s, as Ghana, Kenya, South Sudan, Zimbabwe, Ethiopia, Sierra Leone, and others cross this $6,000 threshold. In 2050, the DRC will be the last of the (current) democracies to cross that threshold.

The next-most-important threshold is $2,000, above which point the risk of democracy dying nearly halves from a range of 4–8% per annum for very low incomes to less than 4%. Nigeria made this transition in 2009. Ghana will join it before the 2016 elections, and Kenya should join before the 2020 elections. Ethiopia, Madagascar and others will become significantly more stable democracies in the 2020s.

This still leaves 12 strong democracies and seven weak democracies in Africa with per capita income below $2,000, which does mean the risk of a coup is a serious 4–8% per annum, and one to two very low-income African states can be expected to lose democracy each year. Indeed, the strong democracies of Mali and Guinea-Bissau were in this group until early 2012, so two of what were 21 democracies did die this year. Of the 19 low-income democracies today, nine will graduate to a safer status this decade, and a further five in the 2020s, including Zimbabwe. Africa's democracies are getting safer with every dollar of GDP growth.

Figure 3.7: Democracies (strong or weak as per Polity IV scale) and when they become less vulnerable

Per capita income level	10,000 +		6,000-10,000		3,500-6,000		2,000-3,500		Less than 2,000	
Risk to democracy	Immortal democracies		Less than 1% chance of losing democracy per annum		Less than 3% chance of losing democracy		Less than 4% chance of losing democracy		Up to 8% chance of losing democracy each year	
Current status in bold	Botswana	Strong	Algeria	Weak	Cape Verde	Strong	Nigeria	Weak	Benin	Strong
	Gabon	Weak	South Africa	Strong	Egypt	n/a			Burkina Faso	Weak
	Mauritius	Strong	Namibia	Strong					Burundi	Strong
	Seychelles	Weak	Tunisia	n/a					Comoros	Strong
	Libya	n/a							DRC	Weak
Dates when countries enter a lower risk period									Dijbouti	Weak
	South Africa (2013)		Egypt (2014)		Nigeria (2021)		Sao Tome and Principe (2014)		Ethiopia	Weak
	Tunisia (2015)		Cape Verde (2019)		Djibouti (2021)		Ghana (2015)		Ghana	Strong
	Algeria (2016)		Nigeria (2029)		Lesotho (2024)		Djibouti (2015)			
	Nambia (2021)		Djiboutie (2029)		Sao Tome and Principe (2024)		Senegal (2015)		Kenya	Strong
	Egypt (2023)		Sao Tome and Principe (2031)		Ghana (2025)		Lesotho (2016)		Lesotho	Strong
	Cape Verde (2026)		Lesotho (2031)		Zambia (2026)		Kenya (2018)		Liberia	Strong
	Djibouti (2035)		Ghana (2033)		Kenya (2027)		Zambia (2018)		Malawi	Strong
	Lesotho (2036)		Senegal (2034)		Benin (2029)		Benin (2019)		Madagascar	Weak
	Nigeria (2037)		Zambia (2034)		Senegal (2029)		Zaimbabwe (2022)		Mozambique	Weak
	Sao Tome and Principe (2037)		Kenya (2035)		Zimbabwe (2029)		Ethopia (2024)		Senegal	Strong
	Ghana (2038)		Zimbabwe (2036)		Ethiopia (2032)		Burkina Faso (2024)		Sierra Leone	Strong
	Senegal (2039)		Benin (2036)		Sierra Leone (2032)		Sierra Leone (2024)		Sao Tome and Principe	Strong
	Zambia (2039)		Ethiopia (2038)		Burkina Faso (2033)		Madagascar (2028)		Zambia	Strong
	Kenya (2040)				Comoros (2034)		Comoros (2029)		Zimbabwe	Weak

Figure 3.7 continued

Per capita income level	10,000 +	6,000-10,000	3,500-6,000	2,000-3,500	Less than 2,000
	Zimbabwe (2040)	Sierra Leone (2038)	Mozambique (2035)	Mozambique (2030)	
	Benin (2041)	Burkina Faso (2039)	Madagascar (2037)	Burundi (2032)	
	Ethiopia (2042)	Comoros (2040)	Burundi (2038)	Malawi (2032)	
	Sierra Leone (2043)	Mozambique (2040)	Malawai (2039)	Liberia (2035)	
	Burkina Faso (2045)	Madagascar (2042)	Liberia (2040)	DRC (2039)	
	Comoros (2045)	Burundi (2043)	DRC (2045)		
	Mozambique (2045)	Malawi (2045)			
	Burundi (2047)	Liberia (2046)			
	Madagascar (2047)	DRC (2050)			
	Malawi (2050)				
	DRC (post-2050)				
	Liberia (post-2050)				

Source: Polity IV database, Renaissance Capital, World Bank, Freedom House

The Next Democratisation Wave

THERE are roughly 23 autocracies in Africa (excluding Somalia) and all except Equatorial Guinea are vulnerable to democratisation at any time. The greatest likelihood of democratisation is when per capita income is in the $6,000–10,000 range. It is at this level when middle-class demands for stronger political representation reach their peak. Tunisia crossed this level in 2000 and from that point on, there was a 6–7% annual chance of its autocratic regime falling to middle-class protests. It took until 2011 before this finally happened. The revolution was predictable. The trigger was not.

The four African autocracies most likely to become democracies, based on per capita GDP data alone, are Angola, Morocco, the Republic of Congo and Swaziland. In their $3,500–6,000 per capita GDP range, the chance is 5% annually. This will rise to 6–7% annually as Angola in 2014, followed by Swaziland in 2015 and Morocco in 2017, as they cross the $6,000 mark. The Republic of

Congo will follow in 2021. We will be very surprised if Morocco and Swaziland are still classified as autocracies within 15 years when their per capita income will be around $10,000. Democracy could of course emerge at any point before then.

Figure 3.8: The spread of democratisation – timing vs per capita GDP

Above 19,000	10,000-19,000	6,000-10,000	3,500-6,000	Less than 3,500
Zero Current status in bold	3-4% chance	6-7% chance	5% chance	3-4% chance
Equatorial Guinea Weak			Angola Weak	Cameroon Weak
			Morocco Strong	Central African Republic Weak
Angola (2044)	Swaziland (2023)	Angola (2014)	Congo, Republic of Weak	Chad Weak
Congo, Republic of (2049)	Angola (2024)	Swazland (2015)	Swaziland Strong	Cote D'Ivoire n/a
South Sudan (post-2050)	Morocco (2024)	Morocco (2017)		Eritrea Strong
	Congo, Republic of (2028)	Congo, Republic of (2021)	Mauritania (2020)	Guinea Weak
	Mauritania (2035)	Mauritania (2028)	Cameroon (2022)	Mali n/a
	Cameroon (2036)	Cameroon (2029)	South Sudan (2023)	Mauritania Weak
	Sudan (2039)	Sudan (2033)	Sudan (2025)	Niger Weak
	The Gambia (2039)	Cote D'Ivoire (2034)	The Gambia (2025)	Rwanda Weak
	Cote D'Ivoire (2039)	South Sudan (2035)	Cote D'Ivoire (2025)	Sudan Weak
	South Sudan (2040)	The Gambia (2034)	Chad (2029)	South Sudan n/a
	Guinea-Bissau (2043)	Chad (2037)	Tanzania (2030)	Tanzania Weak
	Rwanda (2044)	Guinea-Bissau (2038)	Guinea-Bissau (2031)	The Gambia Weak
	Tanzania (2044)	Rwanda (2038)	Rwanda (2032)	Togo Weak
	Uganda (2044)	Tanzania (2038)	Togo (2033)	Uganda Weak
	Togo (2044)	Togo (2039)	Uganda (2033)	Guinea - Bissau n/a
	Guinea (2045)	Uganda (2039)	Guinea (2034)	
	Mali (2046)	Guinea (2040)	Mali (2035)	
	Central African Republic (2046)	Central African Republic (2041)	Central African Republic (2036)	
	Eritrea (2050)	Mali (2041)	Eritrea (2040)	
	Niger (post-2050)	Eritrea (2045)	Niger (2040)	
		Niger (2047)		

Source: Polity IV database, Renaissance Capital, World Bank, Freedom House

The odds of the poorest African autocracies becoming democracies is 3–4% annually, but will rise to 5% for seven countries in the 2020s. These will be Mauritania (from 2020), Cameroon (2022), South Sudan (2023), Sudan (2025), The Gambia (2025), Côte D'Ivoire (2025) and Chad (2029), with Mauritania and Cameroon very likely to democratise before 2030 when their per capita income reaches $10,000. The largest autocracies by population include Uganda and Tanzania. They are likely to be classified as democracies no later than 2040.

The last autocracies in Africa will be energy producers and those countries furthest from advancing their per capita GDP into the $6,000-10,000 range. The latter will consist of just Guinea, Central African Republic, Mali, Eritrea and Niger, which should enter that per capita income range in the 2040s. Renaissance sees no significant chance of any African autocracy that is not an oil exporter reaching per capita GDP of $19,000, so we have included only oil exporters in that per capita income category.

While nearly all of Africa's autocracies will have become democracies by the 2040s, this could of course happen much sooner. We have often seen waves of political revolution start in rich countries and then spread to poorer countries. Examples include the Latin American independence movement in the 1810s, the African independence movements of the 1950s and 1960s, the fall of Eastern European communism in 1989–91, and the Arab Spring, which started in rich Tunisia and engulfed much poorer Syria and Yemen. A similar contagion of political change may spread across equatorial Africa well before 2040.

Renaissance believes the last autocracies will be falling in the 2040s, with the exception of a few energy exporters. The autocracies that have survived the turbulent $6,000-10,000 per capita GDP range, and seen per capita GDP reach $19,000, have so far proved as enduring as democracies above $10,000. They are Qatar, the UAE, Brunei Darussalam, Kuwait, Singapore, Bahrain, Equatorial Guinea, Oman and Saudi Arabia. With the exception of the city-state of Singapore, all are energy exporters. High exports per capita tend to neutralise the "taxation and representation" political debate. This does not mean these countries will always remain autocracies – the exhaustion of energy wealth would change the equation. But for now, we cannot assume democratisation in countries with high energy exports per capita and high per capita GDP, so Equatorial Guinea should prove as stable as Saudi Arabia and Oman, at least until its oil runs out.

Figure 3.9: Net oil and natural gas exports per capita (capped on both scales), 2010, with country political ratings from Polity IV (2009 data)

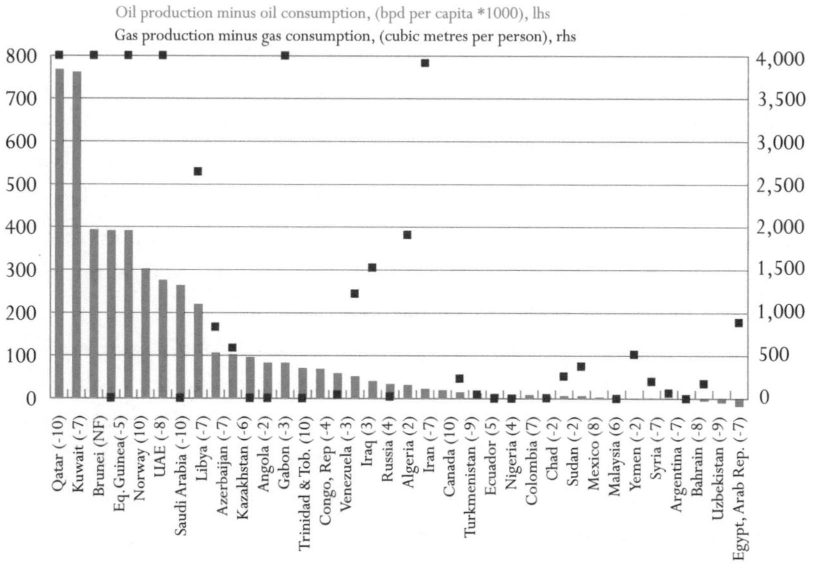

Oil production minus oil consumption, (bpd per capita *1000), lhs
Gas production minus gas consumption, (cubic metres per person), rhs

Source: BP, UN, EIA, Polity IV, Renaissance Capital estimates

Where we are uncertain about the outlook is in countries such as Angola, the Republic of Congo and South Sudan. They do not have Gulf levels of per capita energy exports. But the only strong democracies that export more energy per capita than these three are Norway (like Canada, a democracy before it ever exported energy) and Trinidad and Tobago (a democracy since independence from the UK). Democracy in Iraq and Libya came via external intervention. Russia and Algeria are weak democracies that export amounts of oil similar to South Sudan and Angola. Gabon's transition from weak autocracy to weak democracy in 2009 occurred as it held the first election not contested by the late President Omar Bongo, although it was won by his son. The examples of transition from autocracy to democracy are few and far between. The only guidance we can offer for Angola, the Republic of Congo and South Sudan is that without oil they would likely be democracies within 20 years. With oil, they may remain autocracies for decades.

Providing our growth trajectory for Africa is broadly accurate, we can be confident that two billion Africans will be living in strong democracies by 2050.

Democracy, GDP per Capita and Corruption

Corruption is widespread in Africa. Transparency International gives an annual reminder of how Africa is perceived by its contributors – not all of whom have been to the countries they give scores for. But no one can deny it is a problem. Take a meeting at the Nigerian central bank and you'll see the public information notices decrying the corrosive problem of corruption. Visit Rwanda and the low level of corruption will be cited by all you meet. President Paul Kagame's efforts to emulate Singapore's success in fighting corruption are working, and show what an African country can achieve. But Rwanda is so remarkable because it is the exception rather than the rule.

We do not believe African corruption is special. Financial gain has often accrued to unchecked political leaders, from feudal Europe to the wealthy businessmen (so-called robber barons) who were often accused of excessive power during US industrialisation. Corruption is normal at low income levels, and tends to decrease as per capita wealth rises. The question is how and when will African countries improve their rankings.

Our work suggests that democratisation is not the key driver for reducing corruption, despite the contribution of a free media to rooting it out. The vibrancy of the Nigerian press is widely known. Yet from Romania to the Philippines, the corrupt "solution" to a free press is simply to bribe the journalist, or failing that, to bribe the newspaper proprietor.

What the data show is that the link between political regime and corruption perceptions is weak. Below we group together countries by their Polity IV ratings, and then find the average corruption perceptions index score of that group of countries. If democracy prevented corruption, then the most democratic countries (+10 on the Polity IV scale) should have the least corruption, and there should be a steady rise in corruption scores as we slide down the scale of democracy.

What we find is that the very best average corruption score of 6.6 is indeed the average of the 34 most democratic countries, those that score the maximum +10 on the Polity IV scale. However, once we drop even one notch on the democratisation score to +9, the corruption figure plummets to 3.8. By the time we are at Turkey or Zambia's +7 (i.e. still strong democracy) score on the Polity IV scale, the average corruption figure is a very poor 2.9, which is the same as that recorded by the 11 countries such as China and Belarus whose average Polity IV democracy rating is an autocratic -7. Even more at odds with the "democracy equals low corruption thesis" are the good transparency scores of 5.6 and 5.8 recorded by some of the least democratic countries in the world.

Figure 3.10: Democracy is not strongly correlated with corruption

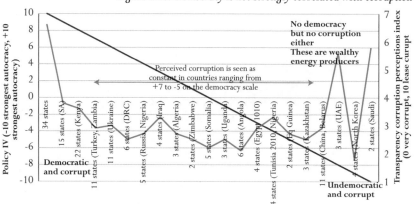

Source: Renaissance Capital estimates, Transparency International, Polity IV

Instead of democracy, a better determinant of a corruption score is the per capita wealth level. African countries generally score worse than richer Western countries in the Transparency International survey because they are poorer than the rich West. This is why rich Gulf countries record good scores on the survey, while poor democracies like the Philippines have low scores.

Figure 3.11: Corruption perceptions index against per capita GDP

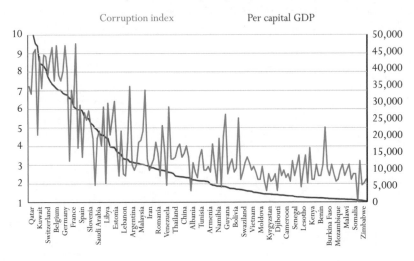

Source: Transparency International, Renaissance Capital

It is no surprise, then, that the African countries scoring best in the Transparency International corruption perceptions survey of 2011 are Botswana (32nd place), Cape Verde (41st place), Mauritius (46th), Namibia (57th), South Africa (64th) and Tunisia (73rd). This is simply a roll call of Africa's richest countries, including some small, rich countries. There are honourable exceptions, such as Rwanda in 49th place despite its very low per capita GDP. But the main message is that as African countries get richer, they will succeed in reducing corruption.

Indeed, between 2001 and 2011, of the SSA countries (excluding South Africa) continuously covered by Transparency International, nine countries improved their ratings by a combined 5.1 points (averaging 0.6 each), while four saw a decline of a combined 2 points. Nigeria showed the third-best improvement of the 90 countries over this 10-year period.

Our analysis suggests that countries with per capita GDP from $0-2,500 in 2011 averaged a corruption score of 2.5, but by the time this entered the $15,000-20,000 range, the corruption score was far better at 4.8. Based on Renaissance forecasts, SSA will not reach this level even by 2050 in constant 2012 dollars. However, there should be a 24% improvement in the corruption score to 3.1 by 2023–35, when average per capita GDP will have risen from $1,670 in 2012 to $2,500–5,000. An additional 10% improvement will be added in the subsequent decade. Governments can support the process; higher growth is not the only reason Nigeria's score has improved so much since 2001. Making it easier to do business and reducing the bureaucratic scope for corruption (as outlined in chapter 4) will help, too.

Corruption and Financial Market Investors

RENAISSANCE concludes that equity investors prefer less-corrupt countries, but debt investors do invest in the bonds of more-corrupt countries. As we have established that corruption perceptions generally track per capita GDP, we can also show when countries are outliers to the average score. There are twice as many African outliers on the positive side (less corrupt than they should be) than the negative side.

Around the world, there are many countries that have a worse corruption rating than their per capita GDP would imply, with Trinidad and Tobago as the most extreme, with a corruption score at 3.2 points a full four points worse than the average of 7.5 for countries with its per capita GDP. Others include Italy, Greece and a number of oil producers, such as Venezuela. They tend to be markets that are normally favoured by debt investors that can sue emerging-market governments in international courts when they default. In Africa, oil producers from Libya to Equatorial Guinea, Angola and Gabon are all seen as more corrupt than their wealth levels suggest they should be.

Figure 3.12: Corruption perceptions score compared with the average of countries with similar per capita GDP (Polity IV democracy rating in brackets)

Minus 3	Minus 2	Minus 1	Average	Average	Average	Plus 1	Plus 2	Plus 3
Libya (-7)	Equatorial Guinea (-5)	Angola (-2)	Tunisia	Kenya	Mauritania	Burkina Faso (0)	Cape Verde (10)	Botswana (8)
	Somalia (0)	Burundi (6)	Algeria	Tanzania	Senegal	Gambia (-5)	Mauritius (10)	
		Gabon (3)	Egypt	Chad	Uganda	Ghana (8)	Rwanda (-4)	
		Sudan (-2)	Swaziland	Comoros	Benin	Lesotho (8)		
			Morocco	Sierra Leone	Mali	Liberia (6)		
			Djibouti	Guinea	Guinea-Bissau	Madagascar (0)		
			Nigeria	Central African Republic	Mozambique	Malawi (6)		
			Niger	Eritrea	Togo	Namibia (6)		
			Congo Republic	DRC	Ethiopia	South Africa (9)		
						Zambia (7)		

Source: Transparency International, Polity IV, IMF, Renaissance Capital

While it may surprise some, there really is nothing special about corruption in the big markets of Nigeria, Kenya, Algeria, Morocco and Egypt, or in Uganda, Ethiopia and Tanzania. They all record corruption scores in line with what their per capita GDP figure implies, a correlation that is paralleled in most developed countries.

Countries that are surprisingly less corrupt than their wealth implies are often favoured by equity investors, including Turkey, Poland, Singapore and Chile in the emerging markets. Presumably this is because fund managers believe that a less corrupt system is likely to treat foreign minority investors better, that companies are better able to get on with business rather than greasing the palms of officials, and that the judicial system may be more reliable when things go wrong.

In Africa, the number of countries outperforming what per capita GDP implies is 14, double the seven that are more corrupt than they should be. At the extreme is Botswana, which is in danger of getting labelled "boringly perfect" in this book. Cape Verde, Mauritius and Rwanda all score very well. This may help explain investor appetite for Rwanda's IPOs of its Bralirwa Brewery and Bank of Kigali in 2011.

Who else do equity investors love? South Africa itself is less corrupt than it should be, though it is testimony to the high standards in that country that South African fund managers probably doubt this is true. Global investors will find it relatively easy to like the South African market, though.

Zambia also scores well, and its ability to launch a previously unknown company, Zambeef, onto the London Stock Exchange again supports this thesis. Ghana is a good performer, too, but this won't surprise anyone, especially not the Nigerians flying to Accra each weekend. The main problem for equity investors is the lack of liquidity in the market.

Fifty Democracies by 2050

WHAT the GDP link shows very clearly is that Africa has to be analysed in the context of its existing wealth levels. It is premature to expect strong, entrenched democracy and low corruption across the continent when the middle class is not yet large enough to ensure either. Yet the growing wealth of the fastest billion is already having an impact and will transform African politics. The same rise in GDP will ensure a reduction in corruption, which is already lower than it should be in 14 African countries. And those countries that outperform in reducing corruption will likely be the winners in terms of attracting equity investors. The 30 or so democracies across the continent today will become less fragile and eventually immortal democracies, with South Africa joining that illustrious group as soon as 2013. Democratisation has been the clear trend of the past 20 years and will spread, with at least two new democracies (Morocco and Swaziland) within a decade and most others to follow by the 2030s and 2040s, giving a total of 50 democracies by 2050.

Notes

1. Freedom House criteria:
- A competitive, multiparty political system.
- Universal adult suffrage for all citizens (with exceptions for restrictions that states may legitimately place on citizens as sanctions for criminal offenses).
- Regularly contested elections conducted in conditions of ballot secrecy, reasonable ballot security, and the absence of massive voter fraud that yields results that are unrepresentative of the public will.
- Significant public access of major political parties to the electorate through the media and through generally open political campaigning.
- Additional note: The presence of certain irregularities during the electoral process does not automatically disqualify a country from being designated an electoral democracy. A country cannot be an electoral democracy if significant authority for national decisions resides in the hands of an unelected power, whether a monarch or a foreign or international authority. A country is removed from the ranks of electoral democracies if its last national elections were not sufficiently free or fair, or if changes in law significantly eroded the public's opportunity for electoral choice.
2. The GBAV omitted the DRC from this figure due to a lack of reliable statistics for the period. Almost certainly, it would have ranked in the top 10 due to deaths during its long civil war.
3. http://www.genevadeclaration.org/the-geneva-declaration/what-is-the-declaration.html.
4. Charles Robertson et al., *Frontier and Emerging Markets: The Revolutionary Nature of Growth*, Renaissance Capital, 22 June 2011.

Chapter 4

Unleashing the Private Sector

While everyone is impatient for change, myself included, we know that it will take time to undo the damage done by generations of misrule and to establish a strong foundation for the future. But we are on our way.

—Ellen Johnson Sirleaf, Nobel laureate, president, Republic of Liberia[1]

By Charles Robertson

WITH all of the advantages that Africa has to offer the investor, business can only flourish if the support is in place for it to do so. Vital factors include a legal framework that can be enforced, ease of entry into the markets, taxation levels that reward endeavour, an infrastructure that provides energy and transport and social policies that ensure people's commitment.

Below we demonstrate the steps that Africa, amidst little fanfare, has already taken. The private sector is being unleashed. The results are quite extraordinary, with examples showing the creation of new businesses across Africa at a rate that has vastly exceeded results over the previous decade, with the role of the entrepreneur being central to this progress. These achievements are not limited to just a few countries: they are an Africa-wide phenomenon. Some of the elements of producing ease of business are a common issue across the continent – energy provision being the most apparent. Transport can run a close second, more so for certain countries. But the continent has improved its position relative to the world in dramatic fashion.

There are two key reasons to assume continued improvement in the coming years. First, Africans proved they can reform as well as anyone else in the world when Rwanda became the first Sub-Saharan African state to top the list for "most improved reformer" in the World Bank's 2010 Doing Business survey.[2] Second, the room for further gains is significant. Since developed markets tend to cluster around best practice (Greece is an exception), there is not much room to improve the business climate and reap productivity benefits as a result. In Africa, even after the progress made in recent years – the World Economic Forum's 2012–13 report saw Nigeria jump 12 places, with Ghana and Zambia also rising 11 places[3] – great gains are there for the taking.

The outlook can only get better, with African nations challenging the best in the world in being open for business. Their success in driving macro and micro reforms in tandem is building opportunities for business that are among the most exciting in the world.

Admittedly, even talking about the "ease of doing business" may sound a little odd if you've ever tried to process a Nigerian visa, sat in a Nairobi traffic jam or had to use the light from your iPad to find the hotel bar as the local generator cuts out in Rwanda. But doing business is getting easier. Nigeria is considering the introduction of "on arrival" visas. The traffic jams in Kenya are partially caused by massive road-building projects that will improve capacity and journey times. The hotel bar in Kigali stays lit for your meeting and the WiFi still enables a candle-lit call home even during a power cut.

As a rule, entrepreneurs persevere. In Lagos, for instance, Aishetu Dozie, one of a growing number of Western-trained businesspeople returning home to set up shop, decided she did not like the child care options she had for her son after school. Having worked as a banker in the US, and with Nigeria's middle class booming, she decided to open a franchise of a US company called Gymboree that specialises in creative child care.

"I gave it a lot of thought and was disappointed with how unimaginative I was being," she wrote on her blog. "Where would local content activities be if I became a Gymboree master franchisee? If you look around Nigeria, we are short on local brands! Coca Cola, 7UP, MTN, PZ Cussons, Apple, Dark & Lovely, Nivea, Chivita, Indomie, Nestlé, Cadbury, and the list goes on. I wanted to actually create something."

Instead, she opened her own successful independent day care facility called Paloo's Place, named after her son.

Then there is Roland Agambire, CEO of RLG Communications, a manufacturer of consumer electronics in Ghana. Born as one of 50 siblings to a desperately poor family in Sirigu, a town in the country's Northern Region, Agambire had a sense of determination early on. His mother was the sixth of his father's 10 wives.

He told an interviewer recently that as a boy, he often scoured the pavements with his siblings outside local bars for dropped coins. But he spent those coins wisely: on education. Later, to pay tuition at Navrongo Secondary School, he spent summers in Accra pushing hand trucks and doing anything he could to augment his savings. But poverty just "toughened him up" and made him determined to succeed.[4]

These are symbolic of more far-reaching changes. In the latest Doing Business survey for 2012, of the top-40 countries, six are Asian emerging markets, six are in central Europe and none is in Latin America. Mauritius and South Africa are the spearhead for Africa. Also among the top 50% of countries globally are Rwanda, Tunisia, Botswana, Ghana, Namibia and Zambia. Each ranks well above China, Brazil, India and Russia.

These rankings are relative, so while they draw attention, they do not demonstrate absolute improvement. If all countries improve by 5%, the rankings will not change, but the economies will be better off. So it is the components of the rankings which warrant more attention, as these demonstrate improvement (or not) over time.

Starting a Business

IT is widely accepted that small and medium businesses are the engine of development, representing entrepreneurism, and job creation. To start a business in Germany in 2004 took some 45 days – today this has been slashed to 15 days, which may be one factor behind Germany's relative strength in the eurozone. In the dynamic US, the figure is just 6 days, as it is in Mauritius, too. But in Rwanda, your weekend dream to set up a business could see it registered three days later, with the completion of just two procedures. In the African population giants of Egypt and Ethiopia, it requires only seven and nine days respectively. Their SMEs are likely to prove dynamos of economic growth.

Figure 4.1: Starting a new business – days required, 2004 and 2012

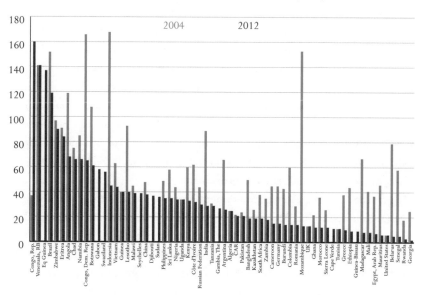

Source: Renaissance Capital estimates

Easier registration of new companies also helps formalise economies, so should lead to better tax collection, while in turn giving government the data it needs to direct investment spending. In Rwanda, reforms that saw the registration period fall from 18 days to three also led to 6,000 new companies being registered in 2011, about equal to the number registered in the previous five years. No doubt rolling out broadband throughout Rwanda has been better directed with the help of these data, and in turn, broadband access will see the birth of many more companies to take advantage of the new opportunities.

There is room for improvement in much of Africa – the average for 32 countries is still 33 days to start a new business. Nigeria requires 34 days, but this has been cut by a quarter from 44 days in 2004. In Kenya, the time has nearly halved to 33 days, in South Africa it has halved to 19 days, and in Sierra Leone it has more than halved to 12 days. Mozambique has managed to slash the time by 90% to 13 days. In Portuguese-speaking Brazil, it still requires four months, but Brazilians need not despair: Angola was at 119 days in 2004 – today the figure is 68.

New businesses will be domestically focused at first, but can eventually challenge on the global stage. Among frontier rivals in Asia, Indonesia still requires

45 days, Vietnam is on 44 and Bangladesh 19. China is on 38, Russia on 30 and India 29. Governments in Africa are making faster progress.

One way governments can incentivise registration is by cutting the requirement for paid-in capital to zero, as recommended by the World Bank. In lower-income countries, any sort of nominal capital requirement may be a hefty sum as a percentage of income per capita, and deterrence to establishing a formal business. To take the West African mining state of Guinea as an extreme example – the minimum was a prohibitively high 41,408% of per capita income in 2004, and the cost of setting up a business was 232% of income per capita. Today the figures are 407% (99% lower) and 118%, respectively. Far better, but clearly there is room for further improvement.

Egypt has cut the capital requirement from 855% to zero, where it joins Nigeria, Kenya, Zambia, Mauritius, Mozambique, Botswana, the DRC and many others. By contrast, China is still at 100% and India is at 150%. The cost of starting a business has also been cut, in many cases by over 90% (including in Angola, Egypt and Ethiopia), but again there is still room for significant improvement.

African states have made impressive leaps to inject dynamism into their economies, and help formalise them, by enabling the registration of new companies. This in turn should improve government delivery of services that a formalised economy needs. SMEs will drive more-diversified growth.

Enforcing Contracts

IS the legal system able to support an investor in Africa? How does it compare to South Asian rivals in the frontier and emerging world? Although many African countries gained independence with few or even no home-grown lawyers, there was an inherited judicial system. We can compare the current processes with the UK, US and Germany, where enforcing a contract may take 300–400 days on average and cost 14–24% of the claim. The process is quicker in Rwanda at 230 days, while it is particularly slow in Egypt at 1,010 days. The average of 32 African countries we've looked is around 600 days, but is 1,000–1,400 days in South Asia. The process is cheapest in Ethiopia, Mauritius and Cape Verde, all at around 15–20%, and most expensive in poorer countries such as Zimbabwe, Sierra Leone and the DRC (all over 100%). The average of 32 African countries is 45%, against 40% in India and 63% in Bangladesh.

There has been little shift in these figures over the past eight years, perhaps because legal systems are tough to change, but what change there has been has generally been for the better. Cases in Rwanda are now one-third shorter at 230 days, and nine months quicker in Nigeria (now 457 days); Zimbabwe is a negative exception, where the cost of making a claim has risen from 32% of the claim to now 113%, making it effectively prohibitive.

Overall the legal system will take 50% longer to deal with than it does in developed markets, and the cost will approach nearly half of the claim itself, compared with a quarter or less in developed markets. Africa's judiciary acts far more quickly than South Asia's, but ranks poorly against potential rivals such as Vietnam. We are encouraged that reforms are happening here, too, but we cannot expect a radical improvement when some of the potential ranking points rely on higher income.

Resolving Insolvency

WHAT happens when a company goes bust in Africa, relative to other countries? Resolving insolvency looks like a nightmare in Asia: the process can take five years in Vietnam, six in Indonesia and the Philippines, and seven in India. Even in efficient countries, it's hardly a fun process unless you're the lawyer. It will take a pretty good two years in Nigeria and South Africa, Ghana, and Botswana; the same as the US. Slow African countries include Kenya, where it is a five-year process. The average of 29 African countries is three years.

Recovery rates from insolvency claims tend to be low in poorer countries, at less than 10 cents on the dollar in Sierra Leone, the Philippines and Rwanda. The average for 29 African countries is 19 cents. The better news is that as Africa gets richer, so do the recovery rates. Unfortunately a seven-fold improvement in Angola since 2004 still leaves the 2012 figure at seven cents on the dollar, but in Kenya it is up six cents to 31 cents, in Nigeria up two to 28 cents, and in South Africa up four to 35 cents. Despite the seven years it takes in India, the recovery rate is still 20 cents. What the data are telling us is that when things go wrong, the judiciary may again be reasonable on speed, but the benefits of using the system will be limited.

Building the Future

THE rapid urbanisation of Africa will be a dominant theme of the 21st century. Governments can impede this or support it. Globally there is great diversity –

with unfortunate Haiti requiring 1,129 days to deal with construction permits, and Zimbabwe a high 614 days. Overall, however, Africa's average processing time, with an average of 218 days across 32 countries, is similar to figures seen in South Asia. It may surprise many that Nigeria is one of the quickest countries in the world – needing just 85 days – less than Germany's 97 days. With Nigerian urbanisation at 50% – the same as China – and rising rapidly, such rapid processing of the 15 permits is evidently helpful and takes half as long as China or India. Another African success story is Kenya, where just eight permits take a below-average 125 days to process. It is little wonder a construction boom has been under way.

Getting construction permits can be expensive and takes too long in many countries, though this, too, is improving. The process looks simplest in Nigeria, South Africa, Ethiopia, Kenya and Mauritius.

Getting Connected

THE World Bank does not try to measure power cuts, but instead the process of setting up an electricity supply to your newly built warehouse in a city. To get supplied in less than three months is good in the emerging-market world – it takes 68 days in the US, 109 days in the UK and 17 in super-efficient Germany. The average for 32 African countries is 122 days. Rwanda at 31 days beats Singapore and Hong Kong, while Egypt (54), the DRC (58) and Ghana (78) all do well, as does India at 67 days. Countries where it takes more than six months include South Africa and Nigeria, while it takes more than a year in Pakistan and Bangladesh. There are only data for 2010–12, but progress has been rapid. In Sierra Leone, the figure has been slashed from 454 days in 2010 to 137, and in Tanzania from 382 days to 109 days.

The cost of electricity in Africa is however very high – at over 2,000% of per capita income in Sierra Leone, over 3,000% in Ethiopia and Bangladesh, and around 5,000% for Rwanda and Zimbabwe. The DRC at 28,800% of per capita income and Burundi at 34,477% are a function of low income, but also highlight that neighbouring Rwanda has done well. Rich Mauritius has the lowest rate of 328.5% in Africa. Overall, Africa compares well with frontier rivals such as Pakistan and Bangladesh, but the continent could still do with an electricity revolution – see chapter 11.

It may be coming. A combination of smart technologies and business opportunity are moving things forward. New solar-powered microgrids pioneered in India and the developed world are bringing power to villages still far from the grid, replacing dangerous, filthy kerosene lamps. Wind-up radios and fans, solar cooking stoves and chemical toilets are game-changing inventions in a region where power is not only unaffordable but unavailable.

But the grids, too, are expanding. Jacqueline Musiitwa, founder and managing partner of a Kigali-based law firm, Hoja Law Group, tells how she helped negotiate a deal to put a mining barge on Lake Kivu, along the Rwanda-DRC border, where it will process the lake's methane to power an electrical plant. "For me the barge was more than just an eyesore," she said. "It was a beacon of hope for Rwanda's future economic development."

Registering Property

AFTER you've constructed your building and hooked up the electricity, the wise businessman will register the property. This is a surprisingly cheap process in Ethiopia, Egypt and Ghana, where the cost will be less than 2% of the property value. It is quick, taking less than a month, in Mauritius, Rwanda and South Africa. What Nigeria gave in speed on the construction permits, it partially takes back with an 82-day wait to register property, and at a high cost of 21% of the reported cost of the property. Africa in general sits in the middle on these issues, with an average of 55 days required to register property, while global extremes range from Bangladesh (245 days) to Georgia and Thailand (just two days). There is evidently room here for governments to streamline and improve the situation, so giving legs to the construction boom required by urbanisation. The data series only exists from 2011, but already countries such as Uganda have been able to demonstrate a cut from 77 days in 2011 to 48 days in 2012.

Low Taxes in Demographically Rich Africa

AFRICA is a continent where taxes on labour are remarkably low and where paying taxes is often quick and simple. In some countries like Romania, companies need to pay over 100 taxes a year. In Africa, none of the major markets are in that camp, with an average of less than one tax per week (33 per year). Some tax systems are so simple that on average there is barely one tax to be paid each month. Mauritius, Tunisia and South Africa are particularly good. Consequently the time spent paying taxes is low – at 200 hours or less in South Africa, Ethiopia, Zambia and others – with the African average of 32 countries at 281 hours. In India it is 254 hours and 398 in China. Countries requiring more than 500 hours include Pakistan, Vietnam (941 hours) and Nigeria (938 hours) – all far better than poor Brazil at 2,600 hours per year. Businessmen are unlikely to find the tax system particularly onerous in this regard.

In terms of profit tax, Africa is roughly in the middle, with an average rate of 19% across 32 countries concealing a range from Zambia's particularly low 2% to Kenya's high 33%, with the DRC seemingly excessive at 59%.

Where Africa stands out is its low rate of labour tax and contributions. The indirect cost of hiring labour is very low – which makes sense in such demographically rich countries. Countries with taxes at 10% or less include Nigeria, Kenya, Zimbabwe, South Africa, and some at zero such as Ethiopia and Botswana. The average is 13%, against 18% in India and a shocking 50% in communist China.

As a result, the total corporate tax burden in Africa is 39% across 32 countries, compared with 62% in India and China at 64%. Even "high-tax" Kenya at 50% and Tunisia at 63% look reasonable.

The benefits of low corporate taxes are obvious. The negative associated with this is the lack of government tax revenue to spend on investment, meaning the private sector has to step in to provide this. It is happening, as we outline in the metals and mining chapter below.

Figure 4.2: Tax rates on the corporate sector, total and by components

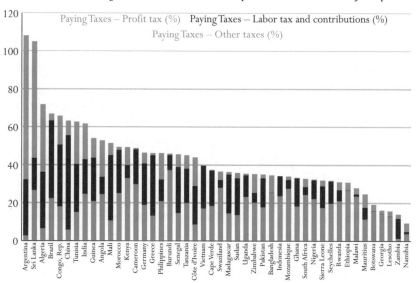

Source: World Bank Doing Business report, 2012

International Trade

WHERE Africa has always been weakest is in trade. In landlocked countries, transportation costs are a huge burden, at around $3,000 per container for exports (Zambia, DRC, Botswana, Rwanda, Zimbabwe), and $2,500–5,000 for imports (the same plus Ethiopia). This contrasts with $1,000–1,500 for many Asian countries. Since 2006, some SSA countries (and Brazil) have seen export costs rise by $1,000 or more per container. Rwanda and Algeria are two exceptions in having seen a fall.

Yet governments are trying to make a positive difference here, too. The World Bank cites research showing that a one-day reduction in travel time inside an exporting country results in a 7% increase in exports.[5] We've seen steep reductions in the time required to export: in Nigeria from 41 days in 2006 to 24 days in 2012, and in Kenya from 45 days to 26 days, while Ghana has slashed the time required to export by 60% from 47 days to 19. Best practice in Africa is the 12–13 days required to export from Egypt, Tunisia and Mauritius (Zimbabwe is worst at 53 days). This may be because Tunisia, Mauritius and Cape Verde require a below-average 4–5 documents to export products, against a more painful 10 in Nigeria.

Exports are clearly associated with higher productivity – as Paul Collier has explained so well in *The Bottom Billlion*.[6] Making it easier to export should not only boost export revenue and open up large markets, but also help improve efficiency in the economy.

Better rail links and more-efficient coastal ports would improve the situation. Infrastructure improvements presently being rolled out as a result of the commodity boom could go a long way towards reducing costs for other traded items. Ideally, the Lamu port project in Kenya would enable the country to slash costs and time required to export by 50%

Given how complicated it is to export, it is no surprise that it is even more difficult to import. Egypt, Nigeria, Ethiopia, the DRC and Zimbabwe all require nine documents for imports (versus e.g. 10–12 in the Commonwealth of Independent States), and it takes over 56 days to import to Zambia, 63 to the DRC and 73 to Zimbabwe. The problem with this is that consumption goods are more expensive, and investment goods, too. There must be significant pent-up demand for cheaper imports, if trade costs could be reduced.

Probably the most important technological change for Africa is the rolling out of the Internet, and the compound annual growth rate in broadband access was over 80% across Africa from 2007–11,[7] which shows how quickly Africa is adopting the latest technology. Exports of services via broadband would presumably be closer to 29 seconds for Rwanda, rather than the 29 days required for goods, and at zero cost rather than $3,275 per container. Services may prove more important for landlocked Africa than for the Philippines or India. The Internet allows those with European language skills, which is most of Africa, to offer everything from back-office financial services – now possible as a result of strong improvement in education – to call-centre support. The 21st century may be the first time in history that many countries can use exports of services to leap-frog the "textiles manufacturing – heavy industry – electronic goods" cycle of manufacturing.

What we show above is that Africa is a low tax environment, and that a broad range of countries are making significant improvements in a number of areas to ease the business burden. The most successful African country in terms of improvement is Rwanda, and below is an extract from a research report we wrote after our first visit in 2011.

A Singapore in Africa – A Rwanda Case Study

A recent visit to Rwanda provided the greatest positive shock in this analyst's nearly 20-year professional career. If you have any doubt that an African country can emulate the best performance seen in emerging Europe or Asia over the past few decades, then a visit to Kigali is required to challenge these assumptions. From the ease of visa-free travel and a well-organized and hassle-free airport, to the reassuring presence of police and security forces, streetlights, low crime, good roads and broadband, there is much to impress (a side trip to see the gorillas is strongly recommended and would be helpful for the country's strong tourism revenues, too).

Renaissance wanted to see if the rumours that something very special was happening in the hills of central Africa were true, and if so, whether this could show that Africa is indeed embarking on a new phase of strong sustainable growth to mirror what Asia achieved in the 20th century.

To be a Singapore of Africa is Rwanda's ambition – and it is succeeding. The country is politically stable, with the next presidential elections due in 2017. There is a zero-tolerance attitude to corruption, and it is effective. Rwanda was the world's best reformer, according to the World Bank's Doing Business survey in 2010; in 2010, 6,000 companies were registered in this country of 11 million people, about equal to the number registered over the previous five years. Keen to dispense with foreign aid by 2020, the country is a darling of many aid agencies, with highly effective implementation and use of foreign inflows. We saw clear evidence of forward planning and a strategy for the country. With access to a market of 130 million people in the East African Community (Kenya, Uganda, Tanzania, Rwanda and Burundi), Rwanda aims to be a hub for investment for both East and Central Africa. Lastly, and much to the distress of any macro/strategist, Renaissance failed to find significant macro-risks for the economy.

Undoubtedly, President Paul Kagame has played a very significant role, and it would not be surprising if Lee Kuan Yew's book From Third World to First *has as well. Singapore in the 1960s had a per capita GDP of around $400, was vulnerable to ethnic and ideological conflict in a region beset by wars, was excessively dependent on foreign aid (primarily UK military bases), and most CEOs could not find it on a map – but it was transformed by vision, infrastructure planning, the creation of an economic development bank, industrial parks to attract investment, and even beautification of the airport and city to give foreign investors a positive first impression, all underpinned by sound macro policies. The Rwandan Development Bank, the use of privatisation proceeds to roll out a fibre-optic broadband network, and the recent launch of a special economic zone for industry, technology and warehousing just a kilometre from the airport might all be seen as following Singapore's example. Like Singapore in its early phase of development, Rwanda is keen to attract investors and is changing its requirement that investors export 80% of production, though an Indian pharmaceutical company's $60 million investment (worth 1% of GDP) is targeted at exports to the region. Renaissance believes that the concentration of GDP in a small area – Kigali, the capital – could be a significant advantage.*

Looking ahead, the government intends to turn Rwanda into a service economy and a conference hub. The ongoing construction of a $300 million conference centre, a planned new airport and the privately funded Marriott hotel will allow continued expansion of the roughly $100 million earned through business tourism (roughly the same value as tea and coffee, or all mining exports). Roads have been upgraded across the country, including to Burundi and Tanzania, with a route to northern DRC to be finished in mid-2012.

The next transport projects include extending the rail line from Tanzania to Rwanda by 2015. The government intends to boost power generation from a sufficient 85 MW to 100 MW in 2012 and as much as 1,000 MW by 2017 through tapping methane gas in Lake Kivu and using peat. It plans to improve energy supplies through extending a 1,200 km oil pipeline from Kenya. Access to Uganda's oil production will be possible from 2015–2016. At present, all petrol is trucked from Mombassa, which is one reason why a litre of gasoline cost $1.67 in Kigali (versus about $1 in the US in 2011); improved access to energy could dramatically improve Rwanda's competitiveness. On the fiscal side, plans are being considered *to introduce a flat 15% income tax rate, for individuals and corporations. To improve the country's skill levels, free schooling has been extended from age 12 to 15, and a German company has been brought in to continue the roll-out of colleges, which will focus on vocational skills. In the meantime, Rwanda is very open to immigration to provide the skills the country needs.*[8]

Unchaining Ambition

SUPPORTING the private sector was not always the top priority for African governments. Nigeria's Ngozi Okonjo-Iweala explains this in *Reforming the Unreformable*,[9] highlighting the interventionist and nationalist ideology of the post-independence era, as well as the constraints on capital that meant many believed the government had the resources and expertise to build the economy. By 2000, few could look at the Nigerian state telecoms company and still believe the state knew best.

This has now changed. In the place of sluggish state monopolies, Africa has a plethora of dynamic private-sector companies expanding dramatically both in domestic markets and across the continent. Successes range from Tullow Oil in the resource extraction sector, to Dangote Cement's investments across eastern and southern Africa, to telecoms companies like MTN. Governments are doing ever more to help accelerate the process, pushing reforms that will see the creation of new business across the booming continent.

Timing is critical, of course. But sometimes simply delivering a quality service and high standards in a market unaccustomed to either can be revolutionary in itself.

Take the Lewis brothers: 45-year-old Andrew and Rob, 41, had both made a bit of money by the time they reached their late 20s. Born in South Africa, Andrew spent some time in the re-insurance business in London, but wanted to come back to Africa. His younger brother had launched an early South African online share-trading platform, U-Trade, and sold it. They had a bit of money, a bit of experience, "but we really were at loose ends," Andrew recalled.

Watching for opportunities, in 2001 they learned that the owner of a small insurance firm in Mozambique, CGSM, had contracted cancer and was eager to sell. Backed by the country's central bank and at a time when the South African rand was in tumult, the Lewises saw a chance to pick up a dollar asset. "The rand was going to hell, so it made sense," Rob said. "We figured, 'What the hell?'"

They outbid a rival, South Africa's Hollard Insurance, and for about $1 million found themselves with an insurance licence, a disastrously disorganized company and the need to find a place to live in Mozambique's capital city, Maputo. Turnover at the firm was about $2 million, and much of the staff – many of them rooting for the Hollard bid – deserted. But the brothers hunkered down, renaming the company Global Alliance, calling on a friend to help them write customised insurance software, and while that was in the works, knocking on the doors of every client and potential client in Mozambique asking them a question they had never heard before: How can we make this better?

"It was amazing, and some of it is timing. Our only real competition was a state insurer, and we found in Mozambique and later in Angola and Ghana that these are bloated bureaucracies, with nonsensical pricing, just bumbling along. Government organizations and state enterprises had to use them – EMOSE, it's call in Mozambique. But we picked up just about everyone else very quickly."

Within a year, Global Alliance was servicing major firms – Vale, SABMiller, Coca-Cola – turning over $8 million and fending off buyout offers. "We were tempted, but our clients in Mozambique encouraged us to expand elsewhere in Africa where they had trouble finding service and promised to back us with business." The biggest hole in the market was Angola, so in 2003, the brothers scraped together $6 million, camped out for two years in Luanda and finally got a licence to compete against Angola's state insurance monopoly, ENSA. As in Mozambique, the oil giants felt compelled to stay with the state insurers. But their servicers – including giants such as Halliburton, Odebrecht and Baker Hughes – all jumped ship, landing on the deck of the Lewises' GA Angola.

Today, from a core of nine employees in Maputo back in 2001, the brothers employ a staff of 250 and agents in both countries, and are branching into retail insurance to tap what Andrew Lewis called "an unbelievable consumer boom. The middle class is exploding, and they have cars and houses and possessions. They'll want insurance, too."

It wasn't easy, of course. Obtaining a licence in Angola took many, many months and several times the company nearly ran out of cash. A move into Ghana in 2006 in an effort to repeat the trick nearly did them in – "it taught us a good lesson. You need to know the market, and we didn't understand Ghana." But they sold out after a single profitable year and refocused on Angola and Mozambique.

The Lewises illustrate an important point that gets lost in all the tales of tech magnates or mining fortunes.

"All we needed to do was do something simple and do it really well," Rob Lewis said. "We didn't mine gold, we didn't sell mobile phones or iPods. We sold insurance, whatever you wanted, in English and Portuguese. People in Africa overcomplicate things. Sell a simple service, sell it well."[10]

Such entrepreneurs still have great scope to make a difference. For European countries trying to reform themselves in the wake of the global financial crisis, the room for improvement in simple business practices is limited. For African countries, even after the gains of the past decade that have seen them top the improvement charts, the opportunity remains to make dramatic improvements in the business climate. Many more are following the leaders, making it quicker to start a new business, register property or deal with construction permits, feeding an urbanisation process that itself is integral to the accelerating growth trajectory.

Additionally attractive for foreign direct investors is a tax system that is relatively simple, and a light burden, particularly in terms of employing labour. Not every country will be the next Singapore, but improvements in the business environment are already under way which show that the impressive performance of Mauritius or Seychelles will be shared across the continent. The result will be the creation of millions of new businesses, hundreds of millions of jobs, and increasingly African corporate and banking giants that will challenge on the global stage.

Notes

1. Steven Radelet, *Emerging Africa: How 17 Countries Are Leading the Way* (Washington, DC: Center for Global Development, 2012).
2. World Bank/International Finance Corporation, 2010, http://www. doingbusiness.org/rankings.
3. *The Global Competitiveness Report 2012–2013*, World Economic Forum, 2012, http://reports.weforum.org/global-competitiveness-report-2012-2013/.
4. "Profile of Mr. Roland Agambire," Regent University College of Science and Technology website, http://www.regentghana.net/events/guests/roland-agambire-profile.php, accessed 11 September 2012.
5. Paul Brenton, Olivier Cadot and Martha Denisse Pierola, *Pathways to African Export Sustainability* (Washington, DC: World Bank, 2012).
6. Paul Collier, *The Bottom Billion: Why the Poorest Countries are Failing and What Can Be Done About It* (Oxford: Oxford University Press, 2007).
7. Stacey Higginbotham, "Norway has more bandwidth than all of Africa & other broadband gaps," *GigaOM* (blog), 18 July 2012, http://gigaom.com/2012/07/18/norway-has-more-bandwidth-than-all-of-africa-other-broadband-gaps/.

8. Charles Robertson, *Thoughts from a Renaissance Man – Rwanda – An African Inspiration*, Renaissance Capital, April 2011.

9. Ngozi Okonjo-Iweala, *Reforming the Unreformable: Lessons from Nigeria* (Cambridge, Massachusetts: MIT Press, 2012).

10. Telephone interview with authors, 12 September 2012.

Chapter 5

Banking on Human Capital

By Charles Robertson

Just to maintain present primary-school enrolment rates, governments will have to increase the number of classrooms and teachers by about 14%. Africa's education and training systems need to be fit for the purpose. Failure to tackle the twin crises of access to school and the quality of learning will not just limit the right to education, undermine prospects for economic growth and waste human potential; it will render countries all the more vulnerable to the political and social instabilities that inevitably accompany urbanisation and youth unemployment.

—Linah Mohohlo, governor of the Bank of Botswana

IF we see education as the bedrock of society, then the remarkable aspect of education throughout Africa is the improvement in the past 20 years and the expected growth over the next 30. Africa is at the same point as India or China in 1990. Those countries enjoyed a surge in growth that corresponded with the entry of that newly educated population into the workplace. All the countries that Renaissance has plotted on the trajectory of growth have many common characteristics. One of the most persuasive is the extent to which surges in growth are mirrored by the advance of education across the population, from primary to secondary and finally to the university level.

Africa has yet to complete all the rungs on the education ladder; so far the main growth has been in primary education, which is now nearly universal. But secondary education has expanded dramatically, from just one pupil in 10 in 1975 to four in 10 (of a far larger population) by 2005. We expect between five and nine out of 10 to be in secondary school by 2020. This means Africa now has the skills it needs to start taking jobs from the global powerhouse that is China. Tertiary education is still far too restricted, but will be the next phase of improvement. The education improvement is pervasive and comprehensive, country to country. We assume that within 30 years the number and diversity of home-grown tertiary-level educated people will meet the demands of the continent in every area.

An educated population is not just essential for supporting growth; it also cements the social structure through the provision of healthcare, schooling, civil administration, services and sales. Africa has all the benefits of the massive surge in schooling still to come in its growth. This will be a major input into not only levering the growth surge up into double figures, but enabling the continent to continue that growth through another 30 years.

If you've ever tried to work out how much damage children will inflict on your savings, then spare a thought for Muyiwa Ajisafe. A successful Yoruba man from western Nigeria will often take a number of wives – three in Ajisafe's case were enough to keep him busy at home and provide him with 12 children. He was kept even busier at work, and not because he was avoiding the dubious pleasure of parenting infants. Ajisafe needed to work to ensure he could pay for the education of his 12 sons and daughters. There is no greater priority for a Nigerian father than the best possible education for his children. He met his goal. His high-achieving children are succeeding in the US, the UK, Nigeria and South Africa, and we are lucky to have Abi Ajisafe working with us at Renaissance Capital today.

We found the same education goals in our survey of the Nigerian middle class in mid-2011.[2] Over 98% of upper-middle-class children complete high school (one-third abroad), and the vast majority head to university. The third-most-cited reason for saving money (after emergencies, and meeting day-to-day needs) was to pay for education. This had higher importance than saving to expand a business, buy property, saving for old age or paying for medicine. Nigerian middle-class parents want their children to become engineers (35%), doctors (34%), lawyers (20%) and accountants (19%) – and a few even suggest banking (12%).

This Nigerian story is of course shared across the continent, and led as much by Africa's women as the men. As generations of women attain higher levels of education, there is often higher enrolment in schools for their childen, leading to declining birthrates among the middle class and greater investment in each individual child. The fruits of this can be now seen in Africa's first female presidents, in Liberia and Malawi, and Rwanda's female-dominated parliament.

An immense improvement in Africa's human capital is under way as a result. It has been greatly needed, as shown so clearly in the examples below from Martin Meredith's *The State of Africa: A History of Fifty Years of Independence*.[3]

When the DRC won independence from Belgium in 1960, there were just 30 graduates in the country. There were no doctors, no secondary-school teachers and no army officers. In the 1959–1960 school year, 136 children completed secondary school in the DRC. The DRC did not have sufficient human capital to run a single government department, let alone the 12th-largest country in the world.

Kenya did not have its first African lawyer until 1956 – a Luo who had to wash dishes in the UK to pay for his education. In Northern Rhodesia (now Zambia), only 35 Africans had pursued higher education by 1959, and in Nyasaland (now Malawi) the figure was just 28. The secondary-school enrolment rate across Africa was just 3% in 1960.

Even the brightest were held back by poverty. Renaissance Capital's Sharon Koimett explains that her Kenyan-born mother "was one of only two students who achieved the required score at her primary school to get admitted to secondary school. At secondary school my mother excelled in both academics and extracurricular activities and topped her class," but in 1975 "she couldn't proceed to her A-levels because my grandmother, affected by bad farming seasons, couldn't afford the fees." In this particular example, it ended well as government funding saw her progress so far that she has since become the most senior woman in the Kenyan treasury. But evidently a great deal of Africa's talent has been lost because of a lack of resources, or even a lack of rain.

Back to Basics

GOVERNMENT policy after independence did not always help; there was an excessive, if understandable, focus on building university education, at the expense of universal primary education. By 1975, when the last African countries were achieving independence, gross primary-school enrolment was 61% across Africa and still just 13% in secondary schools. Given the starting point in 1960, and slow progress in the 1970s, the inadequate education of the population goes a long way towards explaining why so many African economies were in trouble in the 1980s. The educated human capital needed for either good government or vibrant private sectors was simply lacking.

Yet already by 1975, 15 years after the independence wave surged across Africa, the secondary-school enrolment rate compared favourably with the US, where even 115 years after independence (around 1890), just 7% of Americans aged 14–17 attended school. It took another half century after that (i.e. into the mid-20th century) before the US got 90% of its 14–17 year olds into secondary school, and 15% into university.

In the 30 years since 1975, African primary enrolment rates have soared to 96% – with SSA (excluding South Africa) enrolment rates of 93% now comparable to India in 1990. African secondary-school enrolment rates trebled from 13% in 1975 to 39% in 2005. In Nigeria, secondary-school enrolment was 7% in 1975 against 32% in 2005. Kenya is up from 13% to 48%. The richest African countries, including Mauritius, now have 88% enrolment. A rate of 51–90% secondary school enrolment across the continent is likely by 2020.

Multi-party elections and pressure on politicians to deliver secondary school has been key to this expansion. However, the expansion has come at some cost, as teacher numbers have struggled to keep pace with demand. As a result, ambitious African parents have tapped the private sector to ensure better results, a trend that in Kenya was highlighted in David Mataen's book *Africa: The Ultimate Frontier Market*.[4] Governments today still have to ensure both a further expansion in education numbers and quality, too.

Figure 5.1: Secondary-school enrolment rates (1975, 1990, 2005) – SSA in 2005 was ahead of India in 1990, similar to Mexico/Turkey in 1975

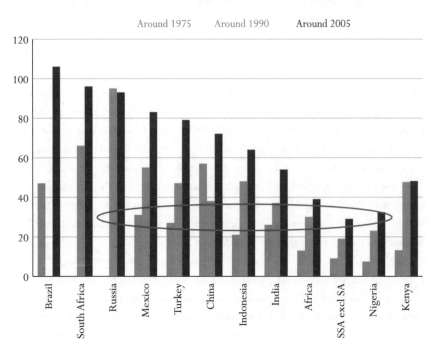

Source: World Bank

Nonetheless, already in 2005, SSA school enrolment rates were equivalent to Turkey or Mexico in 1975, and we doubt the issue of education quality was much different in those countries. Based on current trends, in 2020 Africa's secondary enrolment rates will be considerably better than Turkey, Mexico, or Indonesia in 1990 (47%, 55% and 48%, respectively), and may well rival the 72% recorded by China in 2005. Each of these countries became significant parts of the global economy 15 years later (1990), once these students had entered the workforce. Ghana and Kenya are in stronger positions than China in 1990; and Botswana, South Africa and Mauritius are already ahead of China, Indonesia and India today. Not only has education improved, but there is plenty of anecdotal evidence that well-educated and internationally trained African professionals are returning from the US and Europe, to use their skills in the strong-growth economies in the continent.

Yet the legacy of the 20th century means shortages of skilled labour still exist. When Ngozi Okonjo-Iweala did an internal census of Nigeria's finance ministry nearly 10 years ago, 70% only had high-school education and just 8% had a degree in economics or accountancy. Today, China's phone giant ZTE is shipping 4G equipment to Angola rather than manufacturing in Angola. Its general director Frank Mei says, "the education level is still a bit low...during the war all the educational resources quit the country. So they've only started to build the education system now. In our industry, most of the qualified engineers come from abroad."[5] Once again we see the negative impact of conflict and poor education – in Angola gross secondary enrolment was just 15% in 2006 according to the latest available UN data. But we also see the improvement now under way in the wake of greater political stability and high commodity export revenue, which should allow Angola to invest more in education. That will produce the workers who in 2020 or beyond will be taking the ZTE manufacturing jobs that China could capture in 2005 from European and US firms. To get better value-added jobs, Africa does not have to rival the educational achievements of far richer countries. Instead it has to do better than it did in the past, and this is happening.

African nations – helped by the inflow of the best-educated young workers it has ever had – will be having a similar influence in the world through 2010–30 as Mexico, Turkey, Indonesia and China did from 1990 to 2010. Ajisafe's children should do extremely well – but his grandchildren will do still better. Given the size of the continent, its demographics and the improvement in education, the subsequent (2030–50) generation will not just be global players, but global drivers ready to disrupt the BRIC-dominated global order.

The Impact of Higher Growth on Education

CURIOUSLY the growth trajectory does not imply a big increase in education spending as a percentage of GDP. Low-income countries spend 4% of GDP and high-income countries 5%, according to our analysis of World Bank data.

Figure 5.2: Public spending on education vs per capita GDP (2005 PPP dollars)

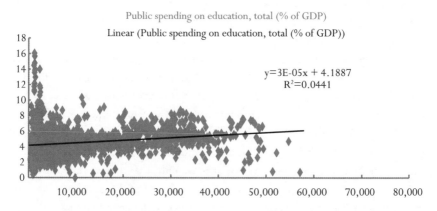

Source: Renaissance Capital estimates

However, higher GDP does of course mean much higher spending in actual cash. Since 2005, the World Bank has two estimates for SSA education spending: at 3.9% of GDP in 2008 and 4.7% in 2010. Renaissance analysis suggests 4.3% of GDP is normal at SSA's per capita GDP level. Using that as a pan-African figure, we estimate education spending in today's money will rise 15-fold, from $93 billion today, via $157 billion in 2020, to total 4.7% of GDP and $1.4 trillion by 2050.

Figure 5.3: Africa's public spending on education

Education (public) – $bn   Education (public) – % of GDP, rhs

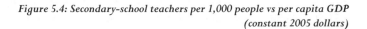

Source: Renaissance Capital estimates

There will be a large impact on teacher numbers, particularly secondary-school teachers. This makes sense, as we expect secondary-school enrolment to continue to rise rapidly, while primary-school enrolment is already nearly 100%.

***Figure 5.4: Secondary-school teachers per 1,000 people vs per capita GDP
(constant 2005 dollars)***

Secondary education, teachers per 1000 people

◆   Secondary education, teachers per 1000 people   ——Linear(Secondary education, teachers per 1000 people)

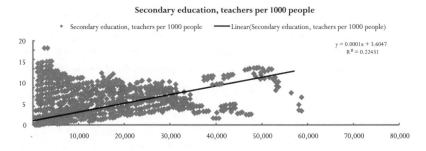

$y = 0.0001x + 3.6047$
$R^2 = 0.22431$

Source: Renaissance Capital estimates

The number of teachers will grow rapidly. Renaissance estimates suggest that Africa's population at its current per capita GDP level would normally have 8.2 million teachers. This should reach 13.5 million by 2030 and 23 million by 2050, for a population of 2 billion.

Figure 5.5: Teachers in Africa

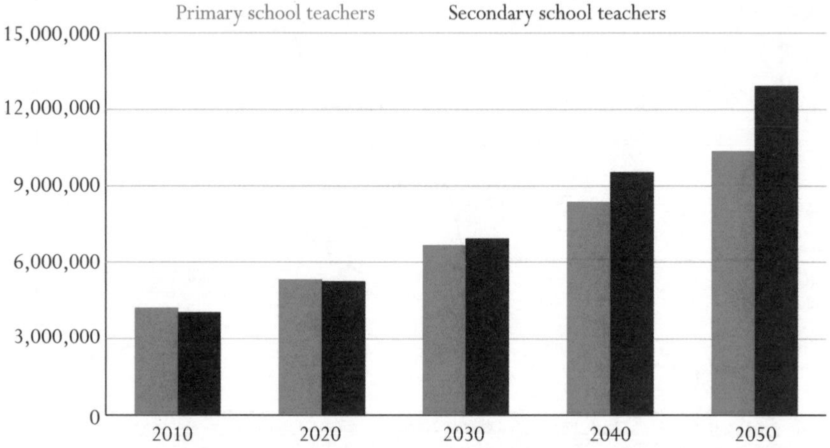

Source: Renaissance Capital estimates

Comparing our data mining – which assesses expected teacher numbers according to per capita GDP – with actual data from various countries, we find the data correspond pretty well in primary education for Tanzania (actual 166,000 in 2008 against the Renaissance GDP-implied estimate of 184,000 in 2010), although Nigeria lags a little at 574,000 compared with our implied figure of 655,000. Where our estimate is way off is in secondary education, where the World Bank estimate of 274,000 Nigerian teachers is far below the 617,000 our data would say is normal at Nigeria's wealth level. This reinforces the point above, that while school enrolment is up, the quality of education may not have risen as fast. Assuming that Nigeria's teacher numbers do catch up with its wealth, Nigeria should have 0.8 million secondary-school teachers by 2020, 1.1 million by 2030 and 2.4 million by 2050 to teach the teenagers among Nigeria's 390 million people. That means a couple of million job opportunities for the generation of Ajisafe's grandchildren.

Most important is that all our statistical work suggests educational achievement will broaden and deepen over the coming decades. Already the improvement in the past 30 years helps explain the stronger economic performance of the past decade. The crucial difference between Africa's prospects in 1980 and today is that the current ongoing demographic surge has experienced vastly more schooling: it has more knowledge and expanded horizons. So not only will Africa provide the young workforce that the world economy will need, but it will become steadily better educated, too, with benefits for direct investors in the country, as well as existing private-sector players and the public administration.

Notes

1. Linah Moholo, "Africa's millions of young people must add up to demographic dividend," *PovertyMatters* (blog), *The Guardian*, 17 July 2012, http://www. guardian.co.uk/global-development/poverty-matters/2012/jul/17/africa-young-demographic-dividend.
2. Charles Robertson, Nothando Ndebele and Yvonne Mhango, *A Survey of the Nigerian Middle Class*, Renaissance Capital, 26 September 2011.
3. Martin Meredith, *The State of Africa: A History of Fifty Years of Independence* (London: The Free Press, 2005).
4. David Mataen, *Africa: The Ultimate Frontier Market* (Petersfield: Harriman House, 2012).
5. Egon Cossou, "Angola's businesses beat most of Europe to 4G mobile services," BBC, 30 April 2012, http://www.bbc.co.uk/news/business-17898861.

PART II

The Massai Market Moment

By Michael Moran and Charles Robertson

Africa's exceptionally robust growth over the last decade is probably understated (informal parts of economies are very big), but not being able to measure this growth precisely shouldn't detract from Africa's potential, which is about much more than resources as it evolves and climbs the consumption, urbanisation and perhaps industrialisation curves that the BRICs have climbed. We believe meaningful opportunities for Western consumer companies exist as Africa's household consumption grows rapidly (it is already greater than some of the BRICs) and that failure to invest now will see others rush in.

—Hugo Scott-Gall[1]

Massai Market: an open-air bazaar in the tradition of Kenya's Massai, where the traditions of village capitalism developed over the course of centuries.

Growth is booming across Africa, from tiny Cape Verde to the demographic giant Nigeria, and from oil producers such as Angola to the hills of Ethiopia. In many of these, as well as strong performers such as Uganda, Tanzania and Seychelles, we cannot attribute the rise of the fastest billion to any single commodity. However, from oil and now gas to mining, natural resources have helped, and below we outline just how dramatic this has been. Oil production has soared in Sub-Saharan Africa and is sufficient to meet all of China's import needs. Oil-related revenue in SSA alone has risen from under $35 billion in the late 1990s to around $235 billion in 2011, and will reach $300 billion even on fairly conservative estimates of prices and production. Yet new discoveries are being made from Ghana in West Africa to Uganda and Kenya in the east. Meanwhile, presently planned iron ore projects across SSA could add over 600 million tonnes of new output within 10 years. More countries could experience the double-digit growth seen in Sierra Leone. Natural resources are still a strong growth story.

The demographic surge is one reason why growth is broader than just commodities. The number of 15–24 year-olds will drop by more than one-quarter in both East Asia and Eastern Europe over 2010–20, while it will rise by 15–20% across SSA for the next three decades. The arrival of new labour should ensure Africa's workforce is competitive with the rest of the world, making it an obvious destination for labour-intensive corporate investment. New jobs will mean higher consumption. Already the consumption boom is dramatic enough that consumer giant Nestlé expects Africa's share of its global sales to double from 5% to 10% in this decade. Global investors can buy headline global stocks that dilute that 100% growth rate, or focus on local companies that capture it all, such as Nestlé Nigeria, PZ Cussons or Guinness Nigeria. The surge in demand will move up the curve from consumer goods such as soap, toothpaste and paint, to white goods and cars. We expect car sales in Africa to soar from 3–4 million now to 8 million by 2020 and to reach current US sales levels by 2030. Industrialisation is likely to meet that demand. The next Geely or Tata may well be Nigerian or Kenyan. Local production will mean local demand for resources – our forecasts imply that steel production will rise from 2 million tonnes in Nigeria today to 115 million tonnes by 2050 – a level that today is exceeded only by China.

Demographics mean that Africans do not need to worry about private pension provision. The even-better news is that from Kenya to Nigeria to South Africa, Africa already has better privately funded pension provision than most other countries around the world. Based on the growth rates we have forecast, pension funds may rise from $260 billion in 2012 to $7 trillion by 2050 (in 2012 dollars) in SSA alone. If managed well, local pension funds could become a strong component in financing the growth of the fastest billion, whilst also becoming the safety net that even Africa will need late in the 21st century.

Notes

1. Hugo Scott-Gall, "Africa's turn," *Fortnightly Thoughts*, no. 27 (1 March 2012), Goldman Sachs Global Investment Research, http://www.fusioninvestmentsltd.com/downloads/gs_research_africas_turn.pdf.

Chapter 6

Oil and Gas in the African Boom

By Dragan Trajkov, Bradley Way and Charles Robertson

Everyone knew the Guinea basin was a very rich deposit for hydrocarbons, but until recently all the attention focused on a small group of countries that were seen as worthwhile investments. But today even countries that were totally off the radar are getting a fresh look.
—Philippe de Pontet, energy analyst, Eurasia Group[1]

WE have already emphasised the helpful role that commodities have played in Africa's growth resurgence, even though oil and gas have not been the drivers for the 7%-plus annual growth rates achieved over 2000–11 in East African countries such as Rwanda and Ethiopia. Indeed, their part in Africa's emergence as a global economic force plays out in spite of, rather than because of, the continent's vast energy wealth. Yet commodities do matter. The rapidly industrialising US economy of the 19th century would have been impossible without the copious harvests and innovative techniques of its huge agricultural sector. Top-10 global economies from Russia to Brazil have benefited from mineral and agricultural exploitation. While Africa's coming boom will be based on macro improvements and growth in many industries, key features will be the well-established and increasingly efficient oil, gas and mining sectors. These are growing fast thanks to innovative government policies that encourage exploration, investment and production – in contrast to lethargic or counter-productive energy-tax policies in OECD countries from Mexico to the North Sea.

In 1965, Africa's oil production of 2.2 million barrels per day (Mbpd) was dominated by North Africa – just 316,000 barrels per day (bpd) and 14% of African production came from Sub-Saharan Africa. The emergence of Nigeria, and then Angola, Chad and Sudan has seen that SSA figure rise to 5.8 Mbpd in 2011 – sufficient to meet all of China's import needs. North Africa has never regained its 4.8 Mbpd peak of 1970. Meanwhile SSA has more than quadrupled its share of

African production, reaching 58% in 2010. Thanks to new production in Ghana, Uganda and elsewhere, Renaissance expects this to reach 66% by 2020.

The consequence of rising production and higher oil prices is dramatic. The value of SSA oil production in 2011 dollars was $1 billion in 1965 but $235 billion in 2011.[2] Assuming no change in oil prices, this will top $300 billion in 2011 prices by 2019, due to new production across SSA.

Figure 6.1: The dollar value of annual oil production in SSA (2011 dollars)

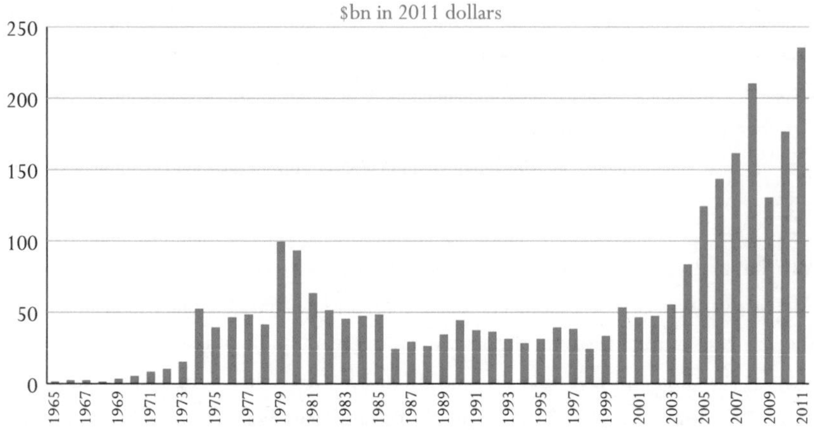

$bn in 2011 dollars

Source: Renaissance Capital estimates, BP

Each year brings new discoveries in SSA, while North African oil production at 4 Mbpd is largely in mature fields. African oil production of 10 Mbpd in 2010 – sufficient to meet all US import demand – should expand to at least 12 Mbpd in 2020–30. This assumes Nigerian oil output at 3 Mbpd, but reforms there may yet lift this to the government's targeted 4 Mbpd. All the growth will come from SSA production, and increasingly from new entrants. By 2020, diversification means "Other SSA" production may exceed that of Angola.

Figure 6.2: African oil production, Mbpd

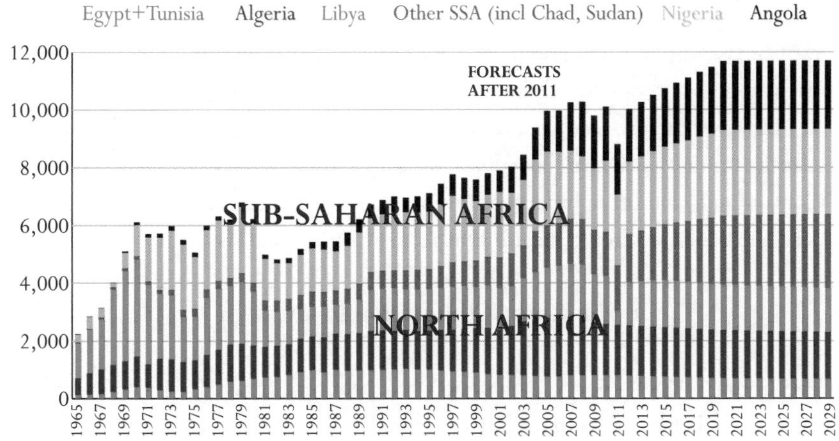

Source: Renaissance Capital estimates, BP, EIA

Africa accounted for 7% of global oil production in 1965, with 6% from North Africa and 1% from SSA. By 2010, of Africa's 12% share, 5% came from North Africa and 7% from SSA. As one Sinopec geologist told us, "SSA, especially West Africa and increasingly East Africa, will soon play a major role in the global conventional energy supply. Globally, the largest discoveries in the past few years occurred on both sides of the Atlantic – Ghana, Angola, Liberia and Brazil. It's not just the discoveries that are important to note – major break-throughs were made in understanding the geology of West African petroleum basins. This will bear fruit in the years to come."

This has had significant geopolitical consequences. In the wake of 9/11, the US was able to shift its import dependency significantly from the volatile Middle East to the more secure supply of Nigeria. Over 1999–2001, 27–29% of US crude oil imports came from the Persian Gulf and 14–15% from Africa. By May 2010, the 12-month rolling total was 18% from the Persian Gulf and 19% from Africa (mainly 11% from Nigeria and 4% from Angola), though since late 2011 there has been a sharp shift back to Saudi imports. The Arab Spring saw SSA again become the secure supplier when Libyan production was disrupted.

Now 30% of Chinese oil imports come from Africa, as China, too, has been keen to reduce dependency on the Straits of Hormuz. In 2010, US Energy Information Administration data show that China imported 893,000 bpd (19% of imports) from Saudi Arabia and 788,000 bpd (16%) from Angola, far ahead of Iran (in third place) at 426,000 bpd (9%), while Sudan took sixth place at 252,000 bpd (5%). As US Energy Information Administration estimates suggest China's imports will rise from 50% of its oil consumption to 72% by 2035, China alone could buy up all the additional oil that Africa might supply.

Africa's total proven reserves have increased. New gas finds off both the Atlantic and Indian Ocean coastlines almost monthly have transformed national balance sheets and brought large infusions of Western capital and investments by Asian and other sovereign wealth funds.

The Right Climate for Investment

THE boom in SSA energy production has been encouraged by savvy governments, which have developed an encouraging investment climate that differs from the rest of the world. In most established oil producers, the tax and royalty regimes take revenue from a project regardless of whether the operator has been able to recoup the capital it has injected. Libya for example has had a reputation for some of the worst fiscal terms globally, with some contracts giving the government 85% of the cash flow from production. The result is that oil production might only become profitable for the investing company many years after production has started. While this regime may work in established oil producers, it means the risk and costs of a new project create a big disincentive for those considering work in new, unexplored regions.

What SSA governments have done instead is only take a share of the profits of energy production after the producers have paid for the costs of the project. This is a key difference that reduces the risk for energy companies. It means that in SSA, it is common to see private-sector independent oil companies (IOC) team up with state-owned national oil companies (NOC). The private companies pay to develop oil and gas in a new and prospective basin, knowing they can start to reclaim capital costs as soon as production starts. Moreover, many of the production-sharing contracts in SSA are not ring-fenced, which means that if an IOC is producing out of block A (for example), and invests in block B, then the investment costs in block B can be used to reduce taxes in block A. Again this front-loads cash flows to encourage investment.

This far-sighted approach has encouraged exploration and subsequent production to spread across the continent. The production-sharing contracts encourage in the first company, which then lays a pipeline and other infrastructure needed to export its production. The area is then considered to be far less risky – as oil has been discovered and produced, and infrastructure is in place to exploit it – so new entrants are encouraged to explore, produce and invest, too. Taken together, this reduces the risks and constraints on financing major infrastructure, cutting the cost of investment and producing quicker benefits for the local economy. A Chevron chemical engineer we spoke to said, "The oil and gas industry has been a major driver of infrastructure investment in SSA over the past decade. While there is still more needed, progress has been impressive."

A curious feature of the African oil boom has been the prominent role of independent explorers. This is partially facilitated by the tax regime that African governments have pioneered. Geologists and petroleum engineers who have gained experience in understanding basin geology while working at a major company have an incentive to enter into higher-risk ventures by forming independent companies. Tullow is an example, having management from ConocoPhilips and Shell who held posts in Africa. Independents take on higher-risk exploration, and when successful typically sell out to larger IOCs once hydrocarbons are discovered. The IOC is happy to buy into a project that has been "de-risked" by the independent, and benefits from fiscal terms that will allow it to invest in developing the project and recoup costs. One recent example is Cove Energy in Mozambique receiving bids from both Shell and Thailand's PTT for a full buy-out.

Increasingly, these independents, at least in Nigeria, are also indigenous companies. In the past year, we have seen a significant number of successful publicly tradeable companies partnering with indigenous companies to develop areas of Nigeria that seem to be forgotten by the majors. These accounted for less than 5% of Nigerian production in 2011 but now include the likes of Afren, Heritage Oil, Maurel & Prom Nigeria, Mart Resources, Eland and Oando Upstream. Within 10 years such companies may represent 20% of total Nigerian production.

There's Something in the Air

ACTUALLY the air is not a problem in Africa. Hurricanes, which are the bane of production in the Gulf of Mexico, and cut production every September and October, are not a feature of the African climate. The temporary falls in output in the Gulf are less problematic than the high development costs in hurricane-prone areas. Maintaining a safe, reliable flow of oil in deepwater projects becomes significantly more expensive. By contrast, for SSA, a simpler and cheaper option is the floating production storage and offloading vessel (FPSO), which receives oil from the seabed well, stores it, and can then directly offload it onto waiting tankers. In Nigeria for instance, a vessel can be a mile out to sea, collect crude, and ship it directly to a UK refinery without even touching a port in Nigeria. The FPSO itself can be moved from field to field.

SSA is one of the few areas where large pools of conventional oil can be found and explored at relatively low cost. We have seen discoveries totalling more than 1 billion barrels with capital (development) costs of about $10/barrel and operating costs also around $10/barrel. For instance, the Jubilee development offshore Ghana has a resource size of 700-1,000 million barrels, and it only took four years to develop, at a price tag of $3.5 billion. In the Gulf of Mexico, much smaller discoveries of 200 million barrels have cost $2.5 billion to develop. Brazil's deepwater plans will prove far more expensive.

Accessible Oil Reserves

AFRICA now has 132 billion barrels of proved oil reserves, equivalent to 36 years of production, and 519 trillion cubic feet of proved natural gas reserves. These represent about 10% and 8% of total world reserves. But for a portfolio investor or in terms of M&A potential, Africa's importance is far greater than those proportions suggest. After all, the reserves in the Middle East (excluding Iraq) and Venezuela are government owned and often unlisted. Africa's oil producers are listed, with access to reserves as large as Europe's or Eurasia's.

Besides the absolute accessible amount of reserves, the annual growth in oil reserves has been better than in any other accessible region in the world. In addition, the production growth in Africa has been faster than in any other region over the past 10 years.

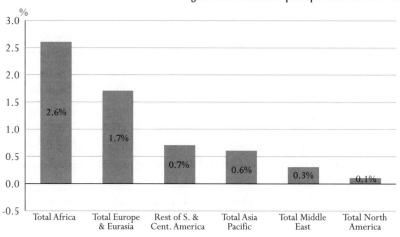

Figure 6.3: CAGR in liquids production 2000–2010

Source: Renaissance Capital estimates, BP Statistical Review

Lastly, the export openness of African energy makes companies here an attractive target for global M&A, especially from Asia and North America, which are long cash but short energy. Net exports from Africa in 2010 were second only to the Middle East. This will change as Africa begins to consume more energy itself, but here at least is one continent that does not need to fear energy shortages in the coming decade.

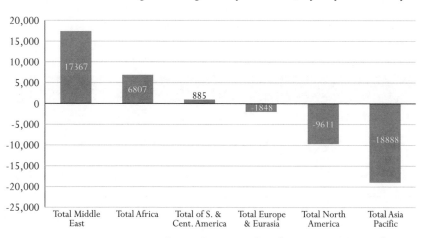

Figure 6.4: Regional export abilities, liquids production surplus

Source: Renaissance Capital estimates, BP Statistical Review

Dragan Trajkov, Bradley Way & Charles Robertson

Nigeria – A Trend of Its Own

WHILE West and East African exploration may have stolen the spotlight, Nigerian indigenisation efforts in the upstream industry could still provide interesting opportunities in this established oil nation. The government is pushing through a Petroleum Industry Bill (PIB) that will unite disparate legislation dating back decades into one single act. The Shell divestiture process is close to completion. Meanwhile three upstream companies with significant Nigeria upstream exposure have had success on international capital exchanges (Afren in London, Mart Resources in Toronto, and Maurel & Prom Nigeria in Paris). Renaissance expects more investment opportunities in the near future.

In addition to these efforts to provide more opportunities to indigenous companies, it has been widely expected that the Nigerian government (through the PIB) will try to encourage the oil majors to relinquish the relatively small undeveloped fields in the Niger Delta region to indigenous companies. Based on IHS data and excluding the already-awarded marginal fields, Renaissance estimates that in Nigeria there are 177 oilfields that were discovered prior to 2000 which have not yet been developed. We believe that about 157 fields (with a resource of less than 50 million barrels) could potentially be in this marginal field category. About 600 million barrels of oil resources are locked in 113 fields that are 1–10 million barrels in size, with an additional 1,000 million barrels contained in 44 fields of 10–50 million barrels. At an average $10/barrel development cost, these 157 fields would require $16 billion of development investment and can potentially produce a combined 250,000-500,000 bpd. This would push up Nigerian oil output by 10-20%, to close on 3 Mbpd.

Figure 6.5: Potential marginal fields

Field size	# of fields onshore	offshore (<170m depth)	Total	total recoverable mmbbls
1-10	64	49	113	572
11-20	9	15	24	382
21-50	10	10	20	652
51-100	10	6	16	1,197
>100	4	0	4	946
Total	97	80	177	3,749

Source: IHS

The Place to Be in the Coming Decade

SINCE a group of oil industry partners (Tullow Oil, Kosmos Energy and Anadarko Petroleum) made the Jubilee discovery in Ghana in 2007, offshore West Africa has become arguably one of the most desirable exploration areas in the world, with most of the super majors already present in the area. While several smaller discoveries have been made since the Jubilee discovery, the hunt for a second Jubilee continues.

The subsequent discovery by Tullow and its partners of hydrocarbons in Uganda expanded the exploration front from offshore West Africa into onshore and offshore East Africa. Headlines in Kenya and Mozambique – formerly thought to be unproductive in terms of oil and gas – now speak of "new petropowers." As the *Financial Times* noted in 2011, at the start of the boom: "East Africa used to be regarded as an oil industry backwater, a poorer relative to the continent's resource-rich north and west. That's changed over the past 12 months as majors and independents invest hundreds of millions of dollars in exploration and compete to snap up licences on the continent's last hydrocarbon frontier."[3]

While the initial exploration results in East Africa were related to smaller natural gas discoveries, 2011/12 witnessed a complete game change in East Africa. World-class natural gas discoveries in Mozambique and Tanzania have changed the thinking of the major oil and gas companies, which now expect to be building LNG facilities with first production in 2018. The offshore East Africa area is now believed to hold more than 100 trillion cubic feet of natural gas resources. This represents 20% of the 2010 year-end proved natural gas reserves of Africa, and such an addition is a remarkable achievement. Furthermore, recent results from Tullow's Kenya well indicating 20 metres of net oil pay (with drilling yet to be finished) has once again revived hopes of significant oil discoveries in East Africa as well.

These recent successes in West and East Africa suggest that exploration activities will continue in the medium term. The chart below depicts the new oil nations, and the hopefuls.

Figure 6.6: New and potential oil and gas nations

Country	Current discovery status	Estimated first production
Ghana	more than 1.3Bbbls of oil discovered	2010
Uganda	more than 1.0Bbbls of oil discovered	2015/16
Mozambique	more than 45 Tcf of gas resources already discovered	2018
Tanzania	more than 10 Tcf of gas resources discovered	2018
Liberia	successful initial discovery (appraisal needed for commerciality)	na
Kenya	successful initial discovery (appraisal needed for commerciality)	na
Namibia	currently drilling	na
Somalia/Puntland	currently drilling	na
Gambia	likely to drill in late 2012 early 2013	na
Ethiopia	likely to drill in late 2012 early 2013	na
Morocco	likely to drill in 2013/14	na

Source: Renaissance Capital, Company data

No End in Sight

AFRICA'S unexplored areas may yet yield new oil and gas fields, but even if they don't, the continent's relative importance as a producer will only grow over the next few decades as some major producers begin to run dry. Of course, oil and gas and hydrocarbons are finite resources. At some point, even giants such as Saudi Arabia and Venezuela will run dry, though each is thought to have reserves that will support hundreds of years of production at current rates.[4] Imagine a time not so far off – 15, perhaps 20 years hence – when other large producers follow. According to EIA data, the US, China, Russia, Angola and Algeria will run out of oil between now and 2034. While reserve lifespan data have proven unreliable in the past, as new technologies such as slant drilling and hydraulic fracturing have come on line, nonetheless the rates of discovery have failed to keep pace with ever-increasing demand. And as scarcity bites, an ever-smaller number of countries will control what by all indications will remain the world's most valuable commodity.

The big producers of the Gulf, along with Venezuela – whose Orinoco field has proven massively larger than anyone expected – will hold their places, as will Kazakhstan and Canada with its vast oil sands. But an increasing percentage of total global production will be located in Africa, with established producers such as Nigeria and Libya joined by newer entrants such as Sudan, Equatorial Guinea, Gabon and Chad. Whether or not these nations are joined by even more recent entrants such as Kenya or Namibia remains to be seen. And some African producers – Angola, in particular, which the EIA estimates has about 19 years of reserves left – will also be depleted. But the fact is, Africa contains more territory yet to be properly explored by geologists than any other continent, so its surprises in energy are very likely to be on the upside.

From Production to Consumption – Refining in Africa

ECONOMIC growth and fuel demand go hand in hand. SSA oil demand has risen 35% in a decade (3% annually). Note however that Africa remains a net importer of fuels, like many prolific crude producers, including Venezuela and Iran. Recent unrest in Nigeria over attempts to liberalise fuel prices shows the difficulty of deregulating fuels in fast-growing emerging markets. However, countries that don't liberalise prices typically see a significant subsidy burden, a lack of refining investment, or both. This is the case with SSA, which exports oil and imports fuel in most regions.

The characteristics of refined fuel supply conditions in SSA can be summarised as: uneven refining capacity throughout the region relative to demand, different rates of economic growth, different rates at which fuels are subsidised, and different access to facilities to receive refined fuel such as pipelines and ports.

Against these varying supply factors, demand for refined products in SSA has risen across the board, reaching approximately the 1.7 Mbpd mark in 2011, with an annualised growth rate of about 2.6% in the previous 10 years. This has had a few natural consequences.

Bunkering and fuel storage facilities have been money makers in Africa over the past decade. As industrial activity picks up in a particular area, demand from ships, trucks and machinery exacerbates constraints on available fuel oil and diesel. These facilities are basically large-scale storage terminals, providing fuels for transportation and industrial activities. Owners of these facilities oftentimes are selling to buyers whose only other option would be to truck or ship fuels from a long distance away, which in addition to high transportation costs leaves no means of storing and providing refuelling services once the fuels arrive. While simple in nature, these investments have provided high returns. We think East Africa, where activity should soon pick up with natural gas development, is well suited for this type of investment.

Also from this disjointed supply and demand, we have seen hubs for fuel transport and intra-regional trading emerge:

- Côte d'Ivoire has historically been West Africa's largest intra-regional exporter and trader of refined products.
- Uganda is a re-exporter of refined fuels, selling into landlocked markets in Southern Sudan, Rwanda and Burundi.
- Benin is gaining share in re-exporting refined fuel products, often from Nigeria to landlocked regions of West Africa.
- Zambia and the DRC also see significant fuel trade over their borders.

Speak to the Saudis in Aramco's Ras Tanura export facility, and they'll tell you that they have been studying two options: as the European crisis grows worse, either buy an existing European refinery, ship oil there, and sell refined fuel; or build a greenfield refinery in Saudi Arabia, and export finished gasoline and diesel to Europe. Why export a raw commodity when you can export a finished commodity at better returns?

Africa accounts for 12% of global oil production, but only around 4% of global oil demand. With demand in the region for refined fuel increasing, and crude production rising substantially, some countries in SSA are approaching a level where they may face a scaled-down version of the Saudi dilemma.

In terms of downstream investments, we see East Africa as ripe for storage and bunkering facilities. We believe Ghana is an example of a country that could refine fuel and be a major provider for West African fuel demand, but this is perhaps further off in the future. The top candidates to build a refinery in the near term are Angola and Nigeria, which could meet burgeoning domestic demand and benefit from exporting finished fuels. Nigeria is the more probable of the two, with CNPC likely to bargain for building a large-scale refinery in the country in exchange for more access to upstream oil. Recently Uganda has also joined the debate over refined versus crude oil exports. While the government appears to be advocating the development of large refining facilities in the next three years (with more than 100,000 bpd capacity), the upstream partners on the project (Tullow, Total and CNOOC) have been advocating smaller facilities that would be big enough to satisfy the needs of the country and potentially some neighbouring countries. The need for new refining capacity in Africa is compounded by the deteriorating performance of existing refineries. The c.75% utilisation rate of African refineries is approximately 10% below the global average.

This is important to watch because refined fuel demand goes hand in hand with GDP growth, but also because it is self-perpetuating, in a sense. Oil and gas investments and related infrastructure are helping to drive economic growth, which is driving fuel demand, fuel trade in the region, and the need to address the issue of heavily disjointed supply and demand for refined fuel in SSA. All eyes are on the more sexy upstream space, but we believe downstream will see large-scale investment in the near future and is key to watch due to its role in fuelling Africa's economic growth.

Next Generation – Investment and Supply

SO far, the most encouraging SSA trends are evident in East and West Africa exploration and development, East Africa LNG development, and Nigerian indigenisation. For its part, North African energy is already recovering from the disruptions of the Arab Spring. For portfolio investors who can only access half the world's oil reserves, Africa will need to be a significant part of their global energy portfolios. Their need to diversify into Africa will provide fresh funding sources for further exploration, which in turn will help ensure that Africa maintains its prime position in terms of the discovery of new reserves and increased production.

SSA has its difficulties, but its hydrocarbon industry is open for business, and boasts a list of investors more diverse than most other areas. Chinese national oil companies have invested throughout the region – in Nigeria, Angola, Chad and Sudan, to name a few countries. Major IOCs such as Chevron and Shell are invested throughout SSA. SSA also is home to a number of independent explorers, such as Tullow, which are some of the real leaders behind the growing oil and gas industry in SSA. Note the recent acquisition of Cove Energy, an independent engaging in high-risk, high-reward exploration in East Africa. A major NOC (PTT) and a major IOC (Shell) both bid for the company after its discovery off of Mozambique. Former members of US oil and gas majors formed Addax Petroleum, with assets throughout Africa, which was later bought by Sinopec International. The diversity of the investors attracted to SSA's hydrocarbon basins is one reason for the rapid increase in investment and production.

The Chevron chemical engineer told us, "We're just getting started. On the oil front, there are massive deepwater areas that have not been explored, with major reserve upside potential. On the gas front, Africa's gas potential is huge

– if governments can work with companies not to flare or abandon gas, exports could pick up tremendously."

The next 5, 10 and 15 years will see distinct waves of new supply coming to market from SSA: first, we'll see established players, primarily Angola and Nigeria, attempting to attract investment and increase their production. The mid-tier players will then follow – we are likely to see significant reserve upside in Ghana and Uganda, and more material production volumes. Following this, we are likely to see large-scale LNG facilities in East Africa, with growing production volumes throughout Mozambique, Tanzania and Kenya. Africa is the only continental area that we think boasts two decades of inventory of major investment and production in oil and gas. SSA's global importance in oil and gas is poised to continue growing at a rapid clip.

Notes

1. Philippe de Pontet, "Africa poised to become energy powerhouse," Ottawa Citizen, April 14, 2011 http://thecitizen.co.tz/magazines/-/9942-africa-poised-to-become-energy-powerhouse
2. Data derived from BP.
3. Christopher Thompson and Katrina Manson, "Oil groups rush to grab slice of East Africa," *Financial Times*, 20 February 2011.
4. Reserve-to-production ratio data from the US Energy Information Administration.

Chapter 7

Mining: The Growth Has Barely Begun

By Jim Taylor, Rob Edwards, Charles Robertson and Michael Moran

With approximately 60% of Africa's population under age 24, foreign investment and job creation are the only forces that can reduce poverty and stave off the sort of political upheaval that has swept the Arab world. And China's rush for resources has spawned much-needed trade and investment and created a large market for African exports – a huge benefit for a continent seeking rapid economic growth.

—Zambian-born economist Dambisa Moyo[1]

Burkina Faso has been stable for 25 years and the country is very under explored. The mineral endowment is a lot more than you see right now. If you look at what's been discovered in Mali and Ghana, it is just a matter of time before something similar is discovered in Burkina.

—Colin McAleenan, president and CEO, Channel Resources[2]

BLAME China. Surely, many do – but viewing the boom in Africa's mining sector that began in 2000 as nothing but the result of China's appetite for raw materials is far too narrow a perspective. Most important is that the continent's resources are finally being discovered, which is related to China's demand. Paul Collier in *The Plundered Planet*[3] writes that discovered sub-soil resources per square kilometre were just 20% of the OECD average in 2000, but now the resources sector reports a major discovery each year. The positive story for Africa's metals and mining sector is driven by a combination of rising commodity prices, an improved investment climate and the high quality of the continent's natural resources. This is a continent whose potential mineral yields are now coming to the world's attention.

Africa is unique from two key perspectives. First, Africa hosts an enormous geological endowment across the whole spectrum of useful mineral elements, but has only developed a fraction of these resources, the presence of which has in some cases has been known about for hundreds of years. For example, the discovery of copper in Katanga province by Europeans was first documented in 1798 by the Portuguese, but the resource had been exploited for centuries before this by local tribespeople. The same can be said for the gold mines of Ghana and ancient Egypt. In the case of the latter, early evidence of their existence predates any other known exploitation of gold in the world. Second, the intensity of use per capita in most African countries of many minerals is much lower than the global average, a manifestation of the developing status of most African economies.

What does the future hold? Latin America's current status as a dominant supplier of iron ore, copper and hydrocarbons could in theory be replicated by Africa, which hosts a comparable geological footprint. The identification of the true scale of African's mineral potential came about largely as a result of the colonization of Africa by Europeans, whose appetite for these metals and other products catalysed the introduction of industrial-scale processes in some regions. Obvious examples are the iron ore industry in Liberia and Sierra Leone, which supplied steel mills in Europe and Japan from the 1950s to the 1990s, and the Zambian and Zairian Copper Belt, which was in its heyday the world's largest copper-producing district. Both experienced a severe decline in output and eventual collapse due to war and lack of investment. During these periods of African decline, other regions such as Latin America and Australia became large suppliers of major commodities, spurred by a phase of initial discovery and government-led infrastructure investment. Gold and diamond mining in Africa (with the exception of Ghana) had always been dominated by South Africa, an effectively industrialised country. Africa's mining development is not only undergoing a renaissance based on what is known, but there is also a considerable focus on exploration to discover the unknowns, hence creating a two-tiered structure of financially strong developers as well as more prospective explorers, which combined will usurp the speculative element that may seek to opportunistically trade mineral rights. The surface has only been touched. The bedrock that will allow development to flourish is similar to what is required in any sector: political and regional stability, workable and fair minerals rights legislation, and broader institutional support for the mining industry. The regional competiveness of Africa relative to other mining jurisdictions can only improve at a time when Brazil and Australia are experiencing heightened levels of resource tax, permitting restrictions and cost inflation, reducing their ability to retain long-term dominance as suppliers of key commodities to global markets.

The industrialisation and gradual urbanisation of China – a country naturally bereft of many commodities that is heavily reliant on imports – has been central to the revival of fortunes of the African mining sector.

It is true that consistent high economic growth by most emerging economies, led by (but not confined to) China in recent years, has resulted in rising prices for most commodities including foodstuffs, oil and gas and metals. China is responsible for over 40% of the world's trade in copper and a staggering 70% of seaborne iron ore trade. In absolute terms, we expect China to spend $130 billion on imported iron ore in 2012. Globally there has been a dramatic increase in wages in the sector – tales abound of Australian truck drivers earning $200,000 a year and policemen leaving jobs paying $60,000 a year to become security guards at mines on $100,000 a year. This has significantly increased the incentives for exploration and development of natural resources around the world – and thanks to historical under-development of a remarkable set of natural resources, the focus is now increasingly on Africa.

Given that Africa covers 20% of the world's land area, it is perhaps unsurprising that it is rich in natural resources. Its huge mineral endowment has been estimated to contain around 30% of the planet's mineral resources, with 40% of its gold reserves, 90% of its platinum group metals and 60% of its cobalt. It also hosts a significant proportion of the world's chrome, diamonds, uranium and bauxite resources.

Yet commodity production levels were for a long period not only low relative to the level of reserves in the ground, and compared with the pace of development achieved in other commodity-rich areas, but were also falling. This followed a period of low investment and exploration during the second half of the 20th century, which can be attributed largely to declining real commodity prices and heightened political risk.

Politics and Minerals

HOWEVER, since the 1990s there have been improvements in the political environment in many Sub-Saharan African countries, together with the adoption of foreign investment regimes designed to attract the capital necessary to explore and develop the continent's resources. In addition, China has sought out greater control over production of the commodities it requires. Initially, new investment was directed at the oil and gas sector in Africa, but the emergence of a new source of large-scale funding has also generally been welcomed by the mining industry. The improved investment environment and the increase in the amount of capital available for mineral development has led to a surge in activity over the past decade in particular.

Steadily increasing gold prices have seen production of the yellow metal skyrocket over the decade in countries such as Ghana, Tanzania, Mali and Burkina Faso, bringing much-needed jobs, foreign exchange and tax revenue. More recently, a new wave of investment has begun in bulk commodities, such as iron ore and coal. Development of these resources often involves the construction of new railway lines, new port facilities and power infrastructure, which is set to benefit the continent for decades to come.

Sierra Leone is on course to record 21% GDP growth in 2012. This is because iron ore production has resumed after a gap of more than 20 years (as it has in Liberia, too). The African Minerals-operated Tonkolili iron ore project shipped its first ore in January 2012. According to our estimates the operation will generate over $3.5 billion in government royalties and over $10 billion in direct tax benefits to the Sierra Leone government over the next 30 years, making this the most significant contributor by far to Sierra Leonean GDP. A combination of Western institutional funders and major Chinese strategic investors shared the cost of construction over a three-year period. The transport corridor associated with moving up to 20 million tonnes per annum (tpa) of iron ore to the coast has also made a significant contribution to national infrastructure. The operation – including construction activities, ancillary port and rail facilities – directly employs over 8,000 Sierra Leone nationals. Not only does this support a considerable skills transfer, but it is worth noting that using common multipliers of indirect to direct jobs supported by mining projects such as this, as well as considering the dependents of these employees, we can assume that the total number of Sierra Leoneans supported in some manner by the development of this operation runs into the hundreds of thousands.

Further expansions under consideration for the next 10 years at these two operations could see $10 billion more in investment and a three-fold increase in the capacity of the mines. GDP in Sierra Leone will leap from $3 billion to $4 billion in 2012, and per capita GDP from $486 to $621, producing tax revenue that could create a virtuous circle of higher investment in education and transport, attracting more foreign direct investment and growth in non-mining sectors.

Iron and Infrastructure

SIMILARLY, in neighbouring Guinea, three of the world's largest mining companies – Rio Tinto, BHP Billiton and Vale – are involved in iron ore projects that are expected to be developed at a cost of over $12 billion, and which will involve the construction of a 700 km railway line. Other similar large-scale iron ore developments are under way or under consideration in Cameroon and the Republic of Congo. In total, if all the potential iron ore developments in West and Central Africa are delivered, iron ore output could reach nearly 600 million tpa within a decade. A weaker global (or specifically Chinese) economy may well extend the timeframe, but we do assume growing demand from India to Mexico to Indonesia will bring many of these projects to life.

Figure 7.1: Iron ore projects, planned output per annum, by country and project initiator

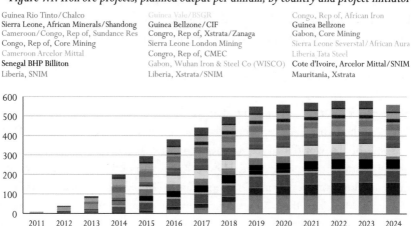

Guinea Rio Tinto/Chalco	Guinea Vale/BSGR	Congo, Rep of, African Iron
Sierra Leone, African Minerals/Shandong	Guinea Bellzone/CIF	Guinea Bellzone
Cameroon/Congo, Rep of, Sundance Res	Congro, Rep of, Xstrata/Zanaga	Gabon, Core Mining
Congo, Rep of, Core Mining	Sierra Leone London Mining	Sierra Leone Severstal/African Aura
Cameroon Arcelor Mittal	Congro, Rep of, CMEC	Liberia Tata Steel
Senegal BHP Billiton	Gabon, Wuhan Iron & Steel Co (WISCO)	Cote d'Ivoire, Arcelor Mittal/SNIM
Liberia, SNIM	Liberia, Xstrata/SNIM	Mauritania, Xstrata

Source: Renaissance Capital estimates

In Mozambique, although the presence of high-value coking coal has been known of for decades, it is only now that investment in refurbished and new rail and ports is being made. Key to this have been not only high commodity prices but also a model transformation of the institutional capacities related to the mining sector as part of a World Bank-IDA-sponsored initiative launched in 2001, after decades of apartheid-era civil war had paralysed the country. The mining code was modernised on par with global best practice in 2003, and a world-class geological database was established and more importantly published.

Lastly, a robust and modern environmental management and permitting system was installed.

As a direct consequence of a reduction in political risk and a commitment to attract investment, private-sector activity in the mining sector flourished. In 1996, there were just 10 private operators in Mozambique. From 2009 until 2011, 112 licences were issues to 45 national and foreign companies in the coal-rich Tete region alone. Real GDP growth is expected to remain at 7.5% per annum on the back of increasing inflows of foreign aid and foreign direct investment into minerals and infrastructure mega-projects. Over $10 billion has been spent and committed by Rio Tinto and Vale alone on acquiring, commissioning and developing their respective coal licences and ancillary infrastructure. The first exports of coal were made late in 2011, will reach 18 million tonnes (mnt) by 2015 and then expand significantly to well over 50 million tpa by 2020. This will still be dwarfed by Australia's roughly 200mnt of projected 2015 exports, but will be equal to half of all North America's 100mnt 2015 exports and may exceed Mongolia's or Russia's exports (around 30mnt each in 2015).

Copper Is Back

SIMILARLY, Africa's copper production is undergoing a resurgence. From 1970–90 the Central African Copperbelt on the border of Zambia and the DRC was one of the world's largest copper-producing regions, with annual output of 1–1.2mnt of copper per year. However, due to political chaos, mismanagement and low commodity prices, production collapsed to less than one-third of this by 2000. Again, the buoyant commodity-price environment since the early 2000s has seen investment return, and copper and cobalt production from the region has surged, having passed previous peaks in 2011. Further developments are under way in both countries, with renewed investment in transport infrastructure to the east. One example is Rendeavour's project to build a city 8 km from Lumbabashi, the capital of copper-rich Katanga province, which reflects and responds to its growing wealth and the requirement for world-class urban infrastructure.

Renaissance is also optimistic about the future of the overall commodity sector. In many cases, commodity prices remain above the levels required to provide incentives to the providers of capital to develop Africa's resources. Encouragingly for the discovery of new deposits, exploration expenditure in Africa has risen steadily over the past decade and is now running at around $1.8 billion per annum, approximately 15% of the world's total.

As a result, the mining industry is not only an increasingly important source of foreign exchange for economies across the continent; it also contributes significantly to governments' tax revenue, and is an important catalyst for education and training of the workforce, while also paying for the infrastructure in ports and other transport links that will benefit other sectors.

It's about Price and Profit

THE main counter-argument we hear is that African minerals are being exploited for the benefit of others, and providing little benefit to Africa itself. Some accuse China of becoming the imperial power of the 21st century in place of the European colonialists of the 19th century, though China itself seems to have shifted from owning and operating mines in Africa, to instead purchasing the product of mines operated by others.

We argue that if resources have value today, there is good reason to sell them. The high price of silk in the Roman era or spices in medieval times was not a promise that such prices would last forever. Resource wealth can be transitory and should be utilised while it exists, providing that an acceptable balance of value and return on investment is found between the purchaser, the miner and the ultimate owner of that resource. Some governments have made resource extraction so unprofitable that investment fails to materialise. In that situation, resources stay in the ground, no transport links are built, no jobs are created, no foreign exchange is provided to fund imports of investment (or consumption) goods and no revenue accrues to the government. Resource nationalism and government efforts to take a larger share of resource profits are inevitable when prices rise. We saw it with the nationalisation of oil companies in the late 1970s. We see it again now from the UK and Australia to South America. The miners argue that the profits are required to counter-balance the barren periods of low commodity prices that were seen in the 1960s and 1990s. So far, Africa is providing more opportunities for new investment than problems.

The benefits to Africa of Chinese investment should be quite different from the impact of 19th century colonial powers. A century ago, all the benefits were expected to accrue to the colonial powers, their companies and their people. Today African governments can and do secure benefits for their countries, jobs for their people and a share of the revenue from the resultant growth. They are determined to preserve their hard-won independence and will use a variety of funding sources, from multi-nationals to the World Bank to China, to secure this. The model for 21st century Africa may be closer to the 19th century experience of self-governing Argentina, Canada, Australia or New Zealand, than what colonized Africa itself experienced in the 19th century or colonized Latin America in the 18th century. Mining can be used to kick-start self-sustaining growth. The key to maintaining political support for foreign investment in the resources sector is to ensure long-term gains from the transparent use of the revenue. Where governments fail to prove this, they will lose power, as happened to Rupiah Banda in Zambia.

"The Chinese are making great investments in various areas of infrastructure all over Africa," says Amanuel Gebremeskel, an Ethiopian-born banker. "But a certain level of local involvement would go a long way to reducing the urban unemployment problem. This is really totally up to local initiative and to expect the Chinese to solve this problem is nonsensical."[4] Such thinking is what has inspired political backing for the new cities being built across the continent, such as Rendeavour's Kiswishi development in the DRC.

African Resources to Become a Domestic Demand Play

BEYOND the next decade, what is striking is that Africa itself will be consuming the resources that come out of the ground. At present, with per capita GDP around $2,000 across the continent, steel demand for example is very low.

Figure 7.2: Steel consumption (kg/capita) against per capita GDP in constant 2005 PPP dollars

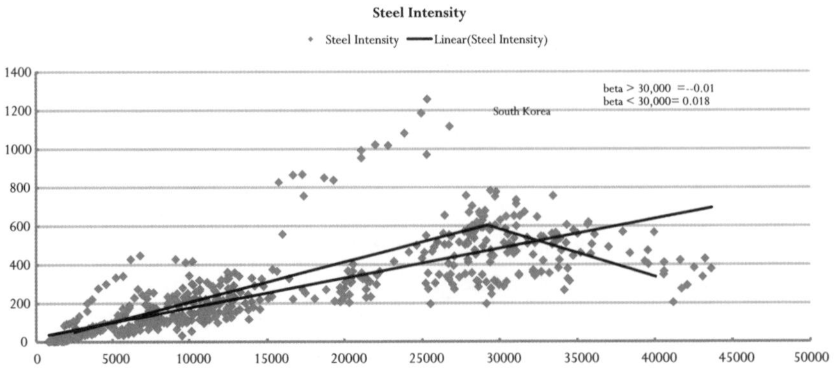

Source: World Steel Association, World Bank, Renaissance Capital estimates

The implication of these charts is that at $10,000 of per capita GDP, per capita steel consumption can be anywhere in the range of 50–350 kg (excluding China). But at $15,000, the range is tighter at 200–400 kg. When Nigeria reaches Indian levels of per capita GDP, around 2018, its steel consumption should be around 50 kg per capita. At South Africa's wealth level of $9,500, per capita consumption may range from 50 to 350 kg, but by the time $15,000 is reached, around 300 kg per capita becomes more plausible.

Domestic Demand Will Grow

AS per capita GDP increases, demand will pick up. At opposite ends of the African continent, both Egypt at $5,000 per capita GDP and South Africa at $9,500 use around 110–120 kg of steel per capita,, compared with less than 20 kg in Ghana, Kenya, Nigeria and Tanzania. The low figure for South Africa may reflect South Africa's concentrated GDP and a Gini coefficient (a measurement of inequality) which is among the most extreme in the world. As a result, the consumption implied by the average per capita GDP figure might not apply, as none of the population is at that average. For the rest of SSA, Egypt may be a better guide to likely trends: overall, Renaissance expects per capita steel demand to more than double to India's level when per capita GDP reaches India's current level of $3,000.

Figure 7.3: Steel consumption (kg / capita) relative to per capita GDP

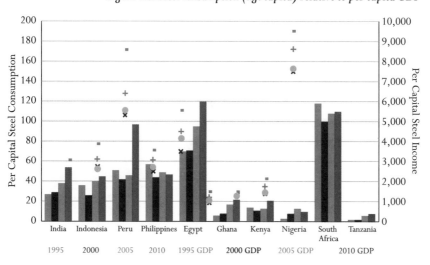

Source: UN, World Steel Association, Renaissance Capital estimates

123

THE chart below shows how Nigeria is currently at the low end of the demand range. It is lagging what an average country at its income level would normally consume, with annual steel demand of 1.6mnt, against an implied 6.5mnt. By 2025, implied data say this should be 25mnt (more than double Indonesia's 11mnt of demand today), and by 2040 70mnt (above India's 66mnt of demand today). By 2050 consumption should be 115mnt, above US demand of 90mnt in 2010, which would make Nigeria the second-largest consumer based on 2010 rankings after China. Assuming a per capita GDP around $15,000 and nearly 400 million people, that number is plausible.

Figure 7.4: Nigerian actual and implied steel demand, against per capita GDP, 1995–2050

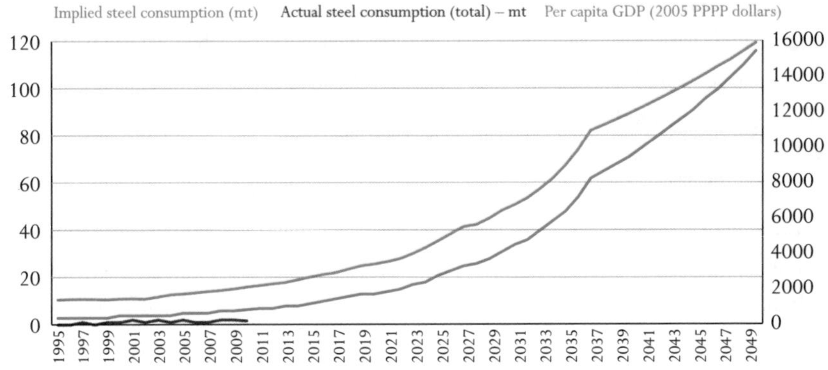

Implied steel consumption (mt)   **Actual steel consumption (total) – mt**   Per capita GDP (2005 PPPP dollars)

Source: UN, World Steel Association, Renaissance Capital estimates

The next decade will also see Africa increase its export supply of the mineral commodities that 1 billion people in China (slowing now) and then India (still rising) will need as they rise up the per capita income charts. Within a decade, new iron ore projects could add 500 million tpa of iron ore output.

But by then, blaming China will be even less justifiable than it is today. Along with the BRICS and other emerging market stars, Africa will increasingly be a consumer of these metals, and a price-maker rather than a price-taker.

Notes

1. Dambisa Moyo, *Winner Takes All: China's Race for Resources and What It Means for the World* (New York: Penguin, 2012).
2. "West Africa Hosts Untapped Mineral Wealth," *Engineering and Mining Journal,*

September 2010, http://www.e-mj.com/index.php/features/530-west-africa-hosts-untapped-mineral-wealth.html.

3. Paul Collier, *The Plundered Planet: Why We Must—and How We Can—Manage Nature for Global Prosperity* (Oxford: Oxford University Press, 2010).

4. Interview with Amanuel Gebremeskel, July 2012, New York.

Chapter 8

The World's Biggest Demographic Dividend

By Charles Robertson

The real key to success for the youth in Kenya is to open their minds to good ideas that can have a multiplier effect. Zero multiplied by zero will always be zero. You can't get something out of nothing. We need to expand our ideas — two multiplied by two is four and four multiplied by four is 16 and so on. That is the true secret to success!

—Manu Chandaria, chairman, Chandaria Group[1]

WHAT is the connection between wages rising 13% in Shanghai in 2011, the eurozone debt crisis and the fact that nine of the ten countries with the highest birth rates in the world are in Africa?

Answer: demographics. We can already see the Chinese pricing themselves out of low-to-medium-wage technology jobs. Africa, with its wealth of job-hungry young people, is well-placed to capture these in the coming decades. In Europe, the pension crisis that has crippled Western budgets is a warning of what an elderly population and unsustainable social-security spending could do to China. It is also likely to spark capital inflows to fast-growing Africa in coming decades as ageing Western populations seek better returns than the 1–2% yields currently on offer in the US or Germany. Africa, with the best demographic profile in the world, is already further advanced on private pension provision than many Asian or European countries. Indeed, Renaissance estimates suggest that Sub-Saharan African pension funds alone will increase from $264 billion in 2010 to $622 billion by 2020 and reach $7.3 trillion by 2050.

Demographics as a Growth Factor

WHEN countries get richer, child mortality rates fall and life expectancy increases significantly. Over the course of a couple of generations, people respond to this by greatly reducing the number of children they have. But during those initial two generations, there is a population explosion. The result is higher demand in the economy but increased labour that helps keep wages down. One factor behind low Chinese inflation in recent decades has been the high supply of young workers. One factor that has been prompting 10–25% wage increases in China is that the supply of young people is in sharp decline.

Figure 8.1: Population of 15–24 year-olds by region, 2000–50

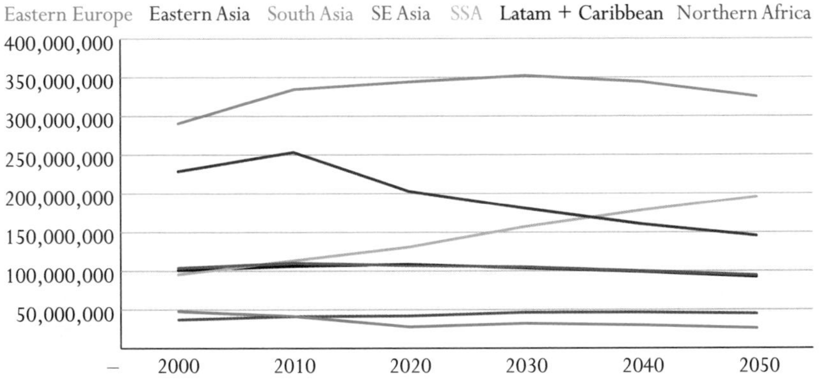

Eastern Europe   Eastern Asia   South Asia   SE Asia   SSA   Latam + Caribbean   Northern Africa

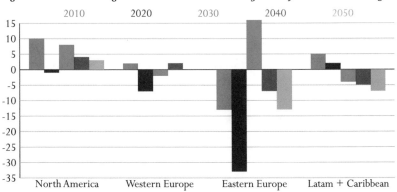

Source: UN

The West is well past this point of decline. The number of 15–24 year-olds is expected to stagnate between 2010 and 2020 in North America, and to decline by 7% in Western Europe. Latin America and the Caribbean will see only marginal growth of 2% before declining over the next 30 years. Southeast Asia is shrinking, too.

Figure 8.2: Percent change each decade in the number of 15–24 year-olds in each region

Source: UN

Eastern Europe is expected to see a dramatic 33% fall in the absolute number of 15–24 year-olds, from 42 million to 28 million over 2010–20, due to emigration by potential parents over 1995–2005 and low birth rates among those who remained in Eastern Europe.

Most shocking of all is that China will see its 15–24-year-old population shrink by 47 million (the US Census Bureau says 67 million), with that 21% decline bringing down East Asian numbers by 20%. So significant is this, that Asia as a whole will see a 6% fall in 15–24 year-olds this decade. The supply of young Asian labour is in decline.

Figure 8.3: Percent change in numbers of 15–24 year-olds in each decade

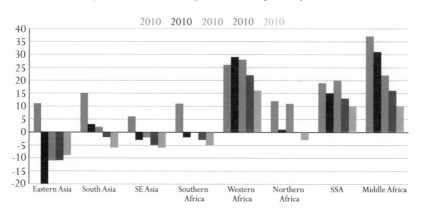

Source: UN

The only continent forecast to experience significant population growth is Africa – and as northern Africa is now relatively rich, the bulk of the growth will be in SSA. Its cohort of 15–24 year-olds will rise by 15% this decade, 20% to 2030, 13% to 2040 and still 10% to 2050. Nigeria alone will become the fourth-most-populous country in the world by 2050, and Africa will have seven of the 20 largest countries.

More Workers, More Consumption

FOR labour-intensive industries such as textiles, or export-orientated services, evidently Africa will look ever more attractive as a location for new factories. While Chinese mobile phones may not be made in Angola today, Chinese clothing and shoe companies do look to Ethiopia as an alternative to expensive domestic production. These industries will entice rural workers on subsistence income out of villages and into cities. By paying their new employees higher wages, these growing sectors should themselves boost consumption.

Indeed, upward mobility, the lubricant of the American Dream and so many successful economies elsewhere, is present throughout Africa. Call it the African Dream. The famous rags-to-riches tales, like those of Nigerian cement magnate Aliko Dangote, the Sudanese telecoms entrepreneur and philanthropist Mo Ibrahim, or Kenya's Ory Okolloh, now Google's Africa policy manager, certainly are not representative. Nonetheless, just as Europe's Rothschilds and Agnellis, or America's Carnegies and Rockefellers, inspired millions of strivers in an earlier era, the lives of Africa's best-known success stories are a driving force behind the expansion of its middle class.

In Accra, Ghana's capital, young Ransford Aning struggled to earn a living cleaning the floors of the popular Champs Bar and Restaurant. He worked hard, watched how the business worked, and got promoted to the wait staff and then management. Today, he earns a solidly middle-class salary as the general manager of a large provisioning firm, Stellar Catering.

In Cameroon, Imane Ayissi, formerly a dancer in the national ballet company, started a successful fashion line popular across West Africa.

Uganda's Gordon Wavamunno began as a taxi driver, founded a bus company to link his village with the capital, and ultimately won the right to operate the country's first Mercedes franchise. Today he is one of Uganda's richest people.

Unity Dow, the first woman on Botswana's high court, changed her country's history and advanced the cause of African women by challenging traditions that reserved inheritance rights exclusively to males.

The young adults who aspire to follow in their footsteps need homes, and items to fill those homes. Consumption will rise and consumer goods sales will increase. This has already begun. Nestlé expects Africa's share of global sales to double to 10% by 2020. Roughly 30% of all Diageo Group capital expenditure in 2011–12 has been in Africa. We read that Guinness sells more in Nigeria than Ireland. But what our growth trajectory tells us, is that this demand will soon be obvious in higher-value-added items, too.

If China became the dream market for the automotive sector in 2010 – which might have looked an unrealistic forecast in 1970 – demographic data coupled with rising GDP mean Africa will be overtaking China's current sales within two generations.

Figure 8.4: Stock of motor vehicles against per capita GDP in constant 2005 dollars

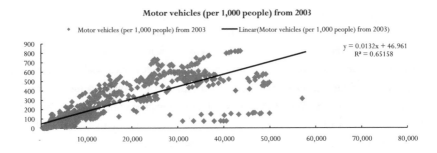

Motor vehicles (per 1,000 people) from 2003

Source: Renaissance Capital estimates, World Bank

Based on the chart above, we can estimate the stock of vehicles in Africa today and make plausible forecasts out to 2050. We assume 5% of the previous decade's stock needs to be renewed each year as 20-year-old cars deteriorate and are replaced. If we add new stock and replaced stock together, we might see African car sales rise from approximately 3 million annually in 2010 to 8 million by 2020. By 2030 they should equal US vehicle sales of 14 million today. Sales will surpass China's current 20 million by the middle of the 2030s, reaching 25 million by 2040. At the end of our forecast period, we expect the stock of vehicles to be 575 million and annual sales to be 40 million.

So while jobs in the near term will be created in the processed agricultural sector, infrastructure development, and textiles, or back-office IT jobs thanks to broadband access, there will be an increasingly significant shift into higher-valued-added sectors in subsequent years and decades. A domestic car industry will require a domestic steel industry. The service sector will continue to expand.

Figure 8.5: Vehicle stock in Africa and annual sales

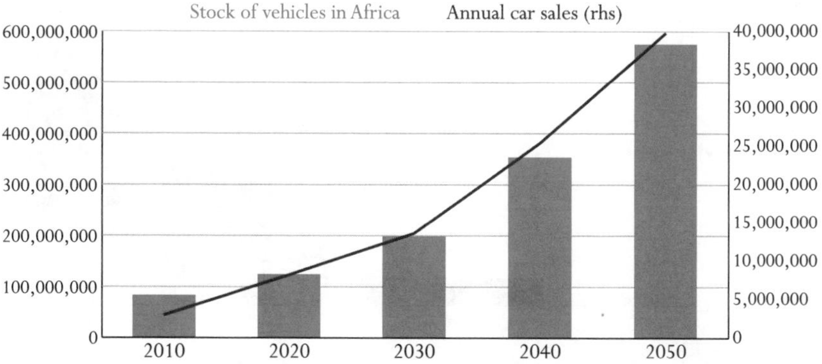

Source: Renaissance Capital estimates

The youth of tomorrow won't just be driving far more. They will also be flying, ideally with their beloved, but increasingly with their 2.2 children, too. Already air-passenger numbers in the top-20 airports exceed 100 million (South Africa and Egypt dominate). Based on Renaissance estimates of air-passenger numbers against per capita GDP, passenger numbers in Africa should be 85 million in 2010. But rising income means that doubles every decade, to nearly 200 million by 2020, 400 million by 2030, 900 million by 2040 and 1.7 billion by 2050. This will hopefully be recognised by Lagos and Nairobi airport developers and helps justify Rwanda's plans to develop a new capital airport. It may be a trend that Stelios Haji-Ioannou, founder of EasyJet (a European low-cost airline) is fully aware of. His next project is to establish FastJet in Kenya, Tanzania, Ghana and Angola.

Figure 8.6: Air-passenger numbers in Africa, 2010–50

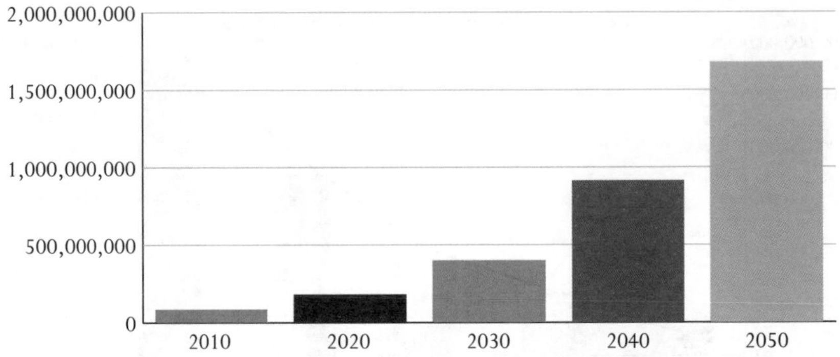

Source: Renaissance Capital estimates

We have much less comprehensive or reliable data to work with on other products. Based on data from India, Egypt and a few others, we can estimate that the stock of TV sets may be around 260 per 1,000 people at Africa's per capita GDP level, and we can assume this will rise to 308 by 2030 and 454 by 2050. Assuming only a quarter of the previous decade's stock is replaced, this implies TV sales rising from 15 million a year in 2020 to 33 million by 2040 and 46 million by 2050 – although they may be called holographic projectors by then.

Based on data from two sources, PC sales will soar, rising from an implied 4 million in 2020 to 11–12 million in 2030, 30–40 million in 2040 and 57–87 million in 2050. Microwave sales should rise from 6 million in 2020 to 11 million by 2030, 21 million by 2040 and 35 million by 2050. Dishwasher sales will begin to take off after 1 million sales in 2030, to 6 million in 2040, reaching 15 million in 2050. Fridge sales should pick up from 3 million in 2020, to 5 million by 2030, 9 million in 2040 and 14 million in 2050.

This consumption explosion will come despite a likely rise in taxation to fund better education and healthcare. If the authorities want to do anything more to limit this, Renaissance recommends encouraging a larger share of wages into private pension funds, so that Africa can avoid the demographic impact of ageing later in the century.

Why Dependency Ratios Matter

WHEN we look at the ratio of working-age adults to pension-age adults, Europe's challenges don't look limited to questions about the ability of peripheral economies to remain in the eurozone. Rather the question is how so few adults will be able to support the growing number of pensioners. The problem looks acute in Japan, which in 2010 had 2.6 working age adults per person aged 65 or more, but will see this fall to 1.9 by 2020 according to UN estimates. The challenge is growing even in China, where the ratio of workers to pensioners will slump from eight to five this decade, implying a slowdown in economic growth.

Figure 8.7: Ratio of 20–64 year-olds per pensioner (aged 65+) in 2010 and 2020

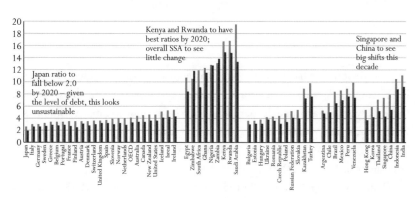

Source: UN 2008 and 2010 database

When it comes to demographic dependency, one continent stands apart, and that is Africa. While richer countries such as Egypt and South Africa will have dependency ratios similar to India's by 2020, most of the rest will have a far better demographic profile.

It will be no surprise to experts on Africa that it will maintain an excellent demographic profile for decades to come, with 10–15 working-age people per pensioner in 2030, and around 10 in 2050. Even Egypt and South Africa will still have around five workers per pensioner by 2050. Yet even with a low pensioner rate, it is amazing to see that African pension fund assets are already among the highest of the emerging markets.

Figure 8.8: Numbers of 20–64 year-olds per pensioner (aged 65+) in Africa

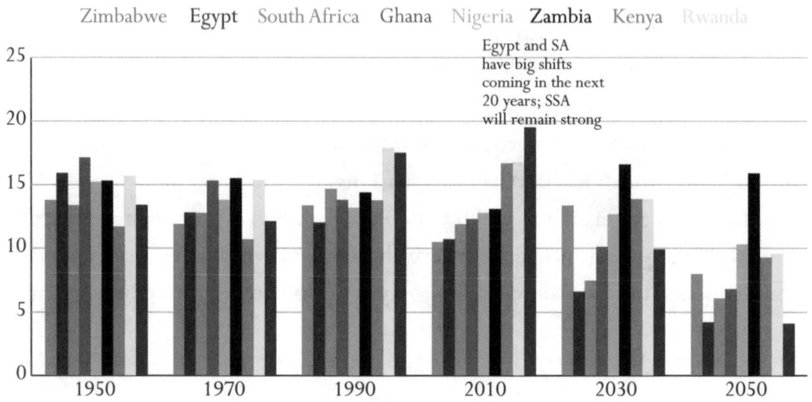

Zimbabwe   **Egypt**   South Africa   Ghana   Nigeria   **Zambia**   Kenya   Rwanda

Egypt and SA
have big shifts
coming in the next
20 years; SSA
will remain strong

Source: UN 2010 database

The region that has recently gone through what Africa is due to experience in the coming decades is, of course, Asia. As recently as 1990, there were more than 10 working-age people per pensioner from South Korea to Indonesia. In 2010, that figure was still above 10 in Asia's favourite equity market, Indonesia, but just 7.9 in China. By 2030, the figure for China will have slumped to 3.8 – equivalent to Japan in 2000.

China's demographic profile today is where Japan was in 1975, which again reinforces the Renaissance view that China's threatened crash (which is always possible) is most likely to occur around 2025. By 2030, Hong Kong and South Korea could have worse demographics than Italy did in 2010 – but Hong Kong has pension fund assets of 35% of GDP today (compared with Italy's 5%); while South Korean pension spending is extremely low and its demographic profile may be bearable if politics does not alter policy. East Asia's strong GDP growth is a fading story.

Figure 8.9: Number of 20–64 year-olds per pensioner (aged 65+) in Asia

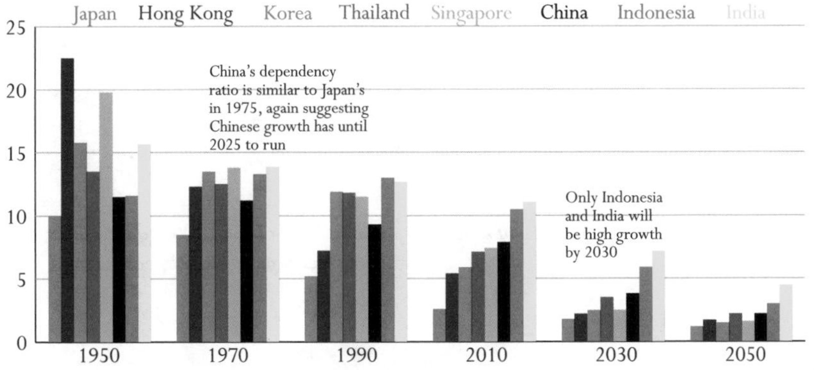

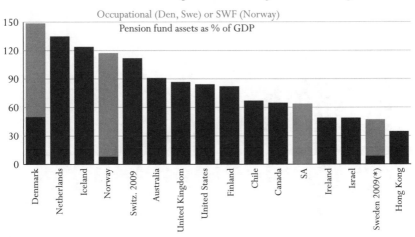

Source: UN 2010 database

Africa's Surprising Pension Wealth

PENSION funds are huge in some of the safest credits in the world – northern European and Anglo-Saxon countries, Chile, South Africa and Israel. The link is not coincidental. Domestic pension funds are often willing buyers of government liabilities, and can be repressed into buying government debt when times are tough. Private pension funds reduce the long-term obligations of governments and provide an ample supply of financing which can drive growth.

Figure 8.10: Pension fund assets as % of GDP in 2010

Source: OECD, including special figures cited for Denmark and Norway

The size of these funds is significant. In the US, pension funds in 2010 were 84% of GDP or $12 trillion, which is nearly enough to cover all federal government debt. Renaissance expects more of this money to enter the emerging market asset class, but where we differ from others is that we see more significant long-term opportunities in Africa – where the time horizon works in favour of pension funds.

Figure 8.11: Global pension fund assets, $ billion in 2010 (Japan 2009) and country total as percentage of global pension fund assets

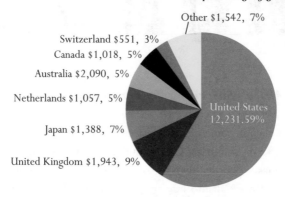

Source: OECD

Figure 8.12: Pension fund assets as % of GDP in 2010, unless otherwise stated

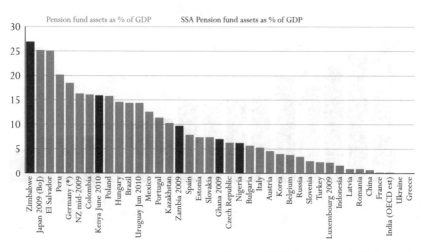

Source: OECD, Renaissance Capital estimates

It is instructive to note how the rest of the world stacks up against Africa. Who would have thought that Zimbabwe is better prepared for future pension needs than Japan? Yes, we can hear faint cries from some suggesting it would be unwise to trust the Zimbabwean authorities to provide pensions over the long term, so private provision is essential. But UN data suggest we should be sceptical about Japan's future public pension provision, too. Other surprises are that Kenya's pension funds are relatively larger than those of Brazil or Poland, and that Nigeria has better pension provision for the future than Austria, Italy or Belgium.

The size of African pension funds is not just impressive relative to many other developed and emerging markets, but also when compared with the scale of financial market assets they can buy.

Figure 8.13: Pension fund assets as % of GDP and as a proportion of total government gross debt (IMF) as % of GDP (rhs; capped at 100%)

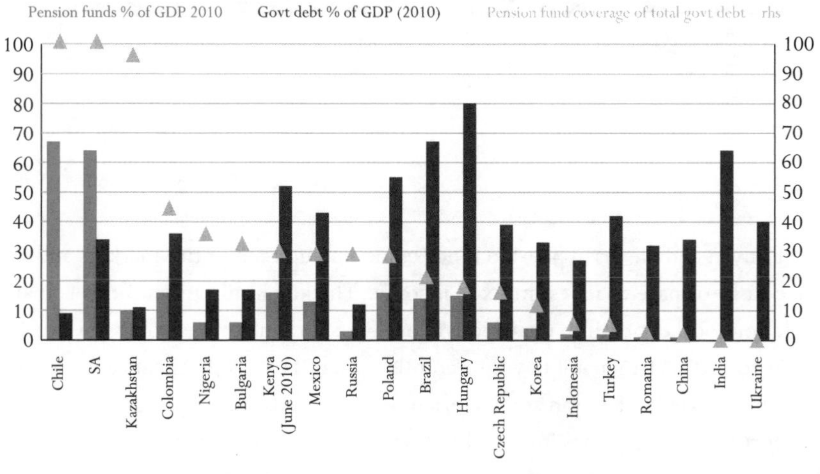

Source: OECD, national sources, IMF

For Nigeria, Kenya and Mexico, pension funds represent some 30% of all government debt, and indeed these funds are very significant players in their respective local debt markets. South African pension funds could buy their entire sovereign debt market.

Some emerging-market pension funds are so big that we have had to cap the scale at 300% coverage of their equity market capitalisation in the graph below.

In both Nigeria and Kenya, pension funds could buy their equity markets outright, while in South Africa they could buy 75% of the market.

Figure 8.14: Figure 8.14: Pension fund assets ($ billion; rhs) in 2010 vs equity free-float market cap in December 2010 ($ billion, rhs) and coverage by the former of the latter(lhs)

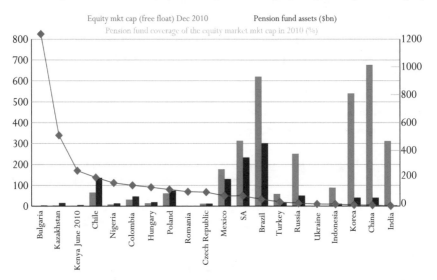

Source: OECD, national sources, MSCI

Kenyan and Nigerian pension funds could buy up their entire markets and still have cash to spare to invest in fixed income. The key implication of this is that if yields on local debt fall to unattractive levels, or if regulators encouraged pension funds to redirect their money into equities, there is a highly significant bid possible from existing Kenyan and Nigerian pension funds. In addition, the domestic support for local equities implied by this means markets may prove less volatile, harder to short, and more akin to what we see in South Africa or Australia than Russia, where small pension assets make local equities highly dependent on the mood swings of global investors.

However, statements from Nigeria and Kenya suggest the authorities would prefer to see their country's funds support long-term infrastructure projects, for example in Kenya by buying the 20-year or 30-year infrastructure bonds issued by the government, and potentially doing something similar in Nigeria in the future. The $18 billion of Nigerian pension fund assets in mid-2012 and the

$5 billion of Kenyan pension funds in 2010 could help to fund the construction of more than a few roads. However, what is most important in the long run is ensuring a good real return for these pension funds.

Not only are local pension funds surprisingly significant in their local markets – Nigeria's funds are roughly double Russia's or Turkey's – but they are also growing faster than GDP (with one exception in Africa being Ghana, where upward revisions in GDP and weakening of the currency may have contributed to the fall).

Figure 8.15: Pension fund assets as a % of GDP

	2001	2002	2003	2004	2005	2006	2007	2008	2009	2010
Czech	2.3	2.7	3.1	3.5	4.1	4.5	4.7	5.2	6.0	6.3
Hungary	3.9	4.5	5.2	6.8	8.5	9.7	10.9	9.6	13.1	14.6
Poland	2.4	3.8	5.3	6.8	8.7	11.1	12.2	11.0	13.5	15.8
Turkey	–	–	–	0.4	0.7	0.7	1.2	1.5	2.3	2.3
Mexico	4.3	5.2	5.8	6.3	10.0	11.5	11.5	10.2	7.3	12.6
Ghana	–	–	–	11.0	9.6	6.4	7.1	7.2	5.4	na
Chile	–	55.1	58.2	59.1	59.4	61.0	64.4	52.8	65.1	67.0
South Africa	55.6	53.8	52.3	57.5	62.4	64.1	66.5	58.5	61.8	64.0
Russia	–	–	–	–	2.1	2.7	2.8	1.7	3.1	3.5
Kazakhstan	–	–	–	7.7	8.6	8.7	9.4	8.6	10.8	10.3
Nigeria	–	–	–	–	–	–	3.9	4.5	6.1	6.9
Kenya	–	–	–	–	–	–	–	–	–	15.9

Source: OECD, IMF, Nigerian Pension Commission, Renaissance Capital estimates

Over the longer term, we should expect SSA pension funds to become ever more significant. The warning from Europe would ideally encourage governments to shift 1% of GDP annually into private pensions. Latin America and central Europe were achieving a similar shift over 2001–10 (see above). We also assume pension funds might manage 5% annual growth in real terms. Taken together, and starting just with roughly $260 billion in pension funds for six SSA countries in 2010 (mostly South Africa), the implication is that SSA pension funds will grow to $622 billion by 2020, and increase to $7.3 trillion by 2050.

Massive Growth Is within Easy Reach

SUGGESTING SSA funds alone will need to find a home for over $300 billion by the end of this decade sounds impressive, but it only implies a rise in pension fund assets relative to SSA GDP from 21% to 26%. Even the estimate of $7 trillion by 2050 is only equivalent to 34% of GDP. This would put SSA in a stronger position than Asia, but not as secure as Anglo-Saxon countries or Scandinavia. The message here is that governments should be pushing their pension fund managers to achieve more than a 5% real return (not hard in such fast-growing economies), whilst incentivising their populations to contribute more than 1% of GDP annually to pension funds.

If we put North Africa into the mix, assuming the same starting point for pension fund size (i.e. zero in North Africa), African pension fund assets would be $10 trillion by 2050, still not as large as US pension funds are today. Nonetheless, what our forecasts suggest is that planning can be done now to help provide an African pension of pot of $10 trillion by 2050 that will go a long way to securing the future of those who will be driving growth in the next few decades. Even with Africa's good demographics, there will still be a need to deliver support for a pensioner population of 167 million in 2050 (against 40 million in 2010), rising to 672 million by 2100.

Such sums will provide a funding choice for Africa that other countries – from southern Europe to Asia – simply don't have. It should reduce the cost of capital and help fuel growth. Most important, we are not expecting Africa to make a significant change here, but simply to do more of what is already being done.

Figure 8.16: SSA pension funds, in $ billion and % of GDP

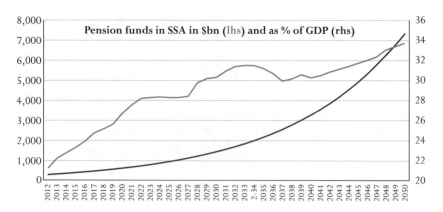

Source: Renaissance Capital estimates

Charles Robertson

Demography Is Destiny

DEMOGRAPHIC trends help explain why southern Europe was booming in the 1950s and 1960s, and why China has been such a success story in the 1990s and 2000s. India and Indonesia still have the best part of a generation to run, demographically speaking, but it is Africa where the future remains bright for the next 40 years. The working-age population will increase by nearly a billion from 574 million in 2010 to 1.4 billion by 2050, supporting the urbanisation trend with the benefits we outline in chapter 12. We will see Africa surge, while Asia matures and China greys.

The demographic impact on consumption will be dramatic. From 3 million car sales annually today, we expect to see Africa buying more cars by 2030 than the 14 million that the US buys today. Within 20 years, there are likely to be well-established African brands in car-making. The coming boom in consumer goods consumption will increasingly be met by supply from factories employing Africa's young adults.

One source of funding for this growth will be the pension funds, which are already more significant than many realise. South Africa rivals Chile in the size of pension funds (as a percentage of GDP) and SSA countries have far better funding than most of Asia, and hugely better demographic profiles, too. Renaissance forecasts that SSA pension funds will rise from around $260 billion today to $7 trillion by 2050, and $10 trillion across the continent.

Africa's demographic outlook means the future of Africa's politics is relatively predictable. In the northern hemisphere we should expect generational conflict in the political arena. Politics will be a contest between the pro-inflation preferences of indebted working-age adults and the pro-deflation preferences of the elderly, with their savings and need for investment certainty. We have yet to see how that plays out over a period of decades. But in emerging markets, and particularly Africa, we will be in the more familiar political territory of class issues driving politics. A rising middle class will demand political accountability, responsive government, and probably higher spending on education and health. It may prove to be Africa's good fortune that its growth trajectory surge is happening after that of Europe and East Asia. Its political leaders and best technocrats will be able to see the 21st century impact on the northern hemisphere of both the welfare-state spending and the savings decisions of the 20th century. Africa will be in a strong position to avoid the same mistakes – by emphasising pension savings now, and avoiding open-ended expenditure commitments that could prove undeliverable in the long term. Getting the balance right will never be easy, but it may be easier in Africa than anywhere else.

Notes

1. "Manu Chandaria: Excellence – Made in Kenya," *GenerationKenya* (blog), 15 May 2008, http://generationkenya.co.ke/manu-chandaria-excellence-%E2%80%93-made-in-kenya/.

Chapter 9

African Banking: The Revolution Is Now

By Nothando Ndebele

Africa is the Silicon Valley of banking. The future of banking is being defined here. The new models for what will be mainstream throughout the world are being incubated here. It's going to change the world.

—Carol Realini, CEO of US-based online banking company Obopay1

Banks have revolving doors and armed security guards. Consumers believe they are for the rich only.

—Gavin Krugel, chief customer strategy officer at South Africa's Fundamo, a pioneer in mobile financial services2

AFRICA has been a continent of the unbanked, but this is changing before our eyes. New technology is delivering banking services to millions – cheaply, simply and more quickly than many in the West have ever experienced. Whereas in the US in the 19th century, banking lagged the agricultural revolution by a century and the industrial revolution by decades, in Africa banking is becoming a key agent of growth in these other sectors. Access to credit is enabling Kenyan farmers to borrow ahead of the next planting season, and helping to smooth fluctuations in income arising from variable weather, while mobile banking ensures that these farmers can move money easily without making laborious and costly journeys to bank branches. This dynamic fusion of technology and entrepeneurship prefigures the revolution in traditional banking that will come as a growing African middle class and more confident corporate sector begin borrowing. We see copious room for expansion in private-sector debt.

Earlier we contrasted the debt crisis in developed markets with the enviable public finance ratios now common across Africa. We did not focus on private-sector debt. It is a rise in private-sector debt that has often helped deliver prosperity in developed markets, as we saw in the US under Presidents Eisenhower and Kennedy in the middle of the 20th century, and again under Reagan and Clinton later in the century. Yet the excessive boom over the past decade, when household and corporate debt reached 200% of GDP in the US, UK and peripheral Europe (seen by Japan in 1990), has been a key contributor to the sovereign debt concerns now shared by those nations.

Figure 9.1: Private sector debt as % of GDP

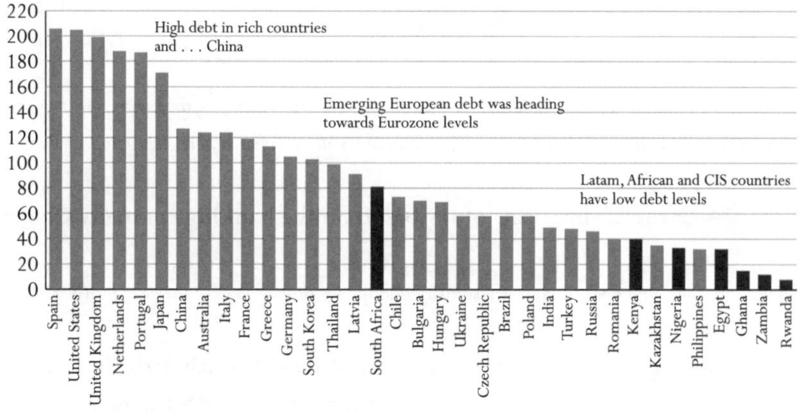

Source: IMF

By contrast, Africa remains the most under-banked continent in the world. Household and corporate debt is usually around 20–50% of GDP, whereas in developed markets the ratio easily exceeds 100% of GDP. If we assume Sub-Saharan African private-sector debt is 35% of GDP across the continent, then it should rise from $500 billion in 2012 to $7.6 trillion by 2050, as GDP rises from $1.4 trillion to $22 trillion. But if debt also rises as a share of GDP, even to the modest 100% of GDP seen in Germany or considerably poorer Thailand, the implications for bank lending across the continent will be dramatically larger. The stock of bank lending will reach $22 trillion (in 2012 dollars) by 2050. That 44-fold rise in bank assets is a self-evidently a bullish story, even if there are boom and busts to manage along the way. Indeed, so confident are we that these crashes will come that we have incorporated them in our long-term forecasts (watch out in 2028, it will be a tough year!).

This should support a very significant rise in asset prices. Housing and land for example tend to be pretty cheap when they can only be bought with cash. In Kenya today there are less than 20,000 mortgages. Once 5–10-year mortgages become available, the price of housing increases dramatically. When 30-year mortgages become available in low-inflation environments, prices rise even more. With the expansion of private-sector debt that we should expect in Africa, growth in house and land prices is likely to far exceed the 15-fold improvement in GDP itself by 2050, even if this growth doesn't match the 44-fold increase in debt levels.

There are clear opportunities here. For African banks, there are new customers to win, and plenty of products to offer them. For the people and corporations of Africa, greater access to credit will provide a means to invest in their own future. For global investors, there is multi-decade boom to come in Africa that they can help finance, in return for which they will likely beat the anaemic returns available from investing in the West. If post-1990 Japan does prove to be the right template for Europe and perhaps even the US, then domestic returns on developed-market assets will be weak, and the incentive to shift capital into emerging markets, and Africa in particular, will be huge.

The right questions to be asking are: when do banking services get delivered across the African continent? What evidence is there that this may have begun already? Is Africa too poor to experience a banking revolution?

FOR many years the international community, both institutions and individuals, has viewed the marginalised poor in Africa with a mixture of pity, guilt and apprehension. The remedy for this confusion of emotions: conditional aid, intended to create a prosperous society. The consequence has been unsurprisingly disappointing. Aid has often failed to make a meaningful and sustainable difference in standards of living. What Africa needs is entrepreneurs more than aid – and what entrepreneurs need is access to credit. To obtain credit we need viable banking and financial markets that are easily accessible, that are user friendly, and that offer well-priced products.

Where are we on banking the continent? According to Financial Access 2010, there are 163 bank accounts per 1,000 adults in SSA. This compares with an average of 635 accounts per 1,000 in developing countries; in other words, other developing countries have five times the number of bank accounts per 1,000 adults. Developed countries have an average of two bank accounts per adult.

Figure 9.2: Deposit accounts per 1000

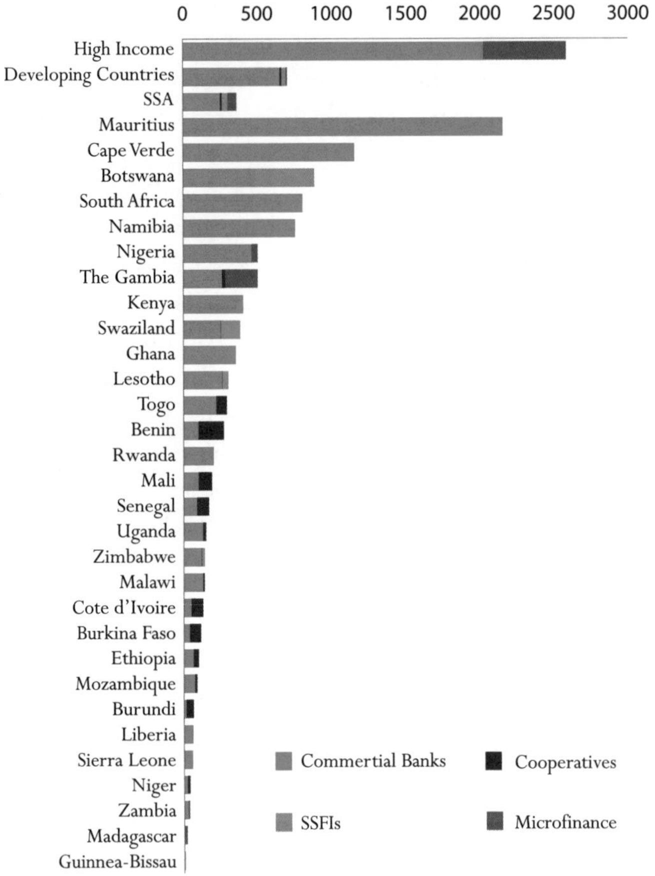

Source: Financial Access 2010, CGAP, World Bank

The picture is just as interesting when we look at access to credit. In SSA there are an average of 28 bank loans per 1,000 adults, which compares with 245 in developing countries and close to 700 in developed countries.

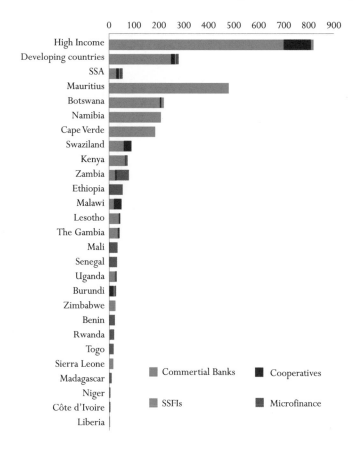

Figure 9.3: Loan accounts per 1000

Source: Financial Access 2010, CGAP, World Bank

In the same way that mobile penetration has continued to outstrip the most bullish forecasts, we believe the scope for further banking penetration in Africa is significant. Renaissance estimates that the ratio of banking assets to GDP for most SSA countries is still below 70%, with loans to GDP even lower at below 45%. This compares with other emerging markets at close to 100% banking assets to GDP and over 60% loans to GDP.

Figure 9.4: Assets/GDP: 2011

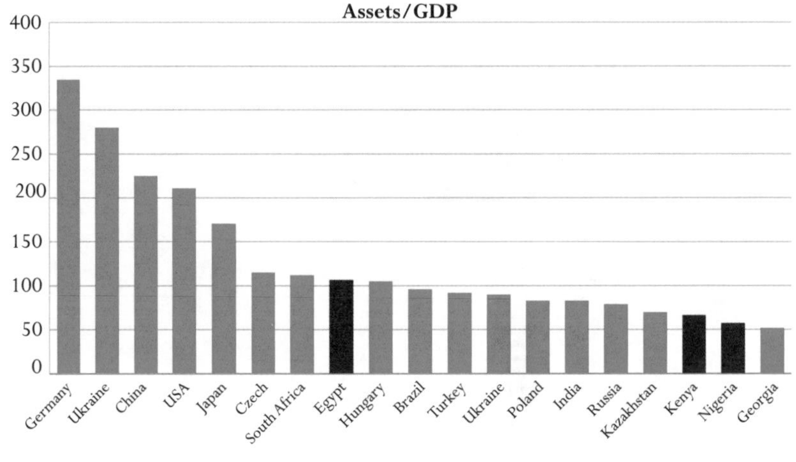

Assets/GDP

Source: IMF

What have been the key developments in the sector?

Despite the current low levels of penetration, banking has come a long way from where it was two decades and even one decade ago. It is sometimes easy to forget the progress that has been made, even as we push for greater penetration and greater growth. SSA has a large number of strong banks, which we believe can be compared to the best in the world. Over the past decade the banking sector has benefited from consolidation, privatisation and regional expansion.

Take Nigeria as an example. In 2000 Nigeria had 88 registered commercial and merchant banks. By the end of 2011 that figure had fallen to 23. Consolidation was achieved primarily through an improved regulatory environment. As bank supervision developed there was recognition that to create a sounder banking system which would be less vulnerable to systemic risks, the minimum capital requirements would need to be raised. This led to a series of mergers and acquisition of weaker players by stronger players. The result is that we now have fewer but stronger banks. In 2004, the top-10 banks controlled 51% of total assets. By the end of 2005 this had risen to 67% of total assets. In 2011 the top-10 banks accounted for a mighty 80% of the industry's banking assets. The benefit of bigger banks is that they have larger balance sheets and hence, can extend larger loans. This helps to feed the growth of big business such as telecoms, power, infrastructure and resource development, which tend to be capital-intensive industries that require large, long-duration loans. In Nigeria banks such as First Bank, Zenith Bank and Guaranty Trust Bank, to name but a few, have played and continue to play a key role in corporate lending. They are, in a sense, helping to fund the growth and development of the country.

The benefits of consolidation have, in some markets, been augmented by the ongoing privatisation of state-owned banks. While state-owned banks played a important role at some point in helping to direct lending to key areas, they were also laden with inefficiencies and poor-quality assets. Partial and full privatisation has allowed these banks to adapt to prevailing market conditions and compete more effectively with competitors. Kenya Commercial Bank (KCB) is a prime example in Kenya. The bank was 100% owned by the government in 1970. Gradually the government has privatised the bank, and its shareholding has now dropped to 18%. While the government remains a key stakeholder and partner, the introduction of private investors has also benefited the bank. KCB has truly transformed itself into a leading commercial bank. With close to 15% market shares in the banking sector's assets and deposits, it has overtaken Barclays Bank of Kenya as the market leader in Kenya. The quality of KCB's loan book has improved, with non-performing loans (NPL) as percentage of total loans falling from 30% in 2004 to current levels of below 6%. Operating efficiencies and returns have also improved. Although most of the banking-sector privatisation is now behind us, there are still some countries where we expect to see further developments on this front. Ethiopia, for example, is one market still dominated by state-owned banks, where there is no foreign ownership of any bank. We expect this market to open up to foreign as well as domestic investors over time.

Consolidation and privatisation have also helped to boost regional expansion. As banks have become bigger and more focused on better servicing their clients, they have started to follow their clients as they expand. In some cases, regional expansion has preceded clients as banks in more-developed markets have sought opportunities in less-developed regions. Most of the big Nigerian banks have subsidiaries in Ghana, for example, a market close to home but offering different opportunities. In East Africa, the Kenyan banks have expanded into Uganda, Rwanda, Tanzania and Southern Sudan. South African banks have headed north of the Limpopo to countries such as Nigeria, Zimbabwe, Zambia and Mozambique and south of the Limpopo to Botswana and Namibia. A few banks – Standard Bank, Ecobank International and United Bank for Africa (UBA) – are pursuing larger pan-African strategies. They are betting on the growing intra-Africa trade links and the emergence of pan-African giants such as MTN, SABMiller and Dangote Cement. With more corporates developing pan-African and regional strategies, we believe more banks will be forced to think beyond their own borders to capture this growth.

How big could the banking sector get over the next few decades? As an example, look at Nigeria – soon to be the biggest economy in SSA. Our forecasts for GDP growth indicate that Nigeria's real GDP could rise to $673 billion by 2020 and to over $5 trillion by 2050 (in today's money). If we assume current (existing) Nigerian banking assets as a percentage of total assets remain around the current level of 50% and that loans and advances conservatively make up 45% of total assets, then we could see the sector's loan book rise from c.$80 billion in 2011 to c.$1.3 trillion by 2050 (in today's money). This would be over $5 trillion if the loans-to-GDP ratio reaches 100%.

Figure 9.5: Nigeria banking sector total loans and advances, NGNbn

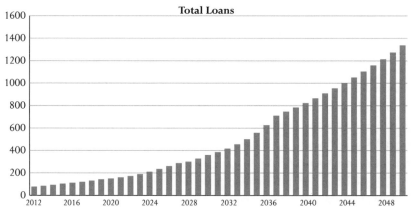

Source: Renaissance Capital estimates

If we also assume that the percentage of loans extended to the retail sector rises from current estimates of around 15% to 40% by 2050, this could put up to $530 billion in the hands of consumers by 2050. Or on the 100% debt to GDP assumption, closer to $2 trillion in today's money.

Figure 9.6: Nigeria banking sector retail loans and advances, NGNbn

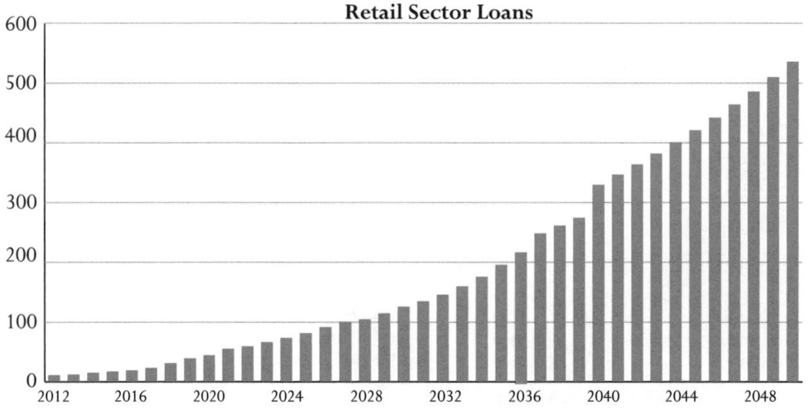

Retail Sector Loans

Source: Renaissance Capital estimates

Another reasonable assumption: that 35% of Nigerians are able and willing to borrow; our potential loan clients rise to around 135 million borrowers by 2050. Given our forecast for retail-sector loans, this implies an average loan per borrower of around $4,000 (in today's money), or $16,000 if the debt-to-GDP ratio rises to 100%. We believe even the lower figure would support our view that the consumption of consumer goods such as white goods, motor cars and property is likely to show very strong growth.

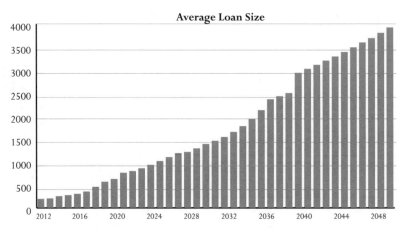

Figure 9.7: Nigeria banking sector average retail loans size, NGNbn

Source: Renaissance Capital estimates

Why has Africa lagged to date? We believe the overriding reason has been the high cost of banking across SSA. Rolling out branches is expensive, although costs vary widely across the continent. New branches can cost from $200,000 to over $1 million. With the cost of capital in SSA in the mid-to-high teens, a branch would have to generate profits of anywhere between $30,000 and $150,000 per year to be value neutral. Away from high-density catchment areas such as large cities and towns, the potential to achieve sufficient scale to generate the needed profits diminishes. As a result most branch networks are concentrated in cities.

New Channels Are Already Evolving

IS this pattern likely to change soon? We think not. As long as banking penetration relies largely on the roll-out of expensive branches and costly products we would expect less densely populated regions to continue being underserved. In Africa, about 60% of the population resides outside of urban areas, which would suggest that a large part of the continent will continue to be under-serviced – if the traditional banking model is maintained. Naturally with urbanisation driving more people into the cities, we would expect banking penetration in cities to continue to rise.

Does this spell a dismal future for the non-urban populace? Not at all. If a branch network is too expensive to rollout then alternative ways of delivering banking services must be developed. One option is to rollout cheaper and more basic branch structures (drop the excessive air-conditioning, potted plants, fresh flowers, fancy counters and revolving glass doors) aimed at providing basic banking services. The other alternative is to forgo fixed branches altogether. We are already seeing both options being pursued in parts of the continent with the advent of low-cost branches, mobile branches (armoured cars designed as branches) and more recently, the growth of mobile phone and agency banking.

Via mobile branches customers are able to deposit and withdraw cash. They can also apply for loans, insurance and other financial services. The benefit for the bank is that these branches can be rotated among different areas during the month to serve communities where a fixed branch may not be viable. The other channel – mobile phone banking – allows customers to access a variety of banking products and services such as making payments, transferring money and making withdrawals – all from the base of the handset. Agency banking goes a step further by providing the much-needed last mile. Agents tend to be local supermarkets, furniture and appliance retailers, service-providers and kiosk owners. The ideal agent is one with a high footfall and the need to handle a large amount of cash. They are in a position to not only receive deposits on the behalf of banks, but also to service withdrawals. As such, customers can transfer money and make payments to one another using mobile telephony. Customers can receive virtual cash and turn it into physical cash with the nearest agent – all without setting foot in a physical bank branch. These are not pipe dreams: the mobile and agency banking revolution is already in motion and driving further penetration of financial services amongst consumers.

Banking the poor and mobile banking have been most successful in Kenya, which we showcase below as an example of how banking is evolving and changing lives.

Kenya Case Study: The Mass-Banking Revolution

KENYA is a country of 43 million people with a substantial rural population that is largely impoverished, despite a diversified economy and range of competitive advantages. Access to financial services in Kenya has historically been low. A number of factors are behind this. Firstly, many in rural areas did not have the financial resources deemed necessary to require servicing. Secondly, the level of financial literacy and knowledge was limited in many areas. And there was also the perception within the financial community that there was very little to be gained by entering into such a market, assumed to be fraught with difficulty and risk.

Yet to the surprise of many observers, new and successful methods of banking have enjoyed significant success in this market. The models are largely premised on 1) respecting and empowering local individuals and trusting them to be worthy debtors; and 2) making use of technology to reach more customers and drive down costs. The explosive success of mass banking in Kenya – the provision of basic financial services in poor communities – has generated substantial interest around the world. The fact that the desperately poor have frequently proved themselves amongst the most reliable repayers of loans has startled observers. The concrete gains in poverty alleviation and the improvement of less tangible social factors such as dignity and self-respect have promoted the establishment of numerous versions and interpretations of mass banking and microfinance throughout the world. In Kenya, the percentage of the population that is banked rose from 26% in 2006 to 41% by 2009. The fact that the business model has demonstrated healthy returns has also helped.

It's a Leadership Story

NEVERTHELESS, in Kenya this was a success born out of failure. In 1993, nine years after the Equity Building Society was formed as provider of small-scale home loans to a low-income clientele, the bank declared itself insolvent. By any financial indicator it was in severe trouble. More than half the loans on the book were non-performing, and accumulated losses exceeded share capital 11 times over. It was against this thoroughly depressing backdrop that the Central Bank of Kenya (CBK) made the bold decision to step in and save the bank by stumping up capital for the business. The CBK took the view that it was valuable for the Kenyan economy to have a bank focused on servicing the lower-income segments of the market, and with central bank support the bank slowly began to turn around its operations and sharpen its strategic focus.

The key to this revival was leadership. As the bank expanded quickly it made some vital hiring decisions, the most important of which was to recruit James Mwangi, initially as finance director and subsequently as CEO of the group. Mwangi's leadership had a revolutionary impact on the company. It expanded its offering, so that instead of focusing solely on mortgages it began to provide an array of credit and saving services. Mwangi also changed the internal culture of the firm, introducing an inclusive ethos which empowered employees to take responsibility for their work and which motivated them to internalise the strategic vision of the firm.

Under Mwangi's guidance, the bank has consistently been involved in various social programmes aimed at improving the lives of the people in its target market. Outreach programmes have entrenched the bank's roots in communities; its most prominent efforts are in education, where Equity Bank awards considerable financial support to talented students, and in agriculture, where the bank has provided an array of support services to many subsistence or fledgling farmers.

Equity's evolution over the past decade has prompted questions such as, "how did Equity do it?" and "what did Equity do differently?" Our key takeaway is that Equity saw an opportunity to service a market that was excluded, overlooked or unwanted by the old-school banks. Opening a bank account – be it transactional or savings – used to be difficult for the average Kenyan. Customers were asked to produce various forms of identification, which many did not have. In addition the retail branches were not conveniently located for low-income customers. There were few branches in high-density neighbourhoods in the cities and even fewer in smaller towns and rural areas. In some instances the "big" banks had gone through a branch rationalisation process which left customers stranded. Equity Bank, on the other hand, developed low-cost, no-frills branches which were rolled out in high-density and rural areas. The bank also rolled out mobile branches to tackle more remote areas. Another key complaint raised by low-income clients was the service levels at banks. Customers felt unwanted and often found the imposing buildings and staff intimidating. Equity Bank allowed customers to "come as you are" – sometimes carrying livestock, sometimes in overalls and muddy boots, sometimes with cooked produce in trays ready for the market. All were welcomed and treated with respect. The chief complaint, however, related to banking charges. People complained about savings being depleted by inexplicable charges and fees. They saw little value added from banking services.

Equity's strategy is focused on banking the underbanked and the unbanked. The bulk of Equity's account holders still reside in rural areas, with the rural/urban mix running at 70%/30%. More than 60% are self-employed, and women dominate the client base. The bank has used its urban and rural reach to grow its deposit book at attractive rates. While the majority of the book resides in "savings products" these do not attract a high rate of interest. Customers use them more as a store of value as opposed to a means of investment. The key for customers is that they understand the fee structures. At the end of June 2012 the bank had about 7.8 million depositors, representing over 60% of the total banked population in Kenya. Regarding lending, Equity lends to 800,000 customers with the average loan size under $2,000 per customer and the average duration for each loan under 36 months. The bank prides itself on growing with its clients from savers to micro-credit to small and medium enterprises, and finally to corporate customers. The distribution of the loan book suggests that a large number of micro lenders have since graduated to SME and corporate loans indicating that Equity is helping to fund and grow entrepreneurs.

Performance Speaks Volumes

IN terms of performance, the company has produced consistently exceptional results. Although its market share is still in the single digits in terms of the value of total loans and deposits in the banking sector (around 8-9%) the bank has returned significant profits. In 2011, profit before tax was KES12,834 million, up from KES2,378 million in 2007 and KES218 million in 2004. Return on equity was 34% in 2011, driven predominantly by outstanding asset margins, with return on assets at 6.1%. The bank has been able to realise an enviable combination: extending much-needed services to previously marginalised individuals, playing a meaningful role in developing communities through enduring outreach programmes and providing solid financial returns to its investors.

The bank has a significant impact on the communities in which it operates. In the late 1990s and early 2000s as the bank sought to move away from its focus on mortgage financing and branch out into other bank offerings, it conducted meetings with communities in the target market. These allowed the bank to explain and educate about various financial products and services but more importantly it allowed the bank to listen and understand what people with lower incomes expected and hoped for from a bank. Here it seemed was a bank that actually cared about its customers and was committed to providing valuable services to them. And despite rapid growth Equity continues to engage in dialogue and feedback sessions in rural communities.

CEO James Mwangi recounts a story about an 80-year-old man who travelled for hours to meet him. The man told him: "When your bank opened a mobile branch in my area, me and my wife, we opened our first savings account. And after some time we went and bought a heifer which was almost ready to calve. And after some time the heifer calved and now my wife, like other women, is able to take milk to the factories. And today we don't have to rely on my children, and we are able to meet our expenses. Three years ago, we struggled. Now we are fine we have even bought a piece of land where we reside."[3]

Targets and Accountability

ALTHOUGH the strategy of targeting the lower-income segment of the market was established prior to Mwangi's arrival, he renewed and refreshed the approach, with a particular emphasis on training staff and aligning their goals with that of the company. He delegated authority and responsibility, making employees more accountable for their actions, giving them a stake in the business, and empowering them to make decisions. One staff member summed it up to management as follows: "before... we just went to work. Now we are going to work to achieve goals. Please make sure we have goals all the time."[4]

Equity Bank rolled out branches rapidly throughout the 2000s. In 2002 ithad 13 branches in Kenya; in 2012 that figure was 135. A serious commitment to serving the most rural communities often requires a willingness to do things differently. Cheaper branches and mobile branches were key in growing customer numbers and driving financial access in Kenya. The next step change for the bank is being driven by the convergence of mobile telephony and banking.

The Mobile Phenomenon

IN tandem with banking the poor, Kenya has also seen phenomenal success and growth in the mobile phone banking market. The movement of money in Africa – both inter- and intra-country – has and will continue to play a key role from a socio-economic perspective. A 2011 survey undertaken by Gallup across 11 SSA countries (South Africa, Kenya, Nigeria, Botswana, Uganda, Tanzania, Zambia, Rwanda, DRC, Sierra Leone and Mali) shows that every month, slightly over half (53%) of all adults in these countries either send or receive payments. This is not only cash flowing from urban to rural areas, but also includes urban-urban, rural-urban, rural-rural and international remittances. What is even more fascinating is that about third of adults sending or receiving payments use only informal cash payments such as bus drivers, travelling relatives and money brokers.[5] This is not only costly but can also be unsafe. Money can be stolen easily and money brokers and bus drivers have been known to charge commissions as high as 20%.

However, in most countries in SSA the options for moving and receiving payments are still limited. The Gallup study showed that remittance payments are highest in Kenya and South Africa, with 76% and 69% of respondents, respectively, having made or received a payment within the month. These two countries also stood out as the most frequent users of electronic channels of transfer. This is not entirely surprising. South Africa is blessed with a high branch network penetration, while Kenya has M-PESA and the agency banking model. In South Africa, the Gallup study indicates that 50% of domestic remiitances were done via bank transfers. In East Africa, Kenyans used mobile money transfers at least 90% of the time and even Uganda and Tanzania showed a preference for mobile payments, at 68% and 60%, respectively.

Figure 9.8: Channels used to send domestic remittances

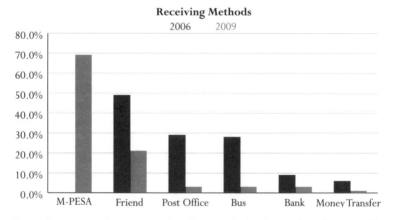

Source: "Payments and Money Transfer Behaviour of Sub-Saharan Africans", 2012 Gallup, Inc.

One cannot talk of mobile money tranfers without a reference to M-PESA. The introduction of mobile banking in the Kenyan market was driven by Safaricom, the country's leading telecommunications company. Launched in 2007, Safaricom's M-PESA mobile phone banking system (developed by UK-based Vodafone and a research arm of the UK government) allows people to deposit and withdraw cash, and transfer it to other people. M-PESA has grown so rapidly that in the past five years, approximately 70% of the Kenyan adult population has used the service. On a recent trip to Kenya, we learnt that "M-PESA" has become more than a Safaricom brand; it has been a nationally recognised verb. People talk about "em-pesaring" someone money as in "I will M-PESA you next week" or "when I M-PESA the school fees."

This success has exploited the fact that while many Kenyans still do not have a formal bank account, penetration in the mobile phone market is extremely high, at about 70%. When you include those with access to a neighbour, friend or family member's handset, Kenya penetration is closer to 90%. Mobile money has had a dramatic impact in many of the world's poorest countries and companies continue to roll out the facility. The Gallup study found 20 nations where more than 10% of adults have used mobile money – and of those 20, 15 were in Africa (Kenya was in the top three).

The system is extremely simple to understand and follow. A customer registers his or her identity and cellphone number with an M-PESA agent (there are more than 23,000 agents around Kenya). The customer can subsequently deposit cash with the agent and have it credited to a mobile account. Customers can then go to any M-PESA agent and withdraw money using their mobile phones as identification. The crucial step is that the money can also be transferred to other M-PESA account holders via text message. Initially this was especially popular amongst migrant workers, who used the service to send money home to family members. However, the ease of transferring money clearly appealed to both unbanked and banked people, as the take-up rate was so high. An intriguing aspect of this service is that Safaricom is not a licensed banking operator and consequently cannot charge fees for rendering specific financial services. Instead the company charges a fee for each transfer, which is scaled to the size of the transaction.

It's a Family Affair

AND as time has passed the service has matured. Initially mobile banking customers were higher-income individuals. But as M-PESA became better known the value of transfers, deposits and withdrawals decreased (until half the transactions were worth less than $10), as lower-income customers realised that this was a way for them to bank. As a result, banks in this market are changing the way they think about making money. Instead of relying only on reinvesting customers' deposits, revenue is now also gained through transactions. Transactional revenue is not a new idea – but the sheer size of this fledgling industry indicates more banks need to re-evaluate the profit potential of low-income customers.

M-PESA transactions between accounts are overwhelmingly between friends and family – over 80% of all transfers. This is more pronounced further down the income ladder. One likely reason is that Kenyans in general (but especially poorer Kenyans) like to get hard-copy receipts of business transactions, as they often need them to prove that a transaction has taken place. As M-PESA only provides soft-copy digital confirmation of transactions, individuals prefer to do mobile exchanges with people they know and trust. This reinforces a key message that has been central to Equity Bank's success: gaining the customer's trust is vital in a market like Kenya, and once gained it can be extremely beneficial in the long run to both the company and the individual.

The table below shows the geographic breakdown of the senders and receivers of mobile money via M-PESA. Urban-to-rural transfers account for more than half of transactions, a strong indication of the attraction of mobile banking in rapidly urbanising economies.

Figure 9.9: Direction of remittances

Sender:	Receiver:	Rural	Urban	Total
Rural		24%	9%	33%
Urban		52%	14%	67%
Total		77%	23%	100%

Reproduced from: Guy Stuart and Monique Cohen, "Cash In, Cash Out Kenya," Microfinance Opportunities financial services assessment (2010), table 6

The rapid uptake of mobile money services in Kenya indicates the immense demand for the service in an economy where until recently physical cash was transferred by bus or taxi drivers, by train conductors or by post, and where cash packages had to be disguised to discourage theft. It is no surprise that within two years of its inception M-PESA became the dominant way to transfer remittances in Kenya.

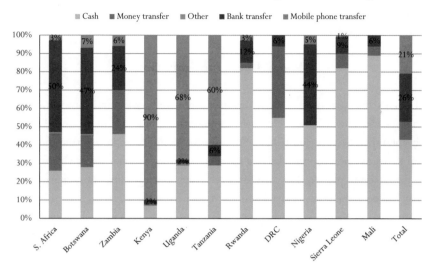

Figure 9.10: Methods of remittance

Source: Isaac Mbiti and David N. Weil, "Mobile Banking: The Impact of M-Pesa in Kenya," NBER Working Paper No. 17129 (June 2011)

The chart above shows how M-PESA has disrupted banking and the informal remittancs business in Kenya. The frequency of remittances has increased as the ease of transferring money has radically improved. However, amongst those that report increased frequency, 87% also report receiving higher-value remittances. Although these data are only a snapshot, this development is important. The fact that individuals are now transferring more money amongst themselves has positive implications for the broader economy. Indeed, the circulation of money has been identified by communities as the most positive impact of mobile money. The increased circulation has boosted local businesses, and thanks to the use of "rescue money" – cash sent to people stuck somewhere without resources – the system has also helped strengthen ties in the community and amongst friends.

An interesting, if somewhat unexpected, consequence of the advent of mobile money has been a considerable reduction in crime (especially in poorer urban areas). There has been a rise in physical safety as muggings are less common. This is because thieves know that people are far less likely to be carrying substantial amounts of cash on their person. There has also been a decline in pickpocketing, which had been prevalent in many areas. Again this is because people keep less money in cash, and more in their M-PESA accounts. Stealing a phone is no use – many people keep their M-PESA SIM-card separate and only put it in to transfer and receive money.

Money Makes the Crops Grow

IT seems that the system may even have improved agricultural production, as farmers can now take care of their administrative tasks far more quickly (and cheaply) then had previously been the case. An M-PESA employee from the Central Kenyan region commented that the speed of mobile money is allowing farmers in the region to place orders early after receiving their own upfront capital quicker than had been the case . And a livestock vendor from Kitui, a rural town 130 kilometres east of Nairobi, described his experiences of M-PESA in the following way: "I am saving a lot because I am not using transport cost like before to buy and sell goats. [M-PESA has] increased financial security. I am not spending more, because after selling I deposit into my account. Also no one is aware when I have money."[6]

M-PESA has also become a means for both banked and unbanked people to save money – indeed, more than 80% of M-PESA users have suggested that they use it to save money. Although M-PESA does not offer interest on deposits (that would be illegal as Safaricom does not have a banking licence) the practical aspects of an M-PESA account make it easier to save. Also, the fact that the average deposit rate in the country is low, at around 1.5% (the lending rate is approximately 17-20%), means that savers with M-PESA are not missing out on a lot.

Thanks to the success of M-PESA, banks such as Equity Bank and KCB have developed their own mobile banking platforms. For example, Eazzy 247 allows Equity Bank customers to transfer and withdraw funds, make loan payments and third-party payments, and check their balance and mini-statements, all via their mobile phones. Essentially it is a comprehensive bank offering from Equity Bank building on Safaricom's M-PESA, and adding more banking services. As with M-PESA, the last mile is serviced by agents tied to the bank. Equity Bank now has over 5,100 agents. KCB has Mobi Bank, which allows customers to make transfers from their bank accounts to any mobile number irrespective of whether the receiver has a mobile money account. The service is not restricted to any one mobile operator – it works with all networks in Kenya, and the last mile is supported by the growing base of over 3,000 KCB agents. While the banks' agencies are expanding, they still lag well behind M-PESA. However, the banks' mobile platforms can offer more services and hence, over time, could see them gaining more market share. Additionally, the banks' agents also operate point-of-sale (POS) devices and hence can issue hard-copy receipts. Data from Equity Bank indicate that while customers are happy to use their phones for deposits, they show a distinct preference for using POS devices for withdrawals in order to get a printed receipt. With time, customers will also be able to use both channels to apply for loans and insurance products, and perhaps even for stock market transactions.

The provision of financial services in Kenya has already changed beyond all recognition. The common theme of the examples of Equity Bank and Safaricom's M-PESA is that the poor have a need and desire for financial services and that servicing this need can be sound business practice. Financial access, prosperity and security of transfer have increased greatly, while both Equity and Safaricom have recognised that there is profit as well as moral value in the provision of their services. With a combination of innovation and commitment, they have both bettered lives, and bettered returns. The potential for a similar revolution in other countries is significant. Take Nigeria, for example, with its population of about 170 million. According to the Gallup study, over half of domestic remittances are still conducted through informal channels. The same can be said for the DRC, another largely untapped market.

To conclude this chapter, we can all see that Africa is underbanked today. Equity Bank is a leading institution on the continent discovering and delivering new forms of banking and helping to fund Kenya's budding entrepreneurs. Safaricom is a leading mobile operator using technology to increase its revenue sources and lock in customers via vital ancillary services. Both Equity Bank and Safaricom show that financial services can be rolled out more quickly in Africa than has been possible in any continent before now. IT advances and innovation have played a key role in this achievement. Improvements in global telephone technology are helping trigger growth in the financial sector, which in turn may boost the agricultural sector and consumer demand. The unprecedented boom in one sector is delivering revolution in another. It is a model that can be replicated across the continent, bringing banking to the fastest billion.

Notes

1. Alex Perry and Nick Wadhams, "Kenya's Banking Revolution," *Time*, 31 January 2011, http://www.time.com/time/magazine/article/0,9171,2043329,00.html#ixzz27TF01lBC.
2. Jane Wakefield, "Mobile banking closes poverty gap," BBC, 28 May 2010, http://www.bbc.co.uk/news/10156667.
3. Garth Saloner and Bethany Coates, "Equity Bank, a microfinance service," Academic case study E260, Stanford University Graduate School of Business (2007), 11.
4. Graham A.N. Wright and David Cracknell, "Equity Bank's Market-Led Revolution," MicroSave research paper (2007), 5
5. Johanna Godoy, Bob Tortora, Jan Sonnenschein and Jake Kendall, "Payments and Money Transfer Behaviour of Sub-Saharan Africans," Bill & Melinda Gates Foundation/Gallup, June 2012, http://www.gallup.com/poll/155132/payments-money-transfer-behavior-sub-saharan-africans.aspx.
6. Ibid.

PART III

The Great Leap

By Michael Moran

I see the opportunity in Africa as greater than anywhere else in the world today not because Africa is different, but precisely because it isn't a special case. The great majority of African countries will transform their economies in the coming decades just as most of Asia, America and Europe have done in their time. The difference with Africa is simply that the scope for catch up and convergence is greater and is likely to happen more rapidly.

——Stephen Jennings, the founder and CEO of Renaissance Group [1]

Great shifts in science, economics or history often take time to digest, particularly when they threaten long-held beliefs or, occasionally, the *raison d'être* of an entire academic or professional discipline. Louis Pasteur drew the ridicule of the medical establishment of his day when he posited in the 1850s that germs might cause disease. Similarly, naval theorists in the early 20th century, smitten with the gun-bristling battleships of the day, pooh-poohed the advent of aircraft carriers until the aircraft carried on those new-fangled vessels sent enemy battleships to the bottom of the sea. In both cases, sceptics cited past experience to disprove the future. These experts, however well meaning, had a clear vested interest in obstructing progress.

A similar kind of resistance confronts any who suggest that Africa's past is not Africa's future. Some development economists, political-risk specialists and aid agencies cling to arguments that rang true during the 1980s when GDP growth in Sub-Saharan Africa virtually collapsed under the weight of varied geopolitical, environmental and policy factors. In today's Africa, as Stephen Jennings implies above, it is simply not true that the lot of the average person is actually worsening. Africa, we strongly contend, is rising, and with it the living standards, expectations, aspirations, health and wealth of its people.

Can we find countries which are failing their people? Yes, of course, and not just in SSA. Scan the globe and you will find much to worry about, not only in Cuba, Fiji, North Korea, Venezuela or Syria, but in Europe, too, and countless other nations where a combination of misfortune and misgovernance threaten to saddle the next generation of citizens with as much or more hardship and destitution as their parents faced.

But this is not the story of the vast majority of today's Africa; far from it. Even previously incompetently managed Zimbabwe has recovered from hyperinflation and grew at 9% last year, while SSA as a whole grew in 2011 at 5%. Sustained over time – as this growth has been in recent years – this has a transformational affect. As part III of *The Fastest Billion* explains, a series of trends are changing the realities of everyday life below the Sahara, almost always for the better, driven by maturing local markets, the availability of global capital, more transparent business practices and improved communications and transportation networks.

In part, as previous chapters noted, this represents SSA's belated arrival as a true player in the global marketplace. But some of this is home grown, too. Kenyan entrepreneurs have delivered mobile telephony to rural areas that were effectively isolated, changing the lives of millions as networks spread across the continent. As we note in chapter 10, very few countries in today's SSA – again, with predictable exceptions – still maintain a state telecommunications monopoly, and the nimble private-sector mobile networks pioneered in Kenya that displaced them have not only connected remote villages, but also jump-started internal and cross-border commerce.

While the roots of a mobile telephone network can be sunk into the soil relatively quickly, the brick-and-mortar tributaries of road and rail systems – and the ports, power plants and urban markets they serve – take more time. The key is the supply of better regulation, commitment from the government, and financing, as the demand is clearly there. Here, too, a combination of loans, credits, foreign direct investment, more-accountable international aid spending and improved governance are beginning to show. While infrastructure continues to lag behind demand, the pace of construction and spending on it has accelerated. As chapter 11 reveals, SSA is on its way to meeting independent estimates that some $90 billion in annual infrastructure spending will be needed for the region to close the gap with other emerging economies.

A virtuous cycle has developed, meanwhile, between expanding SSA agricultural production and the rapid growth of both its urban areas and its middle class. The transition under way is profound and, in some respects, unprecedented. From largely rural, agrarian societies at the cusp of the 20th century, African countries today revolve increasingly around megacities such as Lagos, with over 10.5 million people living within its orbit, Kinshasa (8.7 million) and giant Cairo (home to 11 million).[2] From this, of course, flow problems: water, sewage, power and road systems – not to mention housing stock and city services of all kinds – fail to meet demand from the flood of humanity from the countryside. This is a familiar story, one played out to a reasonably successful end in such diverse places as London, Tokyo, New York, Shanghai and countless other megacities over the years.

But more often than not, the problems of urban overcrowding – while offering low-hanging fruit to myopic Western observers – conceal deeper forces at work. Cities cement national cultures, diluting tribal and ethnic fictions often based on rural traditions. Cities create new constituencies and voting blocs, and community organizations that demand infrastructure spending, access to education and healthcare (all of which are easier to supply to agglomerations than far-flung villages).

Most importantly, cities – large, small, overcrowded or not – create the middle class whose aspirations drive demands for accountability, jobs and social stability. This new consumer class also expects access to foods once reserved for the diplomatic set in African cities. This incentivises local farmers and distributers to meet this demand, creating logistical channels that raise standards all around.

But wait, retort the sceptics: these notional improvements mean nothing if malnutrition and disease continue to stalk the poorest quintile of society. True enough, but again, year after year of strong GDP growth in many of the continent's largest countries and a concerted effort by a growing number of aid groups to stress longer-term health and nutritional solutions over sacks of rice has changed reality – and long-term trends – for the better.

Virtually every indicator of human wellness – infant mortality, infection rates for malaria and HIV-AIDS, life expectancy, the availability of clean water and sanitation – has improved dramatically. None of these measurements presents a full picture of the realities of life in SSA, which in any individual sampling may be better or worse. But the metrics available virtually all point to a brighter future, and in many specific instances, to major opportunities for economic and financial growth in the coming decades.

Notes

1. Stephen Jennings, Special Address to the Global Economic Governance Programme, Oxford University, "Transformational Growth In Africa – Many Paths, One Destination," Oxford, UK, 5 November 2010.
2. UN World Urbanisation Prospects, 2009, http://esa.un.org/unpd/wup/doc_highlights.htm.

Chapter 10

Technology and Timing

By Johan Snyman and Alex Kazbegi

When I visited Nigeria a year ago [in 2001] I had to use a satellite phone out my hotel window. Now when I arrive, my taxi driver is taking calls on one of our new cellphones.

—Zimbabwean businessman Strive Masiyiwa, founder and CEO of Econet Wireless, 2002[1]

NO revolution in Africa has been more obvious than the communications revolution, which has seen 500 million SIM cards sold in the past seven years, Internet users expand 31-fold since 2000, and mobile penetration rates exceed 40%, even in countries where per capita GDP is below $2,000. The spread of the mobile phone defied all those who believed Africa was too poor to get connected; indeed, so significant was the take-up that it forced many economists to upgrade their estimates of African household wealth, and statistics offices to upgrade GDP. The cellphone has not just improved communication – it has created it – and in the process encouraged change in every economic transaction. Agricultural producers can achieve better prices for their crops and animals, companies can manage their logistics more effectively (and therefore stock levels, too), while new services can be built on the back of the humble phone. Trade in goods and services has become easier. To take Somalia as just one example – the mobile phone helps that country sell millions of goats and sheep to Gulf states, while allowing the new pirate industry to collect ransoms. Such a powerful tool has never been so available to so many people in countries embarking on this phase of the growth trajectory.

The fortunes made as a result are legendary among investment professionals. In 2004, for instance, during the height of Zimbabwe's hyper-inflation, a Renaissance client was struck by the fact that, in a country of 12 million people, you could effectively purchase a national phone company for $50 million. The purchase of Econet looks very smart in retrospect: its 2011 market capitalisation was over $719 million. A similar thing happened at about the same time in Nigeria, when another Renaissance client noticed the demand to watch European football – where many top Nigerian stars play these days – was going unmet. The client purchased Naspers, a pay-TV operator, and has seen the value of the asset soar to eight times the initial investment.

But this technology revolution is hardly complete. The arrival of broadband is opening Africa up to the world, and also opening up the continent to itself. Even where roads do not exist, communication is now becoming possible, and when broadband is rolled out across a country, as in Rwanda, medical advice or more responsive government is faster than any could have conceived just a few years ago. Broadband enables Africa to export the services which the Philippines or India have utilised to help drive their expansions, and deliver growth in the services sector which previously would have come only after an agricultural and industrial revolution. Today the communications revolution is allowing Africa to achieve all three at once.

HUMANS have been accelerating for millennia. When ape-men first left Africa, these early colonists travelled at 35 yards a year. When our modern ancestors began to leave Africa about 60,000 years ago, the new wave of human expansion travelled 50 times faster, averaging more than a mile a year.

While our species may not be developing any faster today, we are already experiencing the benefits of faster communication. Ten years ago many of us did not possess a mobile phone. Today we have the ability to sit in Lagos and read Bloomberg and the *Financial Times*. This progress is part of a revolution making it ever easier to do business in Africa electronically.

These are intrinsically accessible technologies. As a result Africa has been able to leap-frog the stage of older communications technologies. The continent today has the highest mobile telephony growth rate and also boosts huge success stories in value-added services, such as mobile money.

Why the success of mobile telephony in Africa? One reason is the lack of fixed-line infrastructure, the result of monopolistic behaviour of governments in the 20th century and a lack of capital. In 2000, only 1.4 subscribers per 100 people in Africa had fixed-line phones. This figure increased to 1.5 in 2007 before falling back to 1.4 in 2008.

Figure 10.1: Mobile subscribers (000, lhs) against SIM penetration (rhs)

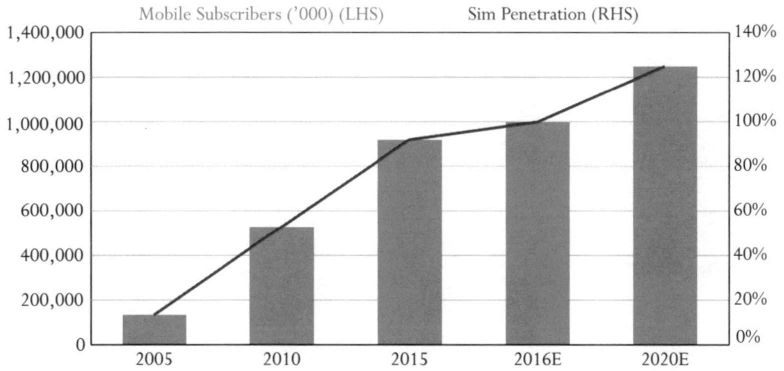

Source: Renaissance Capital

Another reason for success is the changing regulatory landscape – governments have recognised the failures in this sector in the 20th century and allowed the private sector to deliver solutions in the 21st century. Widespread liberalisation of markets and the emergence of competition have greatly increased the performance of the information and communication technologies sector in Africa since the early 2000s. Very few countries in Africa today have less than three mobile network operators (MNO) – and in a few countries, up to six MNOs compete for market share in voice and data. This is a huge shift from the state monopolies set up by so many well-meaning governments in the post-independence era, which mainly served to throttle growth.

Figure 10.3: Competition in mobile markets in SSA, 1995–2010

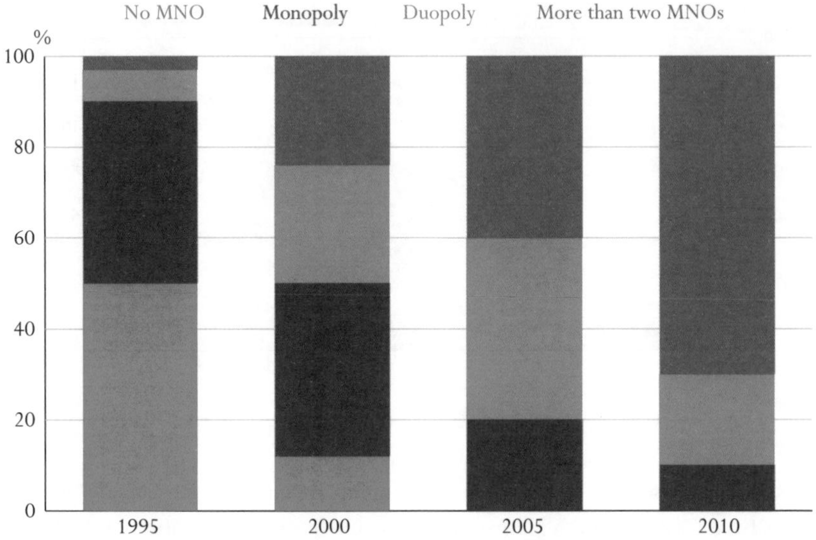

Source: ITU, various regulators and MNOs

Market liberalisation and reforms attracted private-sector participation, and large-scale investments in telecoms took off in the early 2000s. The auction of three GSM licences in Nigeria triggered substantial interest in late 2000 and brought in $285 million per licence. The mobile revolution in Africa had started, and over 10 years later, blended SIM penetration in Africa is between 60% and 65%. The mobile market in Africa has become more evenly distributed, and South Africa's share has declined from 86% in 1998 to 10% in 2011 – while Nigeria's share has expanded from nil in 1998 to 15% in 2011.

Prepaid Made This Market

THE ICT revolution in Africa to date has largely been one of voice communications. More than 85% of total revenue is from voice communications, with access to the Internet and hence contributions from non-voice and non-SMS data still insignificant.

Large-scale access to mobile telecoms received a major boost in the early 1990s with the introduction of prepaid services. Prepaid phones were first introduced (albeit unsuccessfully) in Mexico in 1992, reconfigured successfully in 1993, and later combined very successfully with calling-party pays capability in much of the world. In retrospect, this introduction of prepaid technology, considered a peripheral achievement at the time, has turned out to be the most significant innovation since the development of the original cellular communications concept. Without prepaid technology, which consists largely of storage and billing software, mobile calling might not have reached as many as two-thirds of today's subscribers, especially those located in poor and moderate-income developing countries, where participation in the cash economy is often intermittent.

The African continent is almost 100% prepaid – although there are some pockets such as South Africa (where 15% of the market is postpaid) where a significant base of postpaid business accounts for substantial percentage of airtime revenue.

Overall, GDP per capita reflects the financial capacity of consumers to purchase mobile phones and associated services and accessories, and GDP per capita in Sub-Saharan Africa is low. In the past there has been a strong relationship between mobile adoption and GDP per capita, but that relationship may be breaking down – many countries today with GDP per capita estimated at below $2,000 have attained mobile penetrations of 40% and higher.

To achieve mobile connectivity, consumers in low- and moderate-income countries allocate a larger share of their disposable income to mobile. Mobile spending has grown to 3% of estimated consumer outgoings in developed markets, to 2–4% in emerging markets, and in some low-income markets to almost 10%. These numbers suggest a higher allocation of household budgets to communications than in the past, at the expense of transportation, food, clothing, and possibly housing expenditure. It is possible this level of spending on mobile communications may reflect under-reported income in the national statistical accounts, but there is also an acknowledgement that mobile telephony is now a necessity rather than luxury: hence the remarkable growth in SIM penetration and telecoms spending. Evidently the African consumer places a high value on communications, and a better return on this expenditure.

Another factor is the declining total cost of ownership – lower-priced handsets and declining increments of prepaid minutes that can be purchased, allowing new subscribers to buy a phone and activate service for under $40. As a result, mobile adoption, as reflected in subscriber levels, is now associated with monthly average revenue per user (ARPU) of under $4 in some emerging markets.

The Operators Have Led the Way

AFRICA'S rapid expansion in ICT is being funded by MNOs, governments and banks. Capital markets, corporate bond markets and commercial bank loans have also played a key role in funding ICT. Renaissance calculates that in the past seven years, when 500 million new SIMs were added to mobile networks across Africa, MNOs incurred capital investment of $80 billion. It is interesting to note that MTN, as the leading mobile network operator in Africa, invested $15 billion or almost 20% of total MNO capital investment – probably outweighing all private sector investment except that into resources. The risk-on approach of MTN has been highly rewarding to shareholders – over the 11-year period from 2001, annual compounded growth in earnings of 26% translated into 16% annual compounded appreciation in the MTN share price. The company's network expansion is internally funded and its balance sheet reflects nil net debt

Despite the lack of deep capital markets in many countries, raising local currency debt and corporate bonds for ICT investment has been reasonably successful. Although the corporate bond market in Africa is small compared with the equity market, it plays a significant role in the financing of investment in telecoms infrastructure. And lastly, the role of China in the telecoms sector is growing in importance. Chinese telecoms vendors, such as Huawei and ZTE, are increasingly supplying private and public telecoms operators in Africa with mobile and fibre-optic networks. In Angola, ZTE is providing the equipment for a $1 billion upgrade of Movicel's network, which will see that country roll out 4G ahead of many Western countries.

Beyond the City

THE transformative nature of these advances can be seen on any major African city street. Muathi Kilonzo, a Kenyan-born Africa equity salesman for Renaissance Capital based in London, remembers when it dawned on him that technology had changed even his father's generation.

"It was late December 2010 and our family was on holiday by the coast, but my father had a dilemma. M-PESA (the innovative phone payment system launched in Kenya) had a problem because everyone was trying to use it. My father had to transfer a modest amount of money to a family he had promised to buy a goat so they could celebrate the holiday. What was interesting about this story is the big difference in process between this Christmas and previous ones.

"Previously my father would have rung up his accountant, she would have then written a check, which he would sign, and a messenger would be sent to the bank to cash the check and bring the cash back to his office. Then the recipient of the goat would come to the office and collect the money, or it would be sent by courier. Alternatively the family would have travelled to our farm (at times a few hours journey) and been given a goat by our farm manager. Getting it to the feast was another leg to the saga.

"However, this Christmas it was a very different experience. There was no travelling and the transfer was very simple: phone to phone. Here was a man in his 60s used to delegating such tasks, but now using new technology to make a seamless cashless transfer of money across the country from his chair by the sea. I should add, living in London, I am bemused that this is the 'revolutionary' product a leading high street bank is trying to roll out in the UK only now."

Kenya represents the vanguard, of course, but others are catching up fast. The large-scale investment in telecoms infrastructure throughout Africa has driven SIM penetration to unprecedented levels, and in most cases urban and semi-urban regions can now boast 100%-plus SIM penetration. The urban roll-outs in general have been very profitable, with quick paybacks on invested capital, but now the focus is shifting to the rural areas. As equipment costs not to mention handset costs have declined and targeted marketing has become success-ful, the break-even ARPUs in rural areas have dropped and the investment case for MNOs has improved. The next wave of investing to harvest voice revenues has started, and rural communities should start to enjoy the benefits of mobile telephony.

Figure 10.4: Urban versus rural SIM penetration in Tanzania

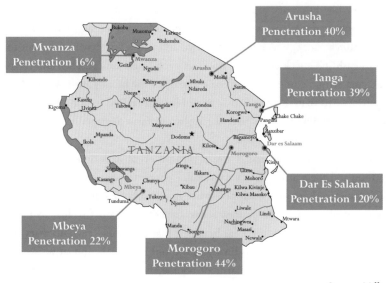

Source: Millicom

The highest-impact development in African telecoms infrastructure in the past few years has been the roll-out of submarine cable systems, driving down wholesale international connectivity prices by over 80%. SSA will have more than 20 terabits of international fibre capacity by the end of 2012, a jump from 200 gigabits a decade ago.[2]

How does the performance of ICT in SSA compare with the rest of the world? Average rates of access in SSA are comparable with South Asia, for example, a region with similar or higher GDP per capita. But around the world, the most important new development in ICT has been growth of broadband Internet. According to the World Bank, 7% of people in 2000 used the Internet, while today it is estimated that 30% of the world's population uses the Internet.

Internet Is Next

INTERNET usage in SSA has begun to take take off, thanks to the emergence of global standards for wireless broadband networks and the increase in availability of international bandwidth.[3] Compounded annual growth in Internet connections is running at 80% over 2007–11. Africa had 4.5 million Internet users in 2000,

more than half in South Africa. By 2011, there were 140 million, led by Nigeria
with 45 million.[4]

Figure 10.5: African undersea cables systems, 2009

African Undersea Cables (2009)
http://manypossibilities.net/african-undersea-cables

Source: Steve Song, http://manypossibilities.net

There can be little doubt that the future of telecoms in Africa is going to be
about broadband. That is the next wave of telecoms development, and it is one
that will massively enhance not only the stature and potential of the African telecoms sector, but also the productive capacity of the continent. As Asian wages
rise and Africa's demographic surge joins the workforce, we expect off-shoring
in services via the Internet to help fuel increasingly rapid economic growth over
coming decades. Africa's leap into the connected world has already been impressive – but the best is yet to come.

Figure 10.6: African undersea cable systems, 2014

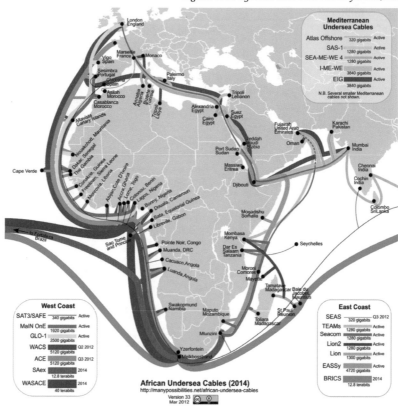

Source: Steve Song, http://manypossibilities.net

Notes

1. Simon Robinson, "Steve Masiyiwa: Founder of Econet Wireless," *Time*, 2 December 2002.
2. www.lightwaveonline.com.
3. Stacey Higginbotham, "Norway has more bandwidth than all of Africa & other broadband gaps," *GigaOM* (blog), 18 July 2012, http://gigaom.com/2012/07/18/norway-has-more-bandwidth-than-all-of-africa-other-broadband-gaps/..
4. http://www.internetworldstats.com/stats1.htm.

Chapter 11

Infrastructure: The Beauty of Starting Afresh

By John Arron

If you give me today $5 billion, I will not invest any abroad, I will invest everything here in Nigeria. Let us put heads together and work.

—Aliko Dangote, founder and CEO, Dangote Cement[1]

The emergence of countries, or in this case a whole continent, into the high-growth phase of the trajectory curve is a defining time, recognisable to few before the event, recognised by everyone afterwards. Renaissance's analysis shows that the combination of factors that triggers dramatic growth does not have absolute ingredients; the headline growth can be in specific fields of commerce or industry. But once started the trajectory encompasses the whole country and every sector.

We have looked at the 'soft' factors: education, the business processes, ease of access to capital, communications and legal structure. But the most visible sign of countries in the trajectory curve is massive investment in infrastructure, which is always a dominant feature to the observer.

To maintain the trajectory requires investment in infrastructure. In India it took a decade of strong Indian growth before this took off. Given the growth trajectory Renaissance can see in Africa, this suggests that Africa should have begun a marked expansion in infrastructure around 2010. It is at this point that governments recognise the need to focus on infrastructure, to improve regulation and to find the financing to make it happen.

This is precisely what we are seeing. The plans are ambitious in scale, as they need to be to facilitate the fastest billion. The demands for infrastructure, which are already rising fast, will accelerate in line with GDP, demand and demographics. Air-passenger numbers will double every decade for the next 40 years, car ownership will multiply more than 10-fold, and electricity demand will soar.

But as we show below, typically in this phase of the trajectory curve, demand is already often in excess of what current infrastructure can supply.

The opportunities for investors are therefore incredibly wide-ranging, from port development to cement for new roads to power generation. The demand for infrastructure improvements will create the most obvious and the most exciting areas of investment; the very appearance of Africa will change. The opportunity for investors and the demand for growth will ensure that across the continent, the extent and scope of infrastructure changes will be one of the most significant and eye-catching aspects of what is happening now, and will be so for the next 40 years. What makes this particularly exciting is not just the sheer scale of the changes that are happening, but also the fact that this is taking place in what are to a large extent greenfield conditions. Planners and developers have the opportunity to create new cities, new transport links and new industrial sites, with all the design and technology of today available from the start.

Financing these long-term projects will be progressively easier, as local debt markets are getting more sophisticated. Eurobond markets have opened up to Nigeria, Ghana and Zambia. For example, 20- and 30-year infrastructure bonds are already offered by the Kenyan government, providing returns that match the needs of pension funds, both local and external. Current investors range from Chinese banks, which lend so that ports and transport infrastructure can be improved, to multi-nationals, which also see the opportunity in Africa, whether it is Dubai World considering port acquisitions, global electricity companies seeking growth markets, or companies such as Lafarge, Athi River Company and Dangote Cement recognising the need for the products they sell.

There is much to be done in Africa. We see every sign that it will be done. Leaders across the continent recognise that political power increasingly depends on providing electric power to their voters – it was a key feature in the Nigerian presidential election of 2011. The incentive for better regulation has grown in line with more responsive government, and so we now see policies that encourage the provision of power, for example Nigeria's moves to bring up the price of electricity production towards economically rational levels. Governments have the incentive to create a new and necessary world for the benefit of everyone.

Imagine the value of a bridge. Not the soaring towers of San Francisco's Golden Gate or the ambitious reach of the new Qingdao Haiwan Bridge in China, which became the planet's longest span at over 26 miles when it opened in 2011.

But rather the simple span crossing a rain-swelled river or a gorge, like so many of the bridges found in Sub-Saharan Africa.

These mundane structures – taken for granted in the developed world as traffic and commerce speed over them – can have a transformative effect in the developing world. Communities cut off by natural barriers suddenly develop local markets, and exchange ideas and knowledge. Rehabilitation of one Moazambique bridge across the Zambezi has helped ease food shortages and moderated food prices when agricultural seasons differ between the north and south of the country.

Bridges also help Africa's nations understand the larger meaning of *Africa* and break down parochial suspicions of outsiders. On the Kenya-Uganda border, for instance, a 60-year-old bridge built under the British colonial administration has been crumbling from the strain of increasing cross-border commercial traffic. The $120 million project to build a new bridge across the Nile at Jinja, funded largely by Japan, will clear long delays at the border – a key leg of the Northern Corridor Route linking Uganda and its landlocked neighbours Rwanda, Burundi and eastern DRC with the ports and markets of Kenya.

Infrastructure Enables the Modern World

NOT only does infrastructure contribute to economic growth, but it remains an important factor in human development. Infrastructure is also a key ingredient for achieving many of the UN's Millennium Development Goals. Access to clean water, the provision of electricity, the provision of road and railway networks and access to a reliable telecommunications network all depend on infrastructure.

As a visitor to SSA, one often encounters traffic jams and power shortages. But traffic congestion is not simply a reflection of a shortage of roads – it is also a sign that existing roads have not been adequately maintained. As in most countries when growth begins to accelerate, the lack of infrastructure is a constraint on growth. For SSA to maintain its accelerating growth pattern requires more investment in infrastructure, just as others required at this stage and indeed still require (as India's power cuts in 2012 demonstrated).

The lack of power remains the primary factor limiting economic growth in the region. Nigeria has been the leading importer of generating sets in Africa for at least the past seven years, and some estimates suggest the country spends almost $10 billion a year running these private sets, which are now the main source of power in the country. If this money was instead spent on electricity, provision could be widened dramatically. The need for power has encouraged governments in Africa to allow 34 independent power producers (IPP) in, investing $2.5 billion in 3 GW of new capacity. More is needed.

A recent report published by the Agence Française de Développement and the World Bank unsurprisingly argues that poor infrastructure has resulted in a number of bottlenecks that result in higher costs, lower intra-regional trade and lower productivity.[2] Another report by the Overseas Development Institute suggests that a stimulus package focused on the delivery of infrastructure would lead to a permanent increase of 2.5% of GDP.[3]

The spending trend line is climbing steadily. While these projects remain complex and politically fraught – Nigeria's electricity-sector privatisation is just one important example – nonetheless hundreds of private-sector companies in Nigeria and elsewhere now bid competitively for such gigantic projects. In East Africa, Kenya is pushing the Lamu port development, which aims for port capacity of 24 million tonnes (mnt) in 2030. That is more freight than Kenya's existing major port (Mombasa) currently shifts, and with Mombasa already a regional bottleneck, the project will bring benefits far beyond Kenya. Among those already lined up to use it are Ethiopia, whose economy is booming, and South Sudan, eager to find a way to bring its oil to market that bypasses its rival in Khartoum. Similar projects, funded by a mix of donors, foreign direct investment and state revenue, are under way in Zambia, South Africa, Senegal, Angola, Sierra Leone and elsewhere.

The Africa Infrastructure Country Diagnostic (AICD) cited by the Ernst & Young 2012 Africa attractiveness survey[4] says that for Africa to close the gap with other emerging markets would require $90 billion annually from 2010–20. We would point out that Africa does not need to close the gap with richer emerging markets: it just needs to invest as much as other emerging markets did when they were at the same point on the growth trajectory. In any case, the figure is already largely met. As Ernst & Young points out, AICD estimates themselves suggest $30 billion is being provided by African taxpayers, while $55 billion is coming from the G8, development finance institutions and the private sector, putting the annual total at $85 billion. Our own calculations, using nominal GDP, suggest that $90 billion annually may be 4% of African GDP in 2012 but just 2% of 2020 GDP (in 2020 prices), which should not be problematic to fund.

John Arron

Road Infrastructure

Waterborne transport is cheap and often a factor in supporting growth – from north-western Europe's Industrial Revolution to the growth on China's seaboard. Africa is no different, with the coast home to many of the continent's urban (and therefore wealth-generating) areas, and the most efficient means to access global markets. Rail and road infrastructure is however essential for land-locked countries and inland regions. The region's trunk road network consists of 10,000 km of road carrying in excess of $200 billion of trade per annum. Between 60,000 and 100,000 km of new road would be required for a Trans-African Highway to become a reality.

Research by the World Bank suggests that in the early 1960s, total road density in Africa was quite similar to that of South and East Asia.[5] However, as others embarked on the rapid growth trajectory earlier, a large gap emerged. Now Africa has 204 km of road (25% paved) per 1,000 km^2 of land area, compared with a world average of 944 km of road (>50% paved) per 1,000 km^2 of land area. This is less than one-third the level in the next-lowest region, South Asia. It has been held back by many factors, not least conflict itself. When Chad's civil war ended in 1987 it had just 30 km of tarmac road – the benefits of peace allowed this to expand nearly 20-fold by 2004 to 550 km.[6]

The World Bank notes that governments recognise the problem and like Chad or more recently Rwanda, many countries have made progress in develop-ing good institutions for funding and bulding road infrastructure.[7] But there is a need to improve maintenance. SSA governments have tended to spend just 70% of their road budgets, meaning there is a near-50% increase in funds available if management of the budget improves. That could markedly improve road infra-structure, as delaying maintenance acts as a drain on the total road budget.

The chart below illustrates the deterioration in the quality of a road over time, based on an initial life span of 20 years. As a road deteriorates, the cost of repairing an unattended road increases exponentially over time. For example, maintenance costs three-to-five years later than the optimal point (A in diagram) increase six-fold. Delaying maintenance by between five and eight years would result in costs 18 times greater than at the optimal point. The World Bank points out that an extra $0.6 billion in road maintenance spending across Africa now would save $2.6 billion in new road expenditure.

Figure 11.1: Cost of maintenance delay

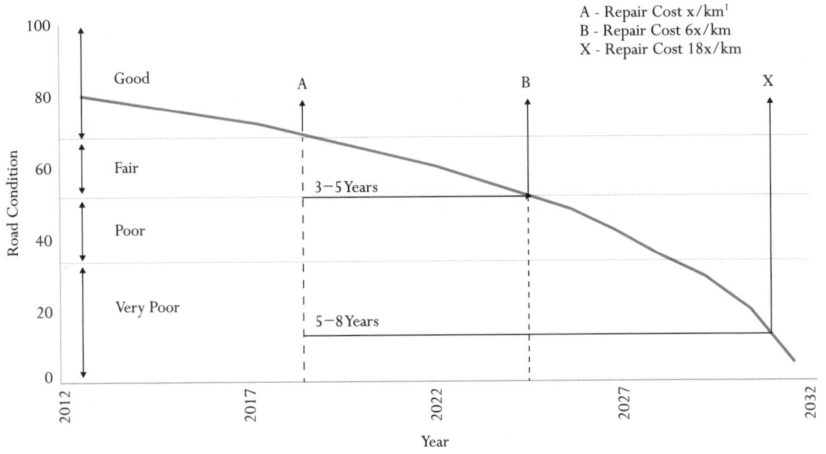

A - Repair Cost x/km[1]
B - Repair Cost 6x/km
X - Repair Cost 18x/km

Source: Sanral

Infrastructure Will Drive GDP Growth

African countries should be spending on infrastructure – because as the figures below suggest, expanding and improving infrastructure is a major growth driver. Infrastructure contributed almost 1% to per capita growth between 1990 and 2005 in SSA as a whole, compared with only 0.8% for macroeconomic and structural policies (such as promoting trade, improving governance and enhancing human capital). Only in West Africa did the effect of structural policies surpass that of infrastructure.

Figure 11.2: Changes in per capita growth caused by changes in growth fundamentals, 1990–2005

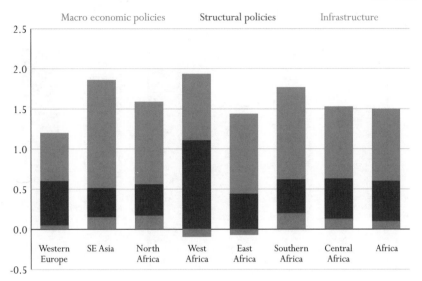

Source: World Bank 2010 report; César Calderon, "Infrastructure and Growth in Africa," 2008.

In a breakdown of the impact of different types of infrastructure, the increased penetration of telecoms accounts for most of the growth. Inadequate power-related infrastructure appears to have retarded growth, reducing per capita growth for Africa by over 0.1%.

Figure 11.3: Changes in per capita growth caused by different types of infrastructure, 1990–2005

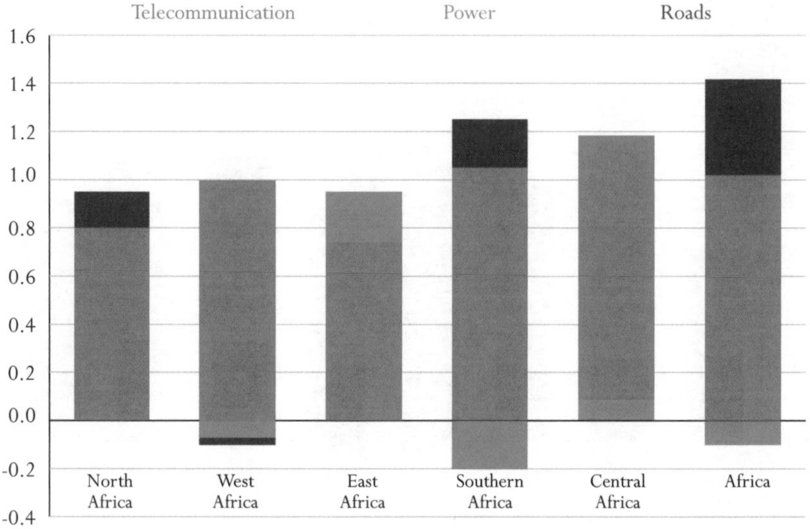

Source: World Bank 2010 report; Calderon, 2008.

Africa Can Do Far More

SSA infrastructure has expanded since independence. Paved road density is up 500%, total road density has doubled and main-line density is up four-fold. However the demands on that infrastructure have soared. A booming population is part of the reason that coverage per person has not improved for electricity or piped water, and both are now ripe for far greater investment. The infra-structural take-off seen in East and South Asia – in terms of electricity, road and main-line density – occurred in 1990. Our growth trajectory suggests we are likely to see the same now in SSA.

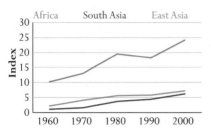

Figure 11.4: Paved road density

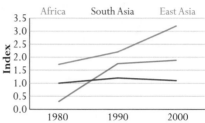

Figure 11.5: Generation capacity

Source: Sudeshna Banerjee et al., "Access, Affordability, and Alternatives: Modern Infrastructure Services in Africa," 2008; Tito Yepes, Justin Pierce and Vivien Foster, "Making Sense of SSA's Infrastructure Endowment: A Benchmarking Approach," 2008.

Source: Banerjee et al., 2008; Yepes, Pierce and Foster, 2008.

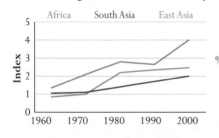

Figure 11.6: Total road density

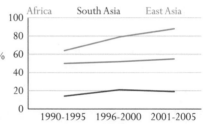

Figure 11.7: Electricity coverage

Source: Banerjee et al., 2008; Yepes, Pierce and Foster, 2008.

Source: Banerjee et al., 2008; Yepes, Pierce and Foster, 2008.

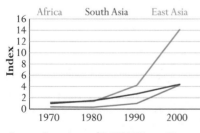

Figure 11.8: Main-line density

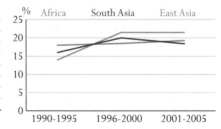
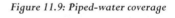

Figure 11.9: Piped-water coverage

Source: Banerjee et al., 2008; Yepes, Pierce and Foster, 2008.

Source: Banerjee et al., 2008; Yepes, Pierce and Foster, 2008.

Note: Road density is measured in km per 100 km² of arable land, telephone density in lines per 1,000 people, and generation capacity in MW per 1 million people.

It is striking that the resource-rich countries lag the others in term of infrastructure capacity. Government corruption in those richer countries remains an issue, but it also appears that much of their additional wealth in recent years has been used to pay off their debt; hence the improvement in the macro-economy.

Why Does Africa's Infrastructure Cost So Much?

Infrastructure in Africa costs more than in other developing countries. Economies of scale, the use of older technologies and the inefficient management of resources are all issues, and the cost of power generation per capita in a small African country will always be much higher than that produced by a thermal or nuclear base-load power station. However, the provision of those services and high prices reflect unnecessarily high margins caused by the lack of competition.

There is scope for a sizeable reduction in electricity, water and railway costs – by up to 99% according to the research data outlined below in Figure 11.9 – and the boost to SSA competitiveness would be dramatic. Fortunately, the positive example provided in the telecoms arena has made clear to many officials that competition can help improve services while reducing costs and bringing in more revenue to the government.

Figure 11.10: The high cost of Africa's infrastructure

Sector	Africa	Other developing regions
Power tariffs ($ per kWh)	0.02–0.46	0.05–0.1
Water tariffs ($ per m3)	0.86–6.56	0.03–0.6
Road freight rates ($ per tonne km)	0.04–0.14	0.01–0.04
Mobile telephony ($ per basket per mth)	2.6–21.0	9.9
International telephony ($ per 3 min call to US)	0.44–12.5	2
Internet provision ($ per mth)	6.7–148.0	11

Source: Banerjee et al., 2008; Anton Eberhard et al., "Underpowered: The State of the Power Sector in SSA," 2008; Minges et al., "Information and Communications Technology in SSA: A Sector Review," 2008; Supee Teravaninthorn and Gael Raballand, *Transport Prices and Costs in Africa: A Review of the Main International Corridors*, 2008.

Research suggests that the costs incurred by Africa's trucking operators are not significantly higher than in other parts of the world.[8] Higher fuel costs; the poor and, in some cases, non-existent road infrastructure; the "facilitation" fees required to cross borders, and the huge queues – all add to the service fees. Partially offsetting these are low wages and in some cases subsidised fuel.

Port inefficiencies add more costs to the final product – as we would expect after SSA trade turnover has quadrupled (albeit in value terms) in little more than a decade – but this should change as ports become privatised. For example, the partial privatisation of the Port of Maputo (Mozambique) has resulted in an impressive 500% increase in port capacity to 12 million tonnes per annum (tpa) since the end of the civil war, with operators having submitted plans to increase capacity to 50 million tpa. The Maputo coal terminal now has 6 million tpa of capacity, up from 1 million tpa five years ago. In addition, the increase in efficiency has allowed the port to compete with the more established Richards Bay port in the export of thermal coal from South Africa.

In our experience covering the African cement industry, the main reason for the high price of cement in the inland countries is the high cost of transport. The cost to produce cement in India and China varies between $50 and $75 per tonne, but after allowing for shipping and port charges, the price of imported cement at the coast rises to $120 per tonne. Given the current low shipping rates for bulk products, imported cement continues to keep the price of locally produced cement competitive, especially in those countries that have zero or low import tariffs on cement (for example, Nigeria has imposed an import tariff of 40% for bulk cement, while importing bagged cement is banned).

Power: The Primary Driver

THE lack of power remains the primary factor limiting economic growth in the region. Installed generation capacity in SSA is currently 68 GW. Excluding South Africa, the figure is closer to 28 GW (of which only 21 GW is generally available), which is barely enough electricity to light one 100-watt light bulb per person for three hours a day. More than 30 African countries experience power shortages and in most SSA countries, less than 30% of the population has access to electricity, although again this is common in countries embarking on the growth trajectory. While the impact of power shortages and power cuts in SSA is partially offset through the use of emergency diesel generators, providing an estimated 6 GW in SSA (4 MW excluding South Africa), the economic cost of power outages is still significant.

Figure 11.11: Economic cost of power outages in selected countries

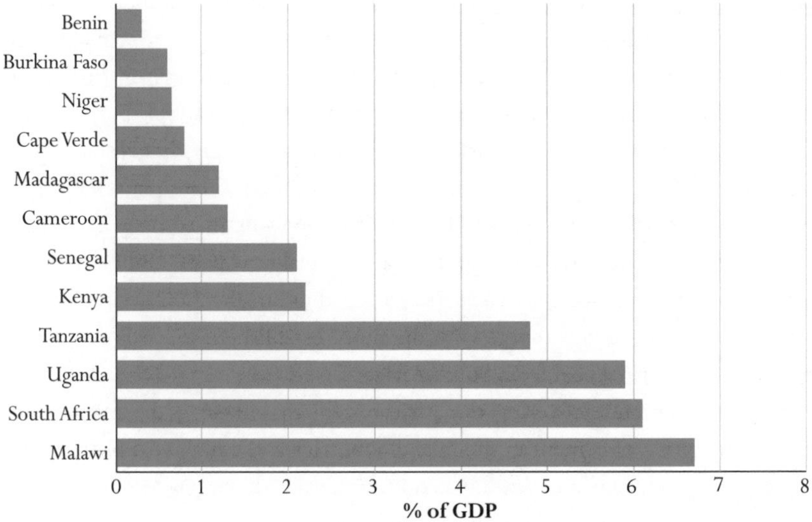

Source: World Bank data; Eberhard et al., 2008

The chart below illustrates which countries in SSA are at risk of power cuts, whether caused by droughts (which reduce hydroelectric capacity), oil-price hikes (which increase generator costs) or conflict (which destroys power infra-structure). Once again, we see that as conflict decreases the risk of damage to infrastructure recedes, which means the incentive to invest in infrastructure is greater.

Figure 11.12: Causes of SSA's power supply shortages

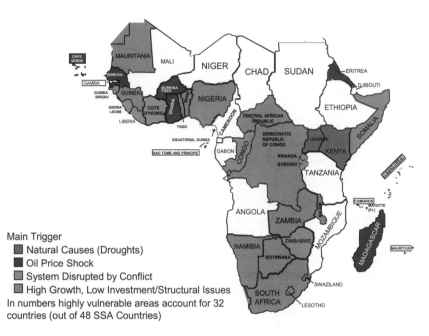

Main Trigger
- ◼ Natural Causes (Droughts)
- ◼ Oil Price Shock
- ◻ System Disrupted by Conflict
- ◻ High Growth, Low Investment/Structural Issues

In numbers highly vulnerable areas account for 32 countries (out of 48 SSA Countries)

Source: IMF

The converse of this is that improving electricity supply would have multiple benefits for an economy, giving a boost to GDP, lowering electricity costs for industry, cutting total power costs for consumers (even if electricity prices rise, diesel generating costs will fall) and raising the popularity of governments. Hence for example the progress being made in Nigeria on electricity reform today. Electricity distributors and generators are to be privatised, and management of the transmission network will be outsourced, with all this occurring within a legislative framework set out in 2005 that is praised by independent experts. Zambia is currently in the process of constructing five new power stations, with funding coming from the Chinese (and using a mixture of IPPs and public-private partnerships [PPP]), and a number of other African countries are currently in the process of evaluating the type of technologies to use. From a pure privatisation perspective, Nigeria leads the way, but as the stream of foreign investment picks up momentum we believe that there will be a significant increase in SSA's power capacity over the next 5–10 years, using a mixture of both IPPs and PPPs.

What else should be and is being done? We summarise the findings of the World Bank.

Improved sector planning: Given the limited resources of the public sector, private participation is and has been sought, typically in the form of IPPs. In the case of Nigeria, the privatisation of state-owned assets continues, but elsewhere in the continent approximately 40 IPPs have been established in 15 African countries over the past 20 years. The function of the IPPs has been to sell electricity directly into the national power grids. Research conducted by the University of Cape Town's Graduate School of Business suggests that IPPs established in North Africa (Egypt, Morocco and Tunisia) have been more successful than those established in SSA.[9] Critical success factors relate to the availability of low-cost fuels, better planning, the endurance of policies and the availability of reliable statistics on the demand for power. Nevertheless, the majority of the IPPs established in SSA (Kenya, Tanzania, Uganda, Côte d'Ivoire, Ghana, Nigeria, Senegal and Togo) have performed and have had their contracts upheld.

Reform of the state-owned utilities: Too often, reform of the state-owned utilities has centred on technical issues, to the exclusion of corporate governance and accountability. To encourage investor participation in the power sector, improved transparency and accountability depend on solid financial management, procurement and management information systems.

Improved cost recovery: A successful power utility must be financially viable, and power tariffs should be set high enough to cover operating costs and contribute to covering capital costs. In many African countries that use a high proportion of expensive emergency power, cost recovery tariffs are unaffordable. However, as regional trade increases, the cost of producing power will decline, making cost recovery more feasible.

Expanding regional trade: Given Africa's considerable and under-exploited hydroelectric, gas and coal resources, the best way to increase power generation at the lowest unit cost is to develop large power generation projects. Since individual countries invariably have neither the demand nor the finance required for these large projects, the World Bank believes that a project finance approach, based on regional power off-take, is required – which effectively requires both donor funding and private participation. Through the creation of power pools, regional trade would increase, which could potentially save up to $2 billion per annum in energy costs. Already four power pools have been formed, the more developed one being the Southern African Power Pool established by the

Southern African Development Community in 1995, with capacity of 56 GW (72 GW targeted by 2025). The West African Power Pool established by the Economic Community of West African States has an installed capacity of 6 GW. The ECCS (central African) power pool has capacity of 5 GW and potential to grow to 59 GW via hydropower schemes, while the Eastern African Power Pool has capacity of 2.5 GW with 5.3 GW targeted by 2025.

Reducing the funding gap: Estimated at $23 billion, the funding gap in Africa's power sector is the largest of any infrastructure sector. Improving the creditworthiness of individual countries could help in accessing capital markets. Already, and in response to the power-sector crisis, donors have increased their emphasis on the power sector, and commitments averaging $1.5 billion per annum between 2005 and 2007 reached a peak of $2.3 billion in 2007. External funding to Africa's power sector has historically been low, but as illustrated below, has increased in recent years.

Figure 11.13: Cement price, $/tonne, 2010

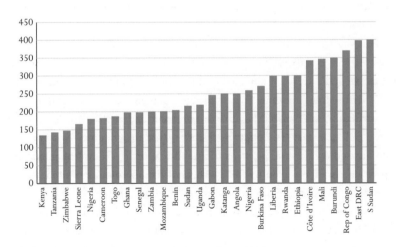

Source: Renaissance Capital

The Investment Boom to Come

THE provision of infrastructure remains the key enabler of economic growth in SSA. There has been improvement over recent decades, and we are now at a point where a jump in infrastructure provision is under way. Electricity generation capacity is reaching record highs in Nigeria, at 5–6 GW, with total capacity of more than 10 GW expected before the next presidential election in 2015. Road-building projects in Kenya have been causing temporary chaos, but will put an infrastructure base in place to serve East Africa's largest urban area – it is no coincidence that many of these projects will be completed before elections in early 2013. These are examples of political leaders responding to popular needs.

To understand the scale of what is coming, consider Dangote Cement, the giant company led by Africa's richest man, Aliko Dangote. This year, his company inaugurated the largest cement plant in Africa at Obajana, and the most modern in the world, with equipment from Japan, Germany, the UK and China. This $1 billion plant alone will produce 10.5mnt of cement annually, and an expansion is planned. With the plant came new roads, an airport, rail and sewage lines and a small city of worker housing.

"When I came to Obajana, you hardly could count 30 zinc roof houses, but today houses are everywhere, while many hotels are coming up in the village," said Attama Lawrence, a small cement dealer in the town, who started as a Dangote labourer.

Dangote has bet big on Africa's infrastructure needs. With operations in 10 other African countries, Dangote's firm turns over $2.5 billion a year – about 1% of Nigeria's GDP. It aims to produce almost 30mnt of cement annually by 2015, from almost nothing five years ago. Cement, the very building block of infrastructure, will enable Nigeria to construct and replace roads, bridges and dams, and kick-start the country's infrastructure programme. Not only is Dangote focused on Nigeria, he plans to establish a further 20mnt of annual cement capacity across the region by 2015. This not from a mine or a Chinese state oil concession, but cement largely used to build within Africa.

Given the degree of investment maturity in the developed world, it is understandable that the focus for investment has shifted to other developing regions, such as SSA. Levels of foreign direct investment flowing into the region have never been so high, and demand from clients representing infrastructure funds for meetings with companies involved in the roll-out of infrastructure continues to increase. Given that roads, power and utilities are the backbone of overall infrastructure development, it is no surprise that more capital is becoming available to finance such projects.

To take advantage of the abundant natural resources suitable for power generation and the increased demand for both residential electrification and industrial development, countries are beginning to liberialise their domestic markets in order to encourage foreign investment. Privatisation (Nigeria), the creation of PPPs and the encouragement of IPPs (across the region) will result in a surge in power capacity.

Investment needs are significant, but the cost of producing power will be reduced through power pools, and already four have been established across the region. Even so, the developing power industry can hardly carry the financial burden alone, and there is an increasing need for private-sector involvement.

Political and regulatory risks continue to be a cause for concern for investors, but through the introduction of PPPs, which have worked well in other countries, levels of transparency are improving, as are levels of regulation and planning.

Investment opportunities, specifically in power, continue to accelerate. From hydroelectric schemes in the DRC (which some suggest could in theory light up all of Europe as well as Africa[10]), Ethiopia and Guinea, to gas-driven projects in both East and West Africa, to nuclear programmes in South Africa and renewable programmes across the region, an increase in the availability of funding will help to boost generation across Africa.

It is estimated that almost $100 billion per annum (65% related to capex and the remainder for maintenance and operation) is required to address Africa's infrastructure backlog, with 40% of this needed for power. This corresponds to 15% of the region's GDP, considerably less than the 20% of SSA GDP provided by oil production alone, let alone other mineral exports. The capital is increasingly available, and that – coupled with the willingness of politicians to put the wellbeing of the people ahead of themselves – means Africa can attain and even surpass the growth rates achieved by any of its Southeast Asian and South Asian peers, by following a path of investment similar to what they began 20 years ago.

Notes

1. Mfonobong Nsehe, "The 10 Greatest Living Business Leaders in Africa Today," *Forbes*, 8 August 2012, http://www.forbes.com/sites/ mfonobongnsehe/2012/08/07/the-10-greatest-living-business-leaders-in-africa-today-2/.
2. *Africa's Infrastructure: A Time for Transformation* (Washington, DC: World Bank, 2010).

3. Ray Barrell, Dawn Holland and Dirk Willem te Velde, "Us or them. Them and us. We are all in it together, stupid. How a G-20 supported fiscal stimulus in sub-Saharan Africa can help the G-20 too," in *A Development Charter for the G-20* (Overseas Development Institute, March 2009), 16, http://www.odi.org.uk/resources/docs/4144.pdf.

4. *Building Bridges: Ernst & Young's 2012 Attractiveness Survey – Africa*, Ernst & Young, http://www.ey.com/Publication/vwLUAssets/EY–2012_Africa_attractiveness_survey/$FILE/attractiveness_2012_africa_v17.pdf.

5. World Bank, *Africa's Infrastructure.*

6. David Mataen, *Africa: The Ultimate Frontier Market* (Petersfield, UK: Harriman House, 2012).

7. http://siteresources.worldbank.org/INTAFRICA/Resources/aicd_factsheet_transport.pdf.

8. Supee Teravaninthorn and Gael Raballand, *Transport Prices and Costs in Africa: A Review of the Main International Corridors* (Washington, DC: World Bank, 2008).

9. Katharine Nawaal Gratwick and Anton Eberhard, "An Analysis of Independent Power Projects in Africa: Understanding Development and Investment Outcomes," *Development Policy Review* 26, no. 3 (2008), 309-338.

10. Mataen, *Africa: The Ultimate Frontier Market.*

Chapter 12

Urbanisation: A Virtuous Circle

By Yvonne Mhango and Arnold Meyer

When we started living in cities, we did something that had never happened before in the history of life. We broke away from the equations of biology, all of which are sublinear. Every other creature gets slower as it gets bigger. That's why the elephant plods along. But in cities, the opposite happens. As cities get bigger, everything starts accelerating. There is no equivalent for this in nature. It would be like finding an elephant that's proportionally faster than a mouse.

—Geoffrey West , theoretical physicist, one of the leading scientists working on a scientific model of cities[1]

The current explosion of growth across Africa's cities presents a transformational moment for African architecture. A vision for the future of urbanism on the continent requires a clear understanding of the historical references – from the empires and kingdoms through to the enforced European encounter and latterly the enthusiastic embrace of modernity that established the image of independence for so many nations. In parallel, a manifesto for urban development demands a contextual language that is distinct from the language of politics. The culture of the African city is hybridised and the African citizen sees himself – reads himself – through his local condition, his ethnic group, which is his history, and through his colonial experience, which is his modernity. People do not operate within a single or a double consciousness, but within a quadruple consciousness. The key is to align this metaphysical fact with the physical fabric of the city. To this end, it is useful to look beyond national borders and instead to seek a more elemental reading of the continent.

—David Adjaye OBE, architect, 2012

Urbanisation is an accelerating trend across Africa, and as we see in other countries on the growth trajectory, it occurs when GDP growth is rising fast. The latest research implies each feeds on the other. The rapid expansion of Africa's cities reflects the continent's best-ever decade for growth, while also providing the foundations that will propel Africa to greater wealth. It is a theme that is a core part of Renaissance Group's work in the continent – as we have begun building new cities from Kenya to Ghana. New urban areas hosting millions of jobs and residents will be a template for the modern African city of the 21st century, and a testament to what private capital can deliver to support Africa's boom.

IF there is a place where most of the positive trends flowing through Africa are collecting, it is the sprawling, heaving cities. These metropolises, varied as the continent that holds them, are hard-scrabble places, often over-populated and beset by many of the same problems that bedevilled Rome at its imperial height, or London in the Victorian era, or New York in its early 20th century adolescence. Petty crime, poor infrastructure, overcrowding and a lack of housing come with the territory. But as these older cities showed, blight is a transitional period on the road to something better. Increasingly, Africa's own urbanisation is leading to the kinds of changes that will ultimately solve the well-known problems that plague not only its cities, but its governments, regions and societies, too.

Africa today is in the grip of rapid and accelerating urbanisation. It is a trend that is transforming the societies of Sub-Saharan Africa: countries that have been largely rural, agricultural and subsistence-based are transforming themselves into urban, industrial, value-added economies. Along with the problems, urbanisation also brings improved productivity, greater wellbeing, higher levels of education and economic skills – and greater demands for accountability and competence on the part of government. These can be met, as Governor Babatunde Fashola is proving in Lagos. Across Africa, a new generation of mega-cities is being born, transforming the oldest continent and laying the foundations of the world's next great growth story.

Africa's population will increase by 60% over the next four decades and the urban population, in particular, will triple to 1.23 billion, according to UN-Habitat. Africa is the world's fastest-urbanising region. In 1990, one-third of Africa's population was urbanised. Today the figure is 40%, and UN-Habitat projects that by 2025 it will reach almost 50%. Rural-urban migration only accounts for 40% of urban growth rates, while higher urban fertility rates account for 60% of growth.

Figure 12.1: Share of population living in urban areas

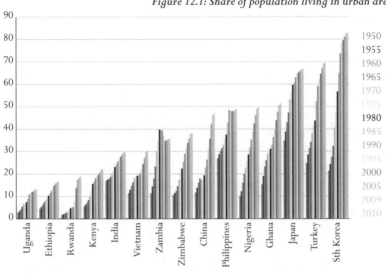

Source: UN

Already, approximately 60% of Southern Africa's population lives in urban areas (see the chart below), compared with 50% in North Africa and just 25% in East Africa.

Figure 12.2: Urbanisation by region, % of total population

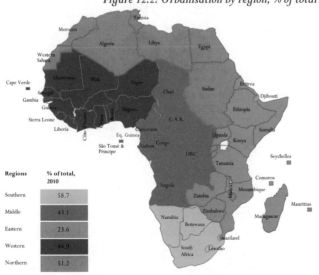

Source: UN-Habitat, Renaissance Capital

When most of Africa was colonised by Europeans in the late 19th century, the continent had almost no urban population. Colonial, commercial and administrative politics catalysed the first wave of urbanisation. The primary objective of the colonists was to export cash crops and minerals from their respective colonies to Europe. Harbour towns were established and railway lines built to transport raw commodities from inland areas to these coastal ports. Central administration functions were often placed in the port towns, which over time emerged as significant urban areas. It is no accident that most of Africa's biggest cities are located along its coastline.

Figure 12.3: Growth of African cities (% increase), 2010–2025 forecast

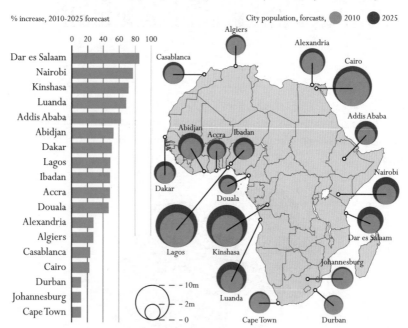

Source: *Economist*, UN-Habitat

When African countries began to emerge as independent nation states, several established centrally planned economic systems. Economic opportunities often stemmed from nascent urban areas – especially capital cities – as these were closest to the seats of power. By one estimate, Nigeria's urban areas have received 80% of total investment in the modern era. In some instances, new cities were built with the intention of decentralising power and investment. For example, Lilongwe (Malawi), Yamoussoukro (Côte d'Ivoire) and Abuja (Nigeria) all arose as planned new capital cities.

Mega-Cities of the Future

SOUTHERN Africa is the most urbanised region in Africa. In South Africa, mining towns, together with ports, drew labour towards urban areas. Moreover, the establishment of large-scale commercial farms by white farmers, which resulted in the displacement of indigenous people from the land, intensified urbanisation. Those who failed to gain employment on these large farms were compelled to work marginal land or migrate to urban areas. A second wave of urbanisation was catalysed by the removal of the laws that restricted free movement of non-whites in the early 1990s. The rate of urbanisation in Southern Africa is now slowing, and the continent's biggest cities in 2025 will not be in Southern Africa. By 2025, according to UN-Habitat, Lagos and Kinshasa will have Africa's biggest urban populations, as the chart below highlights.

Figure 12.4: Africa's most populous cities in 2010 and 2025, million

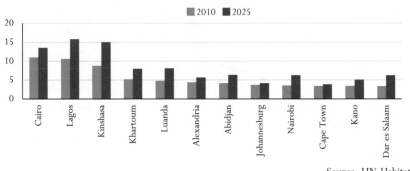

Source: UN-Habitat

North Africa is the second-most-urbanised region in Africa because much of the inland geography is desert and barely habitable. East Africa is the least-urbanised region in Africa. The fact that most of the region's countries are – at least until the recent discovery of gas and oil – resource-light and largely agriculture-based economies partially explains the smaller share of the population that is urbanised.

The New Urban Wave

A host of recent work on the advantages of the city demonstrate that it is more cost-efficient to manage transport, food distribution and most services in urban areas. The availability of labour is greater in cities, and cities are a trigger for faster growth. When Japan was urbanising at its fastest rate from 1950–70, GDP growth was approximately 9% per annum. As China replicated this 40 years later, it too achieved 9% growth. Today it is Africa that is embarking on rapid urbanisation, which implies that the fastest growth is coming over the next few decades.

Figure 12.5: Using Japan urbanisation data for 1950–2010 we can see how others compare

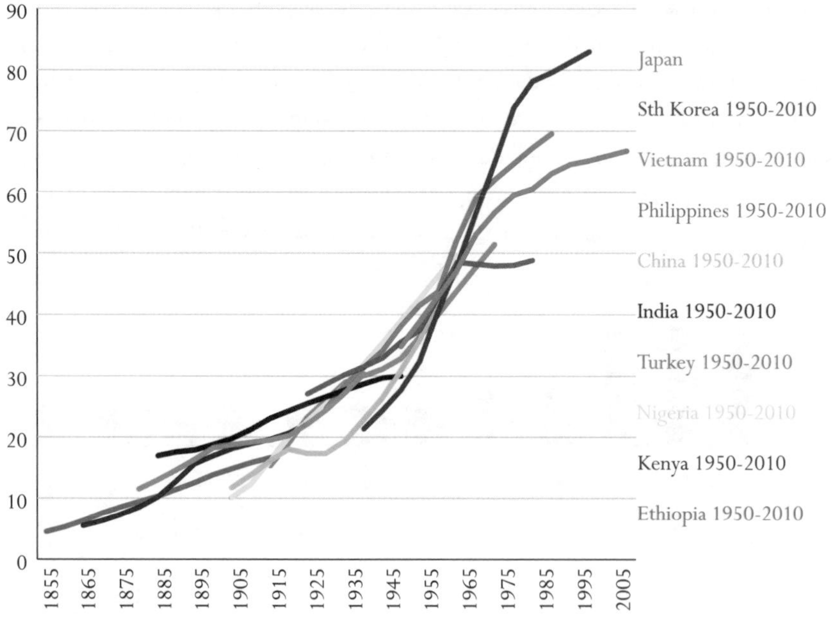

Source: Renaissance Capital estimates, UN

While urbanisation can support growth, it also creates an acute need to build infrastructure – particularly housing. This is no less true in SSA today than it was in China two decades ago.

As we entered the 21st century, real estate developers from the US and Europe were invited to China on fact-finding trips aimed at luring them into a planned construction boom like no one had ever seen before. In what turned out to be an enormous mistake, most of them passed up on the opportunity to get involved in the early stages of the state's plan to build mega-cities around the country, citing widespread poverty, stifling bureaucracy, a lack of serviced infrastructure, an inability to raise local funding, and the challenge of building and maintaining local partnerships.

Fast-forward to 2012 and the same international real estate players who missed the China boom have scouts and fact-finding parties criss-crossing Africa. Their views are not that dissimilar to those voiced in China 10 years ago. Two factors have changed, however. Western developers find diminishing opportunities in their home markets, as the 2008 financial crisis continues to depress housing and construction. Most of all, they appear chastised and regretful at having been invited to help China in an unprecedented spurt of construction only to turn it down. Today, many who had a risk-averse attitude to Shanghai and Guangzhou have quite a different opinion of Nairobi and Dar es Salaam.

Developers appear to understand demographics differently, too – not shying away from what might be seen as daunting growth rates by Western eyes. Today a rapidly expanding population – provided it is fuelling an expanding GDP and middle class – is understood as an engine of housing demand.

Africa's numbers are particularly virile. In 1980 Africa had a population of 400 million people. In 2010 the continent reached the 1 billion mark and in 30 years from now Africa will be close on 2 billion people. If 10% of Africans enter the middle class (estimates are that up to 42% is likely), Africa will have a middle class the size of Europe today, with similar demands for high-quality housing stock.

Take Nairobi, currently the 117th-largest city in the world, estimated to grow in the next eight years to become the 73rd-largest global metropolis.[2] Although unconfirmed, some researchers believe that Lagos has surpassed Cairo as the largest city in Africa, with 11.4 million people. When challenged with a map of Africa, many a global investor would struggle to identify Bamako, Ouagadougou and Lubumbashi. Yet these cities will all expand by at least 1 million people in the next 10 years. If Houston were to grow by 1 million people it would prompt a stampede. Developers and construction-related stocks would soar, mall developers would scramble to secure land and local officials would smilingly adjust their tax-revenue forecasts.

Because it is in Africa, a high degree of scepticism surrounds the opportunities presented by urbanisation. Yet in the vast population explosion of Africa lies its wealth and opportunity. UN-Habitat has stated that many children living today in Africa will reside in cities not yet conceived.[3] Throughout history, cities have been the incubators of innovation, creativity and invention. Africa's cities of tomorrow will be no different; in fact they will evolve much faster, benefiting from changing technology, gains in water treatment and recycling, optimum energy distribution and planned transportation. The old and established cities of the world endured more than 200 years of evolution with constant adaptation, change and innovation at huge cost. Due to the leap-frog effect, African cities will evolve within 10 years of conceptualisation and be able to apply Internet and communications, water and sanitation technology and modern road construction without having to evolve as the older cities did.

So Where Are the Builders?

LARGE areas of land on the urban edge of cities hold the only opportunity for absorbing a significant part of the growth in populations. In designing these new cities, with mixed use as the guiding principle of the new urbanism, not only is housing created, but also employment and the opportunity to bring commerce and industry together with its consumer markets. The resultant infrastructure is utilised 24/7.

Tatu City, 15 km north of Nairobi, just off the new four-lane Thika Highway, is one such initiative. It is a satellite city on the first large piece of unfragmented land outside the capital of Kenya. Tatu City is an initiative of Rendeavour, the development arm of Renaissance Group, and is the first privately developed urban centre in Africa outside of South Africa. Being built in 11 phases on 1,000 hectares, Tatu City will be developed over approximately 10 years and will be home to 70,000 residents and 30,000 day visitors. It is an integrated community with a new financial centre for Nairobi and East Africa.[4]

Manage It, and It Will Grow

WHAT sets Tatu City apart from other large developments is its urban management framework: a privately managed city, where service charges are re-invested in the upkeep of infrastructure, and where owners share in the management and decision making of their city and community.

It is overwhelmingly apparent in just about all of Africa's fast-growing economies that there are sufficient developers to see the top structure development through, although partnering with large international developers would give an execution boost, faster delivery and new technology. What developers are critically short of are serviced land parcels, free from legal encumbrances and with connectivity to good roads, water and electricity. As these become available, from Ghana to the DRC[5], investors are ready to step in, and African governments provide the endorsements needed to secure planning approvals, in some cases in record time.

At the announcement of two new Rendeavour cities in July 2012 in Accra, Ghana's president, John Dramani Mahama, addressed an overflowing hall of officials, businesspeople and tribes representing Rendeavour's partners in those projects.

"We make history here today with this launch," Mahama said. "New cities are going to rise up from undeveloped land through a remarkable partnership between a visionary private foreign investor group and two equally visionary traditional leaders and their communities ... what we are seeking to do with these mixed-use city developments undoubtedly will become a model not only in Ghana but throughout Africa and, perhaps, even further afield."

King City and Appolonia, the new cities under development in Ghana, will each be home to 90,000 residents. The 10-year, phased development will, like Tatu City in Kenya, create hundreds of thousands of direct and indirect employment opportunities. "Our desire as a community is to see developments that will create job opportunities for our people," Nii Tei Adumuah II, chief of Appolonia and a partner, on behalf of his community, in the Appolonia city, told the guests at the Accra event.

Large-scale serviced land investments have the ability to transform Africa's urban landscape, delivering the cities of the future and propelling countries along their fast-growth trajectories. Investors will find that they have the opportunity to reap returns over long periods of development and participate early in the value chain of real estate projects. Thus, private capital will help to lay the foundations of Africa's future metropolises and unlock the potential of the urbanisation boom.

Notes

1. Jonah Lehrer, "A Physicist Solves the City," *New York Times Magazine*, 17 December 2010, http://www.nytimes.com/2010/12/19/magazine/19Urban_West-t. html?_r=1&pagewanted=all.
2. *The State of African Cities 2010: Governance, Inequality and Urban Land Markets* (United Nations, June 2011), http://www.unhabitat.org/documents/SACR-ALL-10-FINAL.pdf.
3. Ibid.
4. See www.tatucity.com.
5. See www.kingcity.com.gh, www.appolonia.com.gh, www.tatucity.com and www. kiswishi.com (DRC).

Chapter 13

Agriculture: The Coming Harvest

By Yvonne Mhango, Michael Moran and Richard Ferguson

Africa is endowed with 60% of the world's unused arable land and millions of dedicated farmers. They simply need the tools, infrastructure, and competence to unlock the continent's tremendous agricultural potential. There is no reason — and no excuse — to leave the survival of millions to unpredictable weather conditions. Rather, countries must take control by drastically improving efficiency and productivity.

—Thierry Tanoh, Ivorian-born vice president, IFC[1]

African [agricultural] productivity is low. If there's an investment then African farmers are very capable of producing enough food not only to feed themselves but also for the export market.
—Professor Calestous Juma, Kenyan-born agronomist, Harvard University[2]

THE dawn of the 21st century has coincided with a surge in global food prices, due to rising wealth in emerging markets, the shift of Chinese rural workers to cities and America's biofuel policies. It also led to a new trend of foreign investment in agriculture, from Gulf states investing in Sudan's Nile valley, to the ill-fated attempt by one Korean company to purchase agricultural land in Madagascar. For the first time in decades, the world has looked to Africa as an exporter of food.

Renaissance sees huge opportunity for Africa to benefit from this growing demand. The UN Food and Agriculture Organization estimates the additional land required to feed a larger and richer world in 2050 at only 71 million hectares (ha). Meanwhile the World Bank believes 400 million ha of unused agricultural land could by tapped by Africa to feed not only itself, but the rising demand of the rest of the world, too.

Productivity improvements are already rising faster than in Asia and have huge room to improve. Nigeria's dynamic new minister for agriculture, with his plans to accelerate investment in agriculture, is indicative of a marked trend across Africa to encourage a sector that was too often ignored in the first decades after de-colonisation.

Below we outline two key themes that give grounds for optimism about Africa's agricultural revolution. First we show how urbanisation itself is often a trigger for a transformation of agricultural productivity. Second, and most encouraging of all, we show that Africa does not have to pioneer an agricultural miracle. That work has already been done in Brazil. Africa is well placed for a productivity surge across the continent, allowing it to rival what China or India has been able to achieve.

Urbanisation and Food Security

NO movement of people and transformation of multiple societies on the scale of what we see in Africa has ever gone off without problems. While urban birth rates are the main driver of city population expansion in Africa, there is a real concern that an exodus from the agricultural sector will reduce food supply. Urbanisation can place pressure on groundwater sources, as we see in Mexico City. Logistics also face greater strain. One Nigerian study estimated that for a city of approximately 4 million residents, food requirements average about 3,000 tonnes per day. This is equivalent to approximately two three-tonne trucks entering the city every three minutes.[3] Food hygiene becomes a serious issue. In Tanzania, approximately 70% of the caloric requirements of low- and middle-income households are met by street food, according to the FAO. In a survey of 559 urban households in Accra, it was found that more than 32% of households' food budgets were spent on street foods.[4] This share was even higher for poorer households. As most of Africa's street stalls are unregulated, and lack sanitation facilities, running water, and adequate refrigeration, there are strong links between the food they produce and the prevalence of gastrointestinal infections.

According to an FAO study in 2009, having sufficient resources to afford a healthy diet becomes the most important dimension of food security in urban areas.[5] According to the earlier Accra study, residents in many developing world cities buy more than 90% of their food. Moreover, the poor spend the largest share of their disposable income on food. As a result, food becomes a political issue.

Sub-Saharan Africa's food density levels (calories/km2/day), which combine per capita food demand and population densities, are generally low compared with Asia. Today, only the cities of West Africa and a few areas around Lake Victoria, in East Africa, have high food density levels. In 2050, food density is projected to increase around the highly populated coastal areas of West Africa, particularly Nigeria. This growth will be driven by urbanisation. If these urban areas are not able to adapt to changing conditions, the risk of food insecurity will increase in places like Nigeria's megacities. The high-population-density areas of rural and urban East Africa will also see an increase in food density, particularly in Ethiopia, Burundi, Rwanda, the DRC and Uganda.

Urbanisation Can Shape Agriculture

HOWEVER, African urbanisation need not necessarily result in higher risks of food insecurity. On the contrary, urbanisation can regenerate agricultural production. Research by Richard Tiffen and Xavier Irz argues that the process of urbanisation is often accompanied by an evolution of farming systems, which sustains food security. This is outlined in the chart below. Over time, as agricultural labourers move into manufacturing and services, farming itself evolves from labour-intensive smallholder practices towards large-scale, capital-intensive and productive farming methods. Meanwhile, the growing purchasing power of urban areas, in turn, provides a ready market for agricultural produce.

In phase A of the chart below, almost all labour is involved in subsistence farming, at low levels of output per labourer, but as the economy transitions to phase C, agricultural productivity increases exponentially. If any chart pinpoints the positive outlook for African agriculture, it is this one.

Figure 13.1: Agriculture, manufacture and service sector labour over time

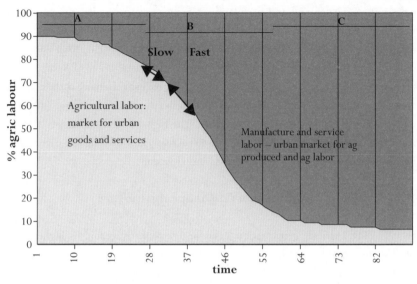

Note: Arrows show positions of low-income and lower-middle-income countries in 1960 and 1980, as given in World Bank (1983)

Source: Mary Tiffen, "Transition in Sub-Saharan Africa: Agriculture, Urbanisation and Income Growth," *World Development* 31, no. 8 (2003).

In effect, agricultural labour and non-agricultural labour form each other's market. The rural area supplies agricultural produce and labour to the urban area, which in turn supplies goods and services to its rural counterpart. Moving out of phase A is slow and a significant challenge, and may last many centuries. However, phase B, where the ratio of the agriculture labour force to the total labour force begins to fall at an increasing rate, can be accomplished in 50-500 years. Today's developing countries are generally making the transition more quickly from phase A to phase B than Britain did during its industrialisation period in the 1700s. Most of Africa is in the early stage of phase B, but as farmers become a local, effective, cash-earning market, this will accelerate the transition and in turn spur the growth of urban areas.

As the manufacturing and service sector's productivity and income increases, it will pull labour out of agriculture. At this stage, the need for additional capital to substitute for labour, in all sectors including agriculture, will grow.

A tendency towards bigger, capital-intensive farms will develop as phase C approaches.

The Transition Is Happening, Now

AS most of Africa is still in the early stage of phase B, the overriding policy objective is to improve productivity in the continent's small-scale farming sector. This requires many repeated, small, private investments, which will be most effective if there are appropriate public investments outside agriculture, including in communications and infrastructure.

African farmers can meet internal demand without increasing productivity only if they transfer resources from export crops (including cocoa, cotton and coffee) to food crops. But there is limited scope to achieve that. In fact most countries on the continent do not export more than 20% of their agricultural production value; 80% is consumed locally.

The increase in Africa's urban population and market over time is already visible in locations such as northern Nigeria. Between 1952 and 1991, Kano state's urban population increased by about 8% per annum, while the rural increase was closer to 1.6% per annum. This strong urban growth explains why Kano will be Africa's 7th-largest city by 2025. To provide for the urban areas, each rural household needed to supply 10 times as much as much grain to urban markets, on average, in 1991, compared with 1952. After decades of under-investment, local supply has not kept pace with demand, resulting in significant food deficits.

But it does not have to be that way. In northern Nigeria, the most efficient farms were concentrated in high-density areas with access to good market facilities, which highlights the importance of public infrastructure. Large-scale farms around Kano increased significantly in the late 1990s, but they only make up about 5% of total agricultural production.

So, the issues are clear: an urbanising Africa is positive for agricultural growth if agricultural investment keeps pace with urban growth. Rising food deficits indicate the agriculture sector has fallen behind in terms of productivity, which Renaissance considers indicative of the scale of the opportunity. Over the long term, a growing population, greater urbanisation, an existing structural food deficit and growing international food needs are four factors which we consider – if addressed with appropriate public policy responses and the intelligent application of private capital – could turn African agriculture into one of the great investment themes of the next few decades. Fortunately the arrival of energetic, visionary ministers, such as Nigeria's Dr Akinwunmi Adesina, suggests that just such thinking has now arrived.

The African Cerrado

IN the early 1960s, the Cerrado region of Brazil, a vast subtropical savanna covering 22% of the country's land mass, was regarded by the governments of the day as something of a wasteland, a zone of wooded grasslands where jaguar, wolf, giant anteater and a handful of subsistence farmers made their home. As large as Germany, France, Italy, Spain and the UK combined, the Cerrado escaped the attention of European settlers largely because its highly acidic soil would not support crops. Thus the Cerrado – the word in Portuguese means "closed" – made little impression on the Brazilian national consciousness. Brazilians seeking their fortune in the great interior – from foreign adventurers to multinationals – were far more likely to head for the fertile, temperate border areas in the south abutting Uruguay, Paraguay and Bolivia, or more romantically, expend their energies in the even-larger Amazonian rainforest.

Yet today, Brazil's position as an agricultural superpower owes much to this "closed" wasteland, and the role of scientists and government policy in transforming the region holds important lessons for SSA. Breakthroughs in horticulture and agronomy, often from Brazil's own researchers, solved the chemical puzzle and ultimately unlocked the region's fertility. The military regime that ruled Brazil at the time then moved quickly to incentivise industrial farming and livestock production with tax breaks, infrastructure improvements and offers of cheap land. They succeeded beyond their wildest dreams – indeed, some think they were a bit too successful. While the agricultural boom transformed Brazil into a leading agricultural exporter, the relatively uncontrolled nature of the transformation led to environmental problems that might have been avoided with a more considered approach.

Half a century later, however, the nations of SSA, faced with fewer scientific challenges and a greater awareness of the importance of environmental balance and sustainability, should be able to apply the lessons of the Cerrado model to great effect as plows, reapers and processing plants begin to exploit the world's most important remaining tract of untilled arable land, the Guinea Savannah.

The Guinea Savannah zone in Africa encompasses approximately 600 million ha of land across a belt of the continent including parts of 27 countries. A recent World Bank study concluded that in spite of its poor soil quality, the warm tropical climate, annual precipitation of 800-1,200 mm and political complexities, some 400 million ha of land is suitable for agriculture. Currently, less than 10% of that land is in agricultural use. Thus, Africa's own Cerrado, with all the upside rewards and downside risks, sits fallow, ready to help bridge the gap between the 21st century's demand for food commodities and current production levels buffeted by the vagaries of climate change, markets, changing dietary habits and surging population growth, particularly in the emerging world.

Figure 13.2: Guinea Savannah region in SSA

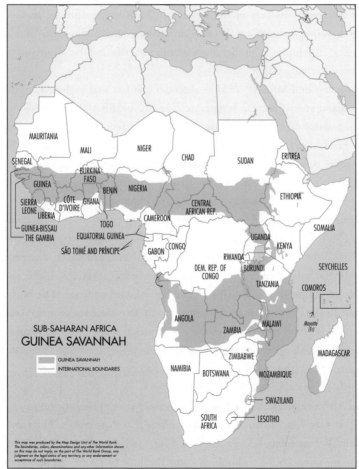

Source: IFPRI via World Bank

The Brazilian Experience

THE transformation of the Cerrado began in the late 1960s, when the government instituted policies to "colonise" the region, encouraging migration and incentivising cultivation. Many agricultural entrepreneurs from the established agricultural zone in the southern regions, attracted by the availability of large tracts of land at a relatively low price, took their investment and farming knowledge with them. Government support included subsidised inputs, credit, price supports and tax incentives.

The national agricultural research organisation, Empresa Brasileira de Pesquisa Agropecuária (EMBRAPA), established in 1973, had a leading role to play in the transformation of the Cerrado. EMBRAPA employed an integrated strategy to raise productivity, through initiatives such as adding lime to neutralise soil acidity, developing high-yielding soybean varieties and the implementation of appropriate farming practices.

To appreciate EMBRAPA's role, consider the fact that soybeans are native to East Asia and grow best in a temperate climate. EMBRAPA developed varieties of soybeans that could grow in the tropical climate of the Cerrado. Similarly, it also bred varieties of nitrogen-fixing bacteria that work best in the Cerrado's soils, reducing the need for fertilisers. To encourage animal husbandry, EMBRAPA developed grass varieties that give higher yields in the Cerrado and designed appropriate livestock-management techniques.

Together with helpful macro-economic developments (a weaker currency in the 1990s helping exports, and then macro-stabilisation), these measures transformed the Cerrado into a dominant agricultural producer. The region accounts for the bulk of Brazil's production of soybeans, sorghum, coffee and beef, and a major proportion of Brazil's production of corn and rice. The best way to illustrate Brazil's transformation over the past five decades is in soybeans and beef – two commodities for which the contribution of the Cerrado is substantial.

The favourable government policies, focus on agricultural technology and migration of ambitious, skilled farmers that successfully opened up the Cerrado are mostly supply-side factors.

Can Africa replicate this success? The answer is a resounding yes.

Will it take four decades, as it did in Brazil? Renaissance Capital and many agricultural economists believe it will not, as vastly improved agricultural techniques, communications technologies and the lure of profits in newly bustling

African cities and international markets beyond spur innovation and investment in SSA's agricultural sector. Most of all, though, it will be the demand driven by continued revolutionary changes in prosperity, population and dietary preferences in emerging markets that ensures regions of Africa already producing and those within the Guinea Savannah yet to be tilled will invariably make their mark on global agricultural markets.

Agriculture in Africa is being reinvented. The Kenyan-born Harvard economist Calestous Juma has noted that innovations in biotechnology, genetics, irrigation and animal husbandry have started to reinvigorate SSA's long-dormant agricultural sector. Combined with the infrastructure improvements driven by urbanisation and the demand created by SSA's growing middle class, this is opening up the possibility that Africa can leap-frog the dream of food self-sufficiency and into the role of an important supplier of agricultural commodities as the next decades unfold.

Scepticism is becoming enthusiasm. Olugbenga Ladejobi, a Renaissance Capital equity salesman in Lagos, remembers the Structural Adjustment Programme years of his youth. Even as an eight-year-old, he remembers, he and his friends had a vague appreciation for the importance (though not yet the fateful distortions) of the acronym SAP.

"Now we have other familiar sound bytes – the Cassava Mix Initiative (CMI), the Agricultural Transformation Action Plan (ATAP), and I would have sworn that it would all go the same way as their ill-fated predecessors. But there's a buzz in the air. People here are actually interested in farming. That's very different."

Driving this interest is the promise of a sustainable occupation, something agriculture has not offered for a long time. Soaring global corn prices have been a boon to maize farmers across Africa, but such successes are vulnerable to market swings. The development of domestic demand across the continent creates a more predictable situation for some farmers, as a growing urban middle class demands a varied and reliable source of retail food.

This has led to shifts in government agricultural policies, but also in the approach donor nations and NGOs are taking. For instance, agribusinesses in Burkina Faso, Ghana, Mali and Senegal are now part of a pilot programme aimed at reducing inflexibility in crop selection, distribution and labour practices. In Kenya, Burundi and Rwanda, a US-based charity, the One Acre Fund, is taking a more micro approach, provide loans of about $75 to small farmers, as well as seeds, fertiliser and even insurance. The training and advice the fund's experts offer has led some to abandon sugar cane as a crop altogether due to its long maturation time and relatively low return on investment.

Stephanie Hanson, a One Acre Fund field officer, says the insurance and training is aimed at ensuring that local farmers have the capacity to survive hard times and react to market demands. "Basically, the idea is to create farmers who think like businesspeople and are less at the mercy of climate or the market. Sometimes, this is a surprisingly simple fix."

Demand and the Middle Class: China's Example

GROWING domestic demand has helped make market forces more real to African farmers, but the greatest drivers remain overseas. For instance, the changing dietary requirements and strategic food needs of China's increasingly urbanised and prosperous population have global implications, and represent a broad trend across the planet.

In 2001 the average Chinese consumed around 44 kg of meat per annum, of which almost 75% was pork. Over the next decade annual per capita consumption rose to approximately 54 kg, a 22% increase. Impressive as this increase may be, further growth is likely. Consider that the average Taiwanese in 2001 consumed around 75 kg of meat annually. In the past decade, the Taiwanese diet has averaged a 4% decline in overall meat consumption, but per capita consumption is still almost 71 kg – over 31% more than the corresponding figure for the average Chinese. If China's per capita meat consumption equalises with Taiwan, it will require approximately 91 million tonnes (mnt) of additional grain – slightly more than the entire corn output of Brazil and Argentina in 2011.

Figure 13.3: Annual per capita total meat consumption, kg

Counrty	2001	2011	2020E	2025E
China	44	54	67	73
Japan	43	46	49	51
South Korea	46	60	70	76
Hong Kong	107	143	151	156
Taiwan	75	71	82	87
EU	73	77	79	80
US	113	108	107	109
Russia	41	58	64	67
India	3	4	4	4

Source: FAPRI

China's shift towards a more protein-based diet is forcing the country into greater dependence on yet another raw material import, soybeans (much to Brazil's delight), to feed poulty. Consider that China imported 10mnt of soybeans in 2001 and by 2011 was importing over 72mnt of the stuff. Note that over the same period, Brazil's soybean output rose from 39mnt to 75mnt and its exports rose from 15mnt to almost 30mnt. Therefore, a large part of Brazil's development across the Cerrado was driven by Chinese demand growth (Argentina and the US also experienced similar levels of export-demand growth). Rising demand for corn to feed pigs meant that in 2011, China finally acknowledged that corn imports are going to rise sharply in the years ahead.

As it has in energy, China inevitably will seek to diversify the sources of its imported foodstuffs. Today, North America or Russia can try and fill this demand, but the weather can hit supply from either or both, as 2012 has shown. Africa offers a southern-hemisphere alternative.

From Basket Case to Bread Basket

THE drivers of food demand – population, urbanisation and income growth – coupled with new factors, such as biofuels, all increase food requirements. While the world is in no imminent danger of societal collapse through a lack of food and capabilities for producing it, spiralling food prices and the scarcity of arable land play their part in fuelling unrest in places such as Sudan's Darfur region and Mali, as well as Egypt, Tunisia and other lands affected by the Arab Spring. Some economists, including Dambisa Moyo, warn that tensions over food and water could be so acute in the future that they may spark inter-state or even regional wars of a kind previously confined to oil (Iraq-Kuwait, 1990) or minerals (Alsace-Lorraine, 1914, or the DRC, 1995).[6] She writes that, "Since 1990, at least 24 civil wars and violent conflicts have had their origins in commodities. Many more conflicts are likely in the coming decades."

Filling this imbalance, she and other economists argue, will rise up the global agenda in coming years, and Africa's unique position as the continent with the largest areas of untilled arable land will loom large.

To get an idea of Africa's potential, consider land. According to the FAO, SSA consists of 2.3 billion ha of land. Nearly 1 billion ha is suitable for rain-fed crop production. Of this 1 billion ha, some 421 million ha is described as very suitable for crop production. In this context, "very" suitable means that the attainable yield in these lands is 80-100% of the maximum theoretical yield.

To put this into perspective, in 2005 the total arable land in use in SSA amounted to 236 million ha, or only about 24% of the total suitable area. Obviously, not all of this land in use would fall into the very suitable category. But, even if we go with that extreme assumption, the land in use would still only be just over half the potential very suitable land.

Figure 13.4: SSA's agricultural potential – Land area, million ha

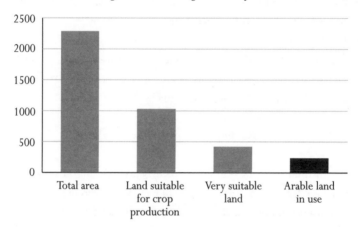

Source: FAO

Clearly, not all 1 billion ha of suitable land can be cropped – and by extension, not all of the 421 million ha of very suitable land can be cropped. A proportion of this land is already under use for non-agricultural activities such as human settlement, economic infrastructure and industrial estates. Also in that figure are forests and protected areas, concepts that would have baffled a 1960s-era Brazilian military supremo but which are recognised as vital resources in their own right today. Even so, the sheer scale of the potential tillable land gives a boost in confidence to those, like Renaissance Capital, that are bullish on the prospects for African agriculture.

"They simply need the tools, infrastructure and competence to unlock the continent's tremendous agricultural potential," says Thierry Tanoh, the vice president for SSA at the World Bank's International Finance Corporation. "There is no reason – and no excuse – to leave the survival of millions to unpredictable weather conditions. Rather, countries must take control by drastically improving efficiency and productivity."[7]

The World Bank study referenced above features several countries, most of which fall within the Guinea Savannah zone, and Figure 13.7 shows the extent to which this fertile belt is underutilised in the countries featured.

Figure 13.5: Extent of Guinea Savannah area in a few African countries, million ha

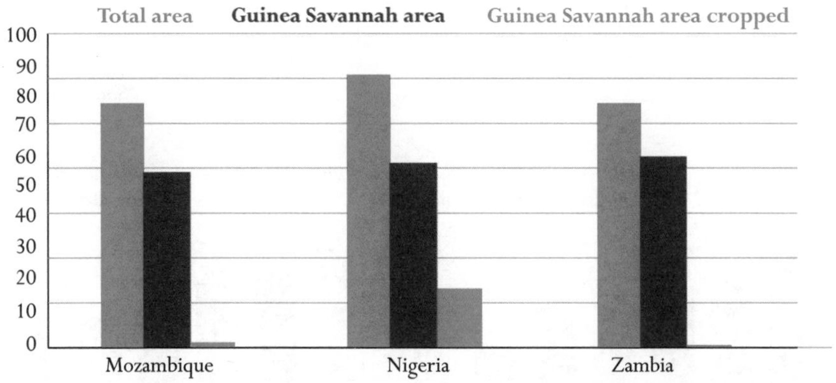

Source: World Bank

To understand the scope for expansion, consider that the FAO estimates the additional land required to feed a larger and richer world in 2050 at only 71 million ha.

As previously noted, land is only one part of the supply equation; an adequate water supply is also essential to ensure that the land can fulfil its potential. Again, mirroring the availability of land and Brazil's experience, Africa is also endowed with sufficient renewable water resources. Of the available water, only around 2% is used for irrigation, leaving scope for expansion.

While the availability of land and water is not an issue, there is an impediment to closing the gap between potential output and actual output: the wide differences in yields obtained in Africa compared with the rest of the world. The figures below compare the average yields from 2000 to 2009 for several key commodities across various regions.

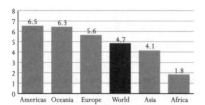

Figure 13.6: Corn yield, 2000-2009 average, t/ha

Source: FAO

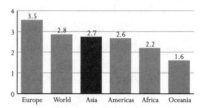

Figure 13.7: Wheat yield, 2000-2009 average, t/ha

Source: FAO

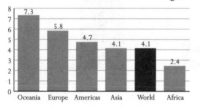

Figure 13.8: Rice yield, 2000-2009 average, t/ha

Source: FAO

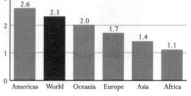

Figure 13.9: Soybean yield, 2000-2009 average, t/ha

Source: FAO

As the evidence above illustrates, African yields are the lowest in the world for corn, rice and soybeans and above only Oceania for wheat. An improvement in African cereal yields to the level achievable with intermediate inputs would imply a huge increase in agricultural output. For some historical perspective, consider the evolution of cereal yields over the past five decades in Africa and Asia. In the 1960s, Asian yields were about 46% higher than African yields. But over the next two decades, as the green revolution spread throughout Asia and skipped Africa, the difference in yields widened. In the 1990s, Asian yields were nearly double African yields.

Yet in the past decade African yields have grown faster than Asian yields, and have begun to narrow the gap. A recent report attributes the improvement to improved efficiency in production, due to changes in output structure and changes in inputs, as well as policy interventions, including fiscal, trade and sector-specific policies.[8] It showed Nigeria accounting for 38% of total factor productivity growth in SSA over 1994–2006, followed by Sudan (14%), Ethiopia (9%) and Tanzania (8%). Individual countries are adopting new policies;

Angola's annual 4.5% productivity gains over 1996–2006 are the best in SSA. In Malawi, after repeated poor harvests in the 1990s and early 2000s, the government began subsidising fertiliser – which prompted criticism from the IMF and World Bank, but turned the country from a maize importer to a maize exporter by 2007. Nigeria appears to be taking a similar course. Already the strong growth trajectory experienced over the past 10 years suggests African agriculture can be transformed if these improvements are maintained over the course of the following decades.

Figure 13.10: Average cereal yields, t/ha

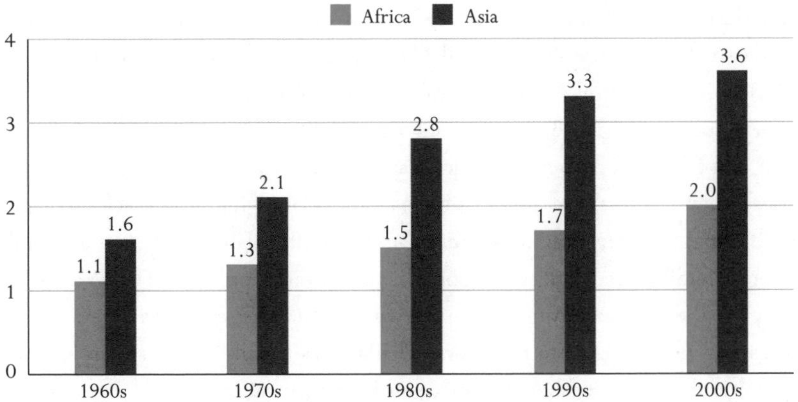

Source: FAO

To get an idea of what these higher yields might mean for Africa, consider the following: Africa's cereal output in 2009 was 108mnt and the average yield was 2.2 tonnes/hectare (t/ha). Increasing the yield to 3 t/ha would increase the output to 148mnt without any additional harvested area. In other words, output would increase by more than one-third. Admittedly even this increased production would not have been sufficient to satisfy demand, as cereal consumption in 2009 was 152mnt.

By 2050, the FAO expects cereal consumption in developing countries to grow more than 60% from current levels. If we assume a similar growth trajectory for Africa, consumption in 2050 would be approximately 243mnt. The FAO also expects 27% growth in arable land in Africa during the same period, implying an additional 63 million ha for cereals. If we assume that African yield growth in the next four decades is similar to Asian yield growth over the past four decades, African cereal yields in 2050 would be approximately 3.5 t/ ha. This would imply production of approximately 219mnt – still some 24mnt below 2050 consumption. Rising productivity would allow growth in exports today, and more supply to meet this African demand in the future.

Africa also has the potential to make an impact in other commodities, such as palm oil and sugar. In these cases, SSA's climate and geography give it a competitive advantage. For example, Malaysia and Indonesia are beginning to face limits to the expansion of palm oil production. A grant of $1 billion from the government of Norway to the government of Indonesia to reduce its deforestation rates might pale against Norway's $20 billion-plus annual investment in its domestic oil industry, but it does give an indication of potential supply constraints in Southeast Asia. Future growth will likely have to come from countries such as the DRC, Côte'Ivoire, Cameroon, Sierra Leone and Liberia.

Lest it appear that we are confusing potential with performance, we acknowledge that it is easier to calculate increases in yields and output than to actually realise them. There are numerous roadblocks, ranging from lack of capital, sub-optimal farming practices and a lack of skilled labour, to non-availability of high-yielding seeds and unfavourable government policies. The World Bank study on the Guinea Savannah region we cited earlier explores a few of these issues, but notes that both Brazil and Thailand were able to transform backward agricultural regions and become successful agricultural exporters.

Finally, SSA's improving physical and ICT infrastructure will help, too. Isobel Coleman, a development expert with America's Council on Foreign Relations, estimates that around $4 billion of its grain harvest out of an estimated $27 billion is lost each year, in good part due to food spoilage associated with poor storage and transportation.[9] This figure is highly embarrassing for agricultural policymakers and is now the subject of priority action by several governments.

In the words of FAO's assistant director-general for Africa, Maria Helena Semedo, "This lost food could meet the minimum annual food requirements of at least 48 million people." Of course, the long-term solution to this problem is improved infrastructure – roads, ports, refrigeration, power generation – requiring significant investments at the national level, investments that African governments are now poised to do. In the meantime, low-cost irrigation techniques allow small farmers to grow crops during the off-season, smoothing out the availability of food and increasing their profits.

Back to Brazil

AS noted, potential remains just that unless a concerted effort is made to unlock it. Brazil is a staggeringly successful example of a nation where an extensive hinterland was transformed into an agricultural stronghold over the course of several decades. However, we note four broad factors to dispel any myths and preconceived notions about the Brazilian agriculture sector:

- This process from the formation of EMBRAPA in 1973 to the point where a wider investor community began to take notice of the Brazilian agriculture sector took more than three decades. Commentators, all too frequently, overlook these lead times. In short, it was not an overnight success story.
- Another factor worth emphasising at the outset is that this was initially a government-inspired plan to develop the country's hinterlands. In addition the success of such a project could be harder under a democratic system then under what was then a Brazilian military dictatorship.
- Brazilian infrastructure and supply are still in poor shape. Some 93% of the country's roads are unpaved, port bottlenecks are the norm, major public infrastructure investment programmes have failed to achieve their original aims, and to get produce from the Cerrado to the country's ports necessitates a 2,000 km journey. Imperfect infrastructure can still be good enough.
- There are both private-sector and public-sector aspects to the Brazilian case study. The success of the Cerrado's development is not fully attributable to either. Instead, it relied on focused strategic aims set out by government, and a resourceful private sector willing to take risks in an area lacking a history of large-scale agriculture.

As noted, the government has played an important role in shaping Brazil's agricultural sector. Government incentives for agricultural producers are wide ranging and have contributed significantly to growth in the sector. These include preferential credit, tax exemptions, financing for agricultural research, marketing and infrastructure improvements as well as an array of federal, state, and local subsidies. Despite that, public expenditure on the agricultural sector is low compared with recent years. Agricultural expenditure in Brazil accounted for only 1.8% of total government expenditure in the period between 2003 and 2005, down considerably from the 1980s.

The lesson from Brazil is that governments cannot ignore the agricultural sector and hope for the best. Greater investment in infrastructure can play a key role in developing the sector. But the experience of Brazil shows it can be done. What would be surprising is if it could be done across all the countries of the Guinea Savannah, at the same time. Inevitably there will be early success stories that happen in specific countries. But as we saw in Europe with its agricultural revolution, success will be replicated.

Africa's Agricultural Opportunity

AT a time of rising global demand, internal constraints on new supply in a number of geographies are becoming apparent. In our view, this is a great opportunity for Africa. We see the example of the Cerrado as a harbinger of things to come, and expect another Cerrado to emerge in Africa. Similar to how the Cerrado benefited from China's growing appetite for soybeans, we believe Africa could benefit from increased global demand for corn, palm oil and other crops.

The inescapable conclusion, at least in the view of Renaissance Capital, is that China and others will increasingly look to Africa to help provide broader food security. And Africa will respond with a combination of agricultural innovation and incentivising policy that will make the Brazilian experience look modest. Taking into consideration the productivity gains that should stem from urbanisation, we are confident that Africa will not only find it ever easier to feed itself, but as a continent can become one of the linchpins of global food security in the decades ahead.

Notes

1. Thierry Tanoh, "Africa's Last Famine," Project Syndicate, 12 September 2012, http://www.project-syndicate.org/commentary/africa-s-last-famine-by-thierry-tanoh.
2. Neil Bowdler, "Africa 'can feed itself in a generation,'" BBC News, 2 December 2010, http://www.bbc.co.uk/news/science-environment-11890702.
3. Akinbamijo Olumuyiwa Bayo, "City Planning, City Growth and Food Security: The Inevitable Trinity in The Nigerian Food Equation," Agricultural Journal 1 (2006), 113-118, http://medwelljournals.com/abstract/?doi=aj.2006.113.118.
4. Daniel Maxwell et al., *Urban Livelihoods and Food and Nutrition Security in Greater*

Accra, Ghana, Research Report 112 (Washington, DC: International Food Policy Research Institute, 2000), http://www.who.int/nutrition/publications/foodsecurity/livelihoods_foodsecurity_ghana.pdf.

5. Ira Matuschke, "Rapid urbanisation and food security: Using food density maps to identify future food security hotspots," Contributed paper prepared for presentation at the International Association of Agricultural Economists Conference, Beijing, China, August 2009.

6. Dambisa Moyo, *Winner Take All: China's Race for Resources and What It Means for the World* (New York: Basic Books, 2012).

7. Tanoh, "Africa's Last Famine."

8. Bingxin Yu and Alejandro Nin-Pratt, "Agricultural Productivity and Policies in Sub-Saharan Africa," Discussion Paper 01150, International Food Policy Research Institute, December 2011, http://www.ifpri.org/sites/default/files/publications/ifpridp01150.pdf.

9. Isobel Coleman, "Food Security and Innovations for Africa's Agriculture," *Democracy in Development* (blog), 8 August 2012, http://blogs.cfr.org/coleman/2012/08/07/food-security-and-innovations-for-africas-agriculture/.

Chapter 14

The Myth of the Equator

By Michael Moran

*The difficulties African states faced as they embarked on independence were daunting. Disease pro-
liferated among humans, animals and plant life. Although modern medicine had tamped epidemic
diseases like smallpox and yellow fever, endemic diseases like malaria and sleeping sickness (trypa-
nosomiasis) took a heavy toll. ... Death rates for children in Africa in 1960 were the highest in the
world; life expectancy, at 39 years on average, was the lowest in the world.*

—Martin Meredith, historian, journalist, biographer, author of *The State of
Africa: A History of Fifty Years of Independence*[1]

Africa is quietly winning the battle against its health challenges, and seeing
dramatic improvements in child mortality rates, as well as rising life expectancy across the continent. The result is that Africa will no longer be held back
by the challenges identified so well in Jared Diamond's *Guns, Germs, and Steel.*[2] In
this century, Africa's success in defeating disease will allow it to at least replicate
the benefits seen from Singapore to Latin America as they achieved the same in
the 20th century. In many cases Africa will do even better. The 50% reduction in
infant mortality in Rwanda to 2010–11 took five years; the same improvement in
India took 25 years.

Deaths from malaria across all of Sub-Saharan Africa dropped by 27% between 2003 and 2009 to 113,000.[3] The disease is being defeated by the simple
and cheap promotion of insect net use. The HIV prevalence rate in SSA among
15–49 year-olds has fallen from 6% to 5.5%, while the number of new HIV
infections has steadily declined for more than a decade. From an annual peak of
2.3 million 15 years ago, the latest World Bank figure shows a decline of 27%
to 1.65 million in 2009. Life expectancy at birth rose from around 40 years in
1960, to 50 years by 1987, where it stagnated for 15 years. From 2002–09 it
has now resumed its steady increase to around 53 years. Some of the biggest
improvements do not come from greater healthcare expenditure, but from a

better focus on healthcare spending, away from expensive capital city hospitals to nurses in rural clinics. Huge health gains can also come without any extra spending on health itself. Improving water sanitation and education can have significant effects, too. Mickey Chopra, UNICEF's chief of health, says, "there's quite a strong correlation between the education of a mother and the survival of her child."[4] The substantial improvements in child mortality rates are apparent to all.

Our growth trajectory tells us that the most dramatic improvements are still to come. Public investment in healthcare should increase the number of healthcare professionals from over 4 million in 2020 to nearly 16 million by 2050, while Africa's population doubles to 2 billion, implying a doubling of healthcare professionals per capita. Life expectancy should reach 60 by 2030 even if there is no acceleration in the current rate of improvement (though we suspect there will be), meaning Africa's fastest billion today will be able to utilise their skills in the workplace for longer. The beneficial impact of the trends we see can only serve to improve the outlook for the continent.

The litany of woe that afflicted many newly independent African nations is well documented, and indeed its hold on the imagination of non-Africans distorts views of the continent to this day. While elements of this picture persist, the progress Africa has made in closing its health gap with the rest of the world too often gets glossed over in the quest for anecdotal journalistic colour or the zeal of a Western NGO to draw attention to its particular crusade.

In fact, Africa's health and wellbeing have steadily improved since the end of the 1980s, and recent statistics suggest that by some important measures this progress has gone into overdrive, including vital macro indicators such as infant mortality, life expectancy and access to improved water sources, as well as more specific measurements such as HIV infection rates and annual deaths from malaria or during childbirth.

Figure 14.1: The SSA HIV new infection rate is falling sharply, and HIV prevalence peaked a decade ago

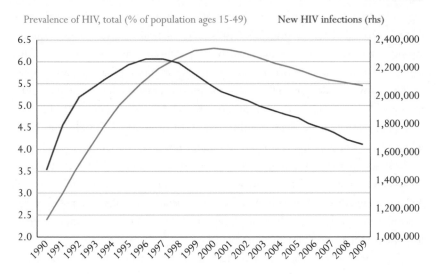

Prevalence of HIV, total (% of population ages 15-49)   New HIV infections (rhs)

Source: World Bank

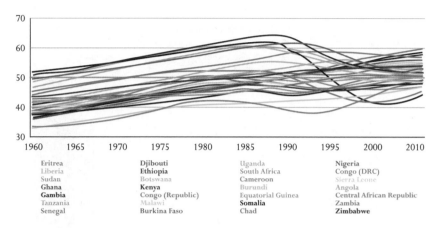

Figure 14.2: Life expectancy is recovering as the HIV crisis subsides

Eritrea	Djibouti	Uganda	Nigeria
Liberia	Ethiopia	South Africa	Congo (DRC)
Sudan	Botswana	Cameroon	Sierra Leone
Ghana	**Kenya**	Burundi	Angola
Gambia	Congo (Republic)	Equatorial Guinea	Central African Republic
Tanzania	Malawi	**Somalia**	Zambia
Senegal	Burkina Faso	Chad	**Zimbabwe**

Source: World Bank

Figure 14.3: The increasing use of insecticidal nets in SSA is driving a fall in malaria incidence

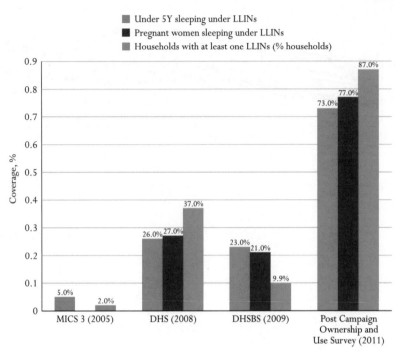

Source: World Health Organization

Key: DHS = Demographic and Health Survey, US AID
         MICS 3 = Multiple Indicator Cluster Surveys, UN
         DHSBS = 2009 World Malaria Report, WHO

Figure 14.4: Trends in Malaria Cases in 39 High Incidence Countries, 2000-2010

More than 50 percent decrease in malaria case incidence	Between 25 and 50 percent decrease in malaria case incidence	Less than 25 percent decrease in malaria case incidence	Unable to assess trends in confirmed malaria cases	
			Recent scale-up of diagnostic testing	Insufficient data
Namibia	Ethiopia	India	Burkina Faso	Angola
Sao Tome and Principe	Senegal		Burundi	Benin
Solomon Islands	Zambia		**Congo**	Cameroon
Suriname			**(Democratic**	Central African
Thailand			**Republic)**	Republic
Viet Nam			Liberia	Chad
Cambodia*			Myanmar	Congo
Gambia*			Sierra Leone	**Côte d'Ivoire**
Tanzania			Togo	Djibouti
(United			Uganda	**Ghana**
Republic)*			Zimbabwe	Guinea
				Guinea-Bissau
				Malawi
				Mali
				Mozambique
				Niger
				Nigeria
				Somalia

*More than 50 percent decrease in malaria case incidence has been reported sub-nationally, rather than nationally.

Note An Inter-Agency Working Group defined these 39 countries as having "extreme" or "severe" malaria burden for the purposes of deciding eligibility to apply to the Global Fund. The countries highlighted in bold appear on the Global Fund's list of "high-impact" countries.
Source WHO, 2011 [3].
Source: Strategic Investments for Impact: Global Fund Results Report 2012

Figure 14.5: Access to improved water and sanitation is also improving

	Population in 2010 (millions)	Water supply coverage in 2010 (%)	Population that gained access to improved sources of drinking water since 1995	MDG progress	Proportion of 2010 population that gained access to improved drinking water sources since 1995 (%)
Malawi	14.9	83	7.2	On track	48.4
Burkina Faso	16.5	79	7.5	On track	45.5
Liberia	4.0	73	1.7	On track	42.8
Ghana	24.4	86	10.3	On track	42.3
Namibia	2.3	93	0.9	On track	40.6
Gambia	1.7	89	0.7	On track	37.7
Rwanda	10.6	65	3.3	Not on track	30.7
Sierra Leone	5.9	55	1.6	Not on track	27.0
Togo	6.0	61	1.6	Not on track	26.1
Sub-Saharan Africa	**856**	**61**	**221**	**Not on track**	**25.8**

Source: WHO/UNICEF Joint Monitoring Programme, 2010

World Bank historical data for Nigeria, for instance, tell a very positive story in spite of Nigeria's political ups and downs. Primary school enrolment, life expectancy and per capita gross national income have all followed an upward trajectory since the 1980s. The percentage of Nigerians living above the UN's official poverty line ($1.25 per day) has improved from 43% in 1985 to nearly 55% today. Similarly, whereas only 30% of the rural population had access to a decent water supply in 1990, 43% are judged to have it today. Significantly, much of that gain is recent.[5]

In health as elsewhere, aggregating the unique and often contradictory trends of SSA's 48 countries risks missing important trends. There is no way to shrug off the extent of the healthcare challenges SSA countries face when they are compared with far richer economies. But many SSA countries now rank favourably when compared with other fast-growing emerging countries. A number of African countries, for instance, now rank above Indonesia in the UN Human Development Index on education and health – these include not only island states and outliers such as Mauritius and the Maldives, but also larger continental economies such as Namibia, South Africa, Botswana and Gabon.[6]

Similarly, even in countries listed at the very bottom of global development tables, slow and steady progress is a general rule. The World Bank in May 2012 released a paper from its Kenya regional office noting a "stunning" decline in infant and under-five mortality rates among 20 African nations, with Kenya leading the infant mortality rate improvement with an annual decline of 7.6% annually, and achieving an even better 8.4% decline in the Under-5 mortality rate.[7] The report's authors debate the causes and suggest some combination of improved access to medical care, higher immunisation rates, a highly successful campaign against malaria, plus GDP growth and higher income levels that have boosted nutritional standards.

Figure 14.6: Annual declines in SSA under-five mortality

Country	Before	After	Annual % decline
Senegal	121 (2005)	72 (2010)	9.9
Rwanda	103 (2007)	76 (2010)	9.6
Kenya	115 (2003)	74 (2008)	8.4
Uganda	128 (2006)	90 (2011)	6.8
Ghana	111 (2003)	80 (2008)	6.3
Zambia	168 (2001)	119 (2007)	5.6
Mozambique	152 (2003)	97 (2011)	5.5
Ethiopia	123 (2005)	88 (2011)	5.4
Tanzania	112 (2004)	81 (2010)	5.3
Madagascar	94 (2003)	72 (2008)	5.2
Nigeria	201 (2003)	157 (2008)	4.8
Benin	160 (2001)	125 (2006)	4.8
Niger	274 (1998)	198 (2006)	4.0
Mali	229 (2001)	191 (2006)	3.6
Malawi	113 (2004)	112 (2010)	2.8
Avereage annual % decline in under-5 mortality			**5.9**

Source: World Bank

This broad picture for human health in SSA, whether measured by the World Bank or the UN's many relevant agencies, confirms a region progressing slowly towards self-sustaining improvements in human health and, ultimately, towards national health systems capable of meeting the demands of populations with higher expectations.

Those higher expectations manifest themselves in many ways. Abiola Adekoya, an equity sales trader in Renaissance Capital's Lagos office, recalls a time when obesity was regarded as a sign of success in her native Nigeria.

"A man that was overweight and had a fat wife was seen as wealthy and a good provider, while an overweight woman was referred to as desirable, attractive and curvaceous," she remembers. "The importance of a woman being curvaceous was so strong that the Efik tribe in Nigeria send their brides-to-be to a 'fattening room.' There, they are fed large amounts of food, massaged and made to sleep for long periods of time in an effort to increase their weight and gain fuller proportions. There were cases where a woman was turned down by her fiancé because she was not full-bodied enough. Clearly, weight was a measure of your economic status and your desirability."

While anyone who has struggled with weight loss may view that as a lost paradise, in truth this is yet another common measure of a society's move towards greater health and prosperity – along with lower birth rates, educational achievement and other metrics that showed steady improvement in places like East Asia and Latin American in the 1980s onward.

Adekoya believes the globalisation of media has played a role, as has a steady exposure to nutritional information through both popular and official channels. "Fat, full-bodied women are no longer the epitome of wealth and beauty; now our billboards are filled with skinny, beautiful women and there is growing pressure in society for women to keep a svelte shape, even after childbirth," she says. "And men are definitely feeling the pressure as they are adjusting their lifestyles to shrinking their potbellies and making efforts to achieve a 'six-pack'-like figure."

The democratisation trend of the past two decades has also reinforced this improvement by injecting accountability into many African countries. These political trends have required national governments to subjugate tribal, ethnic or other loyalties to electoral considerations that require a broader definition of "public interest." Experts, including Steven Radelet, the chief economist of the US Agency for International Development, argue that this is bound to lead to further improvements in health delivery and force even reluctant governments to solicit investment for major improvements in healthcare technology, infrastructure, staffing and systems from global capital markets.[8] Among the destinations where foreign direct investment inevitably will be needed:

- **Medical infrastructure**: The undercapitalised national healthcare infrastructures found across the region are increasingly open to private investment or public-private partnerships, and the healthcare sector is one in which outside players can make a difference while securing a good return on their investment. The demands for infrastructure – medical and otherwise – implicit in SSA's burgeoning population growth should provide ample vehicles for FDI, as well as jobs in the engineering and construction sectors, and associated manufacturing and service industries.

- **Insurance markets**: SSA's private healthcare insurance market is largely untapped. The private sector – fee-charging physicians and clinics – already accounts for about 50% of healthcare expenditure across all income levels, according to World Bank figures. This suggests fertile ground for the expansion of both public and private health insurance schemes. Indeed, in Ghana, Nigeria, Kenya and Uganda, government insurance plans are being expanded, and private offerings have recently been introduced, though still focusing on the very highest end of the market.

Figure 14.7. Public/private breakdown of SSA healthcare expenditures, 2008

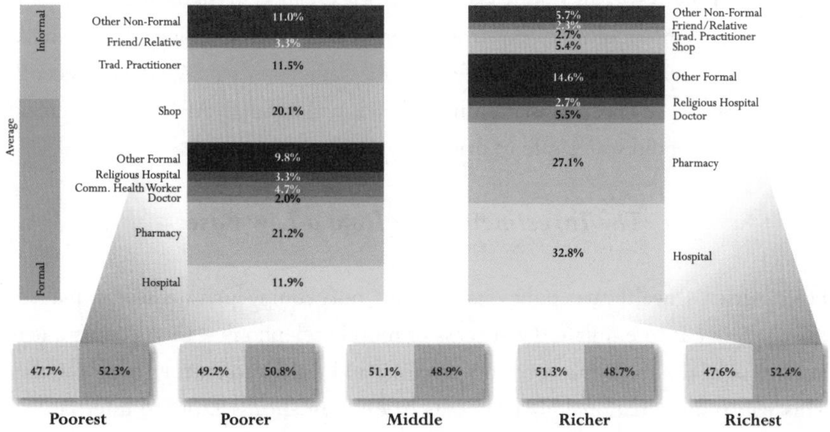

Source: Demographic and health surveys conducted after 2000, http://ps4h.org/globalhealthdata.html

- **Training and staffing**: The gap between trained African medical staff and demand is exacerbated by low salaries that encourage emigration or, within SSA borders, lead to the best doctors seeking employment with siloed programmes funded by international donors rather than national health systems. The demand for capacity at Africa's medical and nursing schools is enormous, and as governments begin to address the pay-scale issues, they will increasingly view private and public funds devoted to medical training as a source of stable employment for millions of people. And if fiscal constraints continue in Europe and the US, the private sector may find a market for medical administrative consulting as Western donor organizations retrench.

• **Technology**: With the expansion of SSA healthcare infrastructure and capacity will come greater demand for medical technology. Some of this will be on the high end – capital-intensive therapies like kidney dialysis, radiation and advanced diagnostics. But, in keeping with the trend in Africa's telecommunications and financial infrastructure, much of this spending will be directed towards simpler, more mobile technology. In Kenya, for instance, Mashavu Networked Health Solutions has started deploying mobile healthcare kiosks in remote districts. Hand-held diagnostic instruments, still rare even in Western hospitals with ample resort to traditional laboratories, can help medical staff in more spartan conditions leap-frog a generation of technology. And some of this upgrade will be home-grown: Cameroon's government recently deployed cheap biosand filters, developed in South Africa, to help make household water safe to drink.

The Investment Case from a Low Base

FOR Africa's healthcare policymakers and burgeoning private-sector players, the challenge is to emulate the success of mobile telephony – to skip over a generation of health infrastructure and practice, and right into cutting-edge systems. This will require national governments to open medical sectors to international investment, if not competition.

A study by the International Finance Corporation, an arm of the World Bank, estimates that there will be demand for up to $20 billion in FDI for infrastructure, training and insurance programmes in SSA's health sector by 2016. "Around 550,000–650,000 additional hospital beds must be added to the existing base of 850,000. An additional 90,000 physicians, about 500,000 nurses, and 300,000 community health workers will be required over and above the numbers that will graduate from existing medical colleges and training institutions," the report concludes.[9]

By our estimates, another 300,000 physicians and over 600,000 nurses and midwives are likely to be added in SSA between 2010 and 2020, as a function of the economic growth we have outlined.

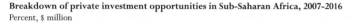

Figure 14.8: Private investment opportunities, SSA healthcare sector, through 2016 (%, $ per million)

Breakdown of private investment opportunities in Sub-Saharan Africa, 2007-2016
Percent, $ million

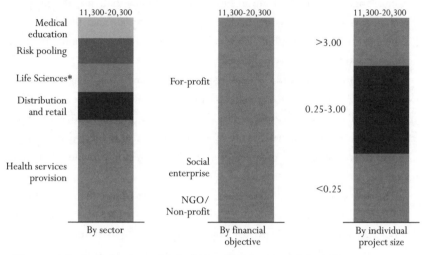

*Pharmaceutical and medical products include South Africa. All other areas exclude South Africa

Source: Ministries of Health; National Accounts; country interviews; McKinsey analysis

Using East Asia's successful public-private systems as a model, some governments have already begun creating vehicles for this investment.

Rwanda, for instance, uses community-based health insurance (CBHI) coverage to provide prenatal care. Each household pays a fee of $5 per year, up from $2 when the system was first introduced in the late 1990s. While the higher price has caused some drop-off in participation, health services are almost free and almost 91% of Rwandans were insured as of 2010, according to the Africa Progress Panel, a Geneva-based non-profit organization. The programme was modelled on a successful plan launched in Ghana in 2004 and has since been emulated in Uganda and, with some adjustments, in Mauritania.[10] In all four cases, the benefits are redeemable at public or private facilities – resulting in a small boom among those who provide these services.

The mobile healthcare kiosks deployed in Kenya are a case in point. The pilot project of Mashavu Networked Health Solutions installed two such kiosks, in Nyeri and Ngong, that use wireless technology to transmit vital signs to central sites for evaluation.

Kenya's government, meanwhile, has launched a data transparency initiative aimed at helping provide the kind of indicators that will measure policy effectiveness – and also give foreign investors a view into the sector. While this initiative ran into opposition in the Kenyan bureaucracy, Bitange Ndemo, the project's director, says there is no going back. "We need to explain that the data won't just be used to audit them, but also to build Kenya, build apps, support the right healthcare and food-security policies."[11]

Success breeds imitation – and regret, too. Many African policymakers, even as they continue to cite the effects of neo-colonialism and internal conflict, are aware of their own responsibility for the lost opportunities of the post-independence years. This vital attitude correction is also helping drive changes in government policy and greater access to private-sector providers that offer promising returns on investments.

"The deficiencies of health systems in Africa are not wholly the result of Bretton Woods policies. Africans must share the blame," writes Dr. Ebrahim Malik Samba, the WHO's former Africa regional director. "[Governments] did not make proper use (through sound investment) of the monies borrowed, although they started on more or less the same footing as other countries, e.g. Korea, India, which have performed significantly well. They failed to argue the case for supporting social services on the continent. They are now paying dearly for the trends of the 1970s and 1980s."[12]

Most appear intent on reversing these mistakes. Where East Asia's nascent Tigers invested in vast national health and insurance networks in the 1970s and 1980s, Africa – to the extent it pursued any national policy template – was at the mercy of the era's Structural Adjustment Programme, a macro-economic overlay of austerity prescriptions that the World Bank and IMF required for loans during those years.

The Silo Effect

ANOTHER reason to think Africa may soon open its healthcare sector more comprehensively to FDI is the risk associated with the continent's continued dependence on foreign donors – whether public or private. With both the US and Europe facing their own fiscal problems, official aid disbursements will almost certainly fall over the next decade.

EU aid, once vying to outdo aid from Washington, is dwindling at an alarming rate, primarily as a result of the eurozone's sovereign debt crisis. For instance, Italy's Ministry of Foreign Affairs reduced its aid to SSA by 56% in 2010, and by a further 45% in 2011. Since the Millenium Challenge Goals were instituted in 2000, Italy had regularly donated more than EUR1 billion annually, much of that going to SSA. The figure for 2011: EUR179 million.[13]

Laurie Garrett, an American global health scholar whose work is funded by the Bill and Melinda Gates Foundation, says the trend is clear. "In 2009, 94% of all global health promises made by the EU and its member countries were actually disbursed, but by the end of 2010 only 78% were, and the gap appears to have widened further in 2011."[14]

Already African recipients are working with NGOs and other global health experts to cushion the blow, and to ensure that the programmes funded by large Western transfers and directed at HIV/AIDS, malaria, tuberculosis and prenatal care since the mid-1990s are absorbed into national budgets.

Garrett is one of several Western experts who argue that unidirectional aid funding is already undermining the hard-won gains of the past several decades. Foreign aid, she says, should be divorced from particular diseases and directed instead towards expanding the capacity, staffing and technical competence of national health systems.

The Supply Side

THE need to stress systems over silos will become more important in coming years as ageing developed nations require more and more trained medical staff per capita. Already, the medical "brain drain" has taken its toll on African countries, which struggle in the best of conditions to train and graduate enough physicians, nurses and qualified aides to fill available positions. In 2008, the British medical journal *The Lancet* published a paper from veteran Western aid workers and their African colleagues asking, "Should active recruitment of health workers from SSA be viewed as a crime?" Draconian, perhaps, but not if the trends they project come true.[15]

"High-income countries, such as Australia, Canada, Saudi Arabia, the US, the United Arab Emirates and the UK have sustained their relatively high physician-to-population ratio by recruiting medical graduates from developing regions, including countries in SSA. In contrast, over half of the countries in SSA do not meet the minimum acceptable physician-to-population ratio of one per 5000 – WHO's Health for All standard. Nurses, pharmacists, and other health workers are systematically recruited from a region struggling with the greatest burden of infectious and chronic illness and the specific challenge of HIV/AIDS."

Indeed, the report suggests that the doctor-to-patient ratio may go as high as one per 25,000 in some countries if trends continue. Furthermore, some of the disease-specific programs have lured the best and brightest out of public hospitals into the Western-funded specialty clinics.

At the micro level, this translates to fewer sick people seeing a doctor for preventive care or early diagnosis and more of them resorting to hospitals too late for effective intervention.

McKinsey & Company, a consultancy, along with the non-profit Touch Foundation, commissioned a study in Tanzania in an effort to determine how best to shore up local healthcare failings – and to extrapolate those results for the rest of the region. The WHO, the report said, estimates that a country the size of Tanzania should require a medical workforce of about 92,000. The present number is 24,500. Low salaries, inadequate incentives and poor working conditions contribute to a high turnover among active staff, too.

"Tanzania has fewer than 100 training institutions, which produce fewer than 4,000 graduates a year. Up to 30% of the country's health workers leave the system within a year after training," the report found.[16]

But McKinsey also found signs that policy solutions exist and that private sector investment has a role, too. Taking a page from other developing countries, the report said, "Tanzania could offer student loans and incentive packages, as well as an increased commitment from local districts to maintain the quality of healthcare facilities."

Based on Renaissance estimates, a country with Tanzania's population and GDP level in 2010 should have 79,000 nurses and and 54,000 physicians: clearly today's numbers are too low. But these figures should rise with increased wealth. By 2040, based on the same population, higher GDP should support 143,000 nurses and midwives as well as 70,000 physicians.

Figure 14.9: Rising wealth implies more health-sector employees

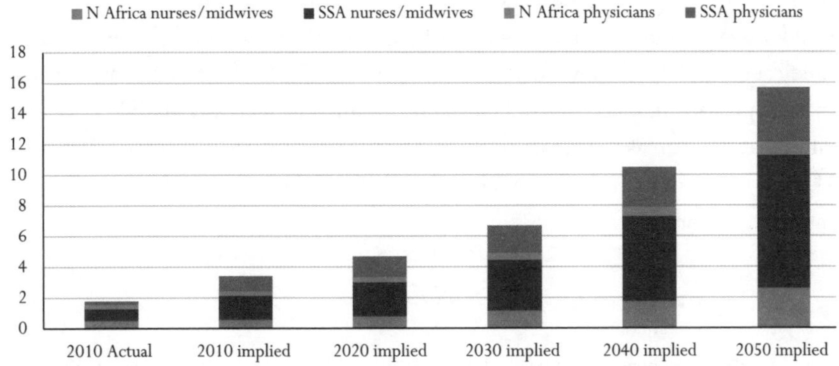

Source: Renaissance Capital estimates

Again, Asia provides some examples – this time not among its Tigers, but rather in Cambodia, a country which has remained saddled with many of the same problems that have traditionally been associated with SSA. A study by Stanford University's Asia Health Policy Programme found that inadequate salaries, along with poor training, hindered the surveillance of infectious diseases in Cambodia and Indonesia in the wake of the outbreak of the SARS virus in 2005.

"Subjects who mentioned this issue as a barrier frequently made reference to the fact that technical capacity far exceeded human capacity, and that the lack of skilled staff was in fact preventing the efficient use of donor-funded equipment," the report said. "At the same time, incentives were such that skill itself was not rewarded in government service. As one international doctor bluntly stated: 'In Cambodia, like anywhere in the world, if you pay people, they do their job. If you don't pay them, they won't. They've got to feed their kids.'"[17] And that's the most powerful incentive of all.

Yet despite the challenges, what is most striking is that health indicators are improving across the board. The vast majority in Africa are living longer and better than ever before, and given our assumptions for the economic boom in coming decades, there will be more resources than ever allocated to accelerating these trends. We expect public health expenditure to top private health expenditure by 2023, but both to soar from our estimate of a combined $120–145 billion today to $1.9 trillion in today's money by 2050. The number of healthcare workers should rise dramatically, particularly in SSA. Life expectancy in SSA is up from 50 a decade ago to 53 now, and should reach 60 no later than 2030. In brief, to paraphrase Diamond, we expect Africa to produce more steel, to require fewer guns, and face fewer challenges from germs. And this assumes no medical breakthrough, although recent reports of a 50% effective vaccine against malaria perhaps in place by 2020 could be a game-changer. Meanwhile new vaccines that used to take 20 years to reach Africa now do so in 2–5 years.[18] Progress like this does not provide the shocking headlines of the past, but does surely warrant celebration.

Notes

1. Martin Meredith, *The State of Africa: A History of Fifty Years of Independence* (London: The Free Press, 2005), 150-151.

2. Jared Diamond, *Guns, Germs, and Steel: The Fates of Human Societies* (New York: W. W. Norton & Company, 1999).

3. There is a huge divergence of estimates regarding both malaria and HIV – for both we use the World Bank's database of African Development Indicators.

4. David Brown, "Child mortality falls more than 40 percent in the past two decades," *Washington Post*, 12 September 2012, http://www.washingtonpost.com/.

5. http://data.worldbank.org/country/nigeria.

6. *Human Development Statistical Annex*, in *Human Development Report 2011: Sustainability and Equity – A Better Future for All* (United Nations Development Programme, 2011), 160, http://hdr.undp.org/en/media/HDR_2011_EN_Tables.pdf.

7. Gabriel Demombynes and Sofia Karina Trommlerová, "What Has Driven the Decline of Infant Mortality in Kenya?," Policy Research Working Paper 6057, Poverty Reduction and Economic Management Unit, Africa Region, World Bank, May 2012, http://www-wds.worldbank.org/external/default/WDSContentServer/IW3P/IB/2012/05/03/000158349_20120503152728/Rendered/PDF/WPS6057.pdf.

8. Steven Radelet, *Emerging Africa : How 17 Countries Are Leading the Way* (Baltimore: Center for Global Development, 2010).

9. *The Business of Health in Africa: Partnering with the Private Sector to Improve People's Lives*, International Finance Corporation, 2008, http://www.ifc.org/ifcext/healthinafrica.nsf/AttachmentsByTitle/IFC_HealthinAfrica_Sec3/$FILE/IFC_HealthInAfrica_Sec3.pdf.

10. *Maternal Health: Investing in the Lifeline of Healthy Societies & Economies*, Policy Brief, Africa Progress Panel, September 2010, http://www.africaprogresspanel.org/files/1412/8523/5171/APP_Maternal_Health_English%20FINAL.pdf.

11. Elana Berkowitz and Renée Paradise, "Kenya's open-data plan," *McKinsey Quarterly*,

September 2011. The Kenya Open Data Initiative can be accessed at https://www.opendata.go.ke/.

12. Ebrahim Malick Samba, "African health care systems: what went wrong?," Editorial, News-Medical.Net, 8 December 2004, http://www.news-medical.net/news/2004/12/08/6770.aspx.

13. "Italian ODA in 2011: Another cut," *Italian Aid at glance* (blog), Action Aid International, Italian branch, http://actionaiditaly.blogspot.com/2010/10/italian-oda-in-2011-another-cut.html, accessed 2 October 2012.

14. Telephone interview with the author (Michael Moran), 12 June 2012.

15. Edward J Mills, William A Schabas, Jimmy Volmink, Roderick Walker, Nathan Ford, Elly Katabira, Aranka Anema, Michel Joffres, Pedro Cahn and Julio Montaner, "Should active recruitment of health workers from sub-Saharan Africa be viewed as a crime?," *The Lancet* 371, no. 9613 (28 February 2008), doi:10.1016/S0140-6736(08)60308-6.

16. Lowell Bryan, Michael Conway, Tineke Keesmaat, Sorcha McKenna and Ben Richardson, "Strengthening sub-Saharan Africa's health systems: A practical approach," McKinsey Quarterly, June 2010, https://www.mckinseyquarterly.com/Strengthening_sub-Saharan_Africas_health_systems_A_practical_approach_2591.

17. Sophal Ear, "Emerging Infectious Disease Surveillance in Southeast Asia: Cambodia, Indonesia, and the Naval Area Medical Research Unit 2," Asia Health Policy Programme working paper no. 27, Stanford University, Stanford, CA, 22 January 2012, http://iis-db.stanford.edu/pubs/23591/AHPPwp_27.pdf.

18. David Brown, "Child mortality falls more than 40% in the past two decades," *Washington Post*, 12 September 2012, http://www.washingtonpost.com/.

Chapter 15

Conclusion: This Is Africa's Moment

The best way to predict the future is to create it.
—Abraham Lincoln, 16th President of the United States of America

IN the last cycle of emerging-market development, Africa was not there. But in the cycle now under way, Africa will be the biggest winner. Of all the potential fast-growth regions of the world, Africa has the best resources, the best demographics and the best finances. And above all, it has the best trends.

Investors don't ask 'where do we stand right now?' They ask, 'what is the trend?' Will tomorrow be better than today? And how much better can better be?

On those counts, Africa is arguably the world's best investment case. The trend in governance and democratisation is up. The trend in official finances and macro-economic stability is up. The trend in health and education is up. And above all, the story is now Africa's story. After a century of subservience to prescriptions from outside – whether colonial or post-colonial, whether well-intentioned or not – Africa is now providing its own solutions to its own challenges, and showing that it can meet those challenges rather better than anyone else.

What a contrast to the Africa of just a few decades ago. In the 1970s and 1980s, as the Asian Tigers were building their industrial economies, as China and India were beginning their different paths towards globalisation, and as Eastern Europe was feeling its way out of its Cold War-era stagnation, Africa looked moribund.

One reason was debt. In Sub-Saharan Africa, virtually every country was saddled with debts that could never be serviced, but never – it seemed – be erased either. Export revenues from cocoa beans to copper were falling or stagnant. Real investment levels fell from their post-colonisation highs, and infrastructure capacity contracted while population growth still required rapid expansion.

As for governance, this was the era of Mobutu in Zaire and Idi Amin in Uganda, of kleptocracy in West Africa, stagnation in East Africa, and conflict in Central and Southern Africa. There was oil, in Nigeria, Cameroon and Angola for example, but it seemed only to make things worse. Where there is no governance, and no purchase for the real private economy, oil and other resources become a treasure chest to be looted.

But no trend is without its counter-trend. The first signs that something very different could happen in Africa came quite early. In Ghana, for example, when in 1981 yet another coup brought Flight Lieutenant Jerry Rawlings to power. Did Africa really need another military government full of revolutionary zeal and rhetoric? To the surprise of everyone the Rawlings government began introducing rational economic policies designed to foster business, not hinder it. Slowly but surely the Ghanaian economy began to grow, to the point where it became a model for regional economies attempting to foster accountability and growth. In 2011 it joined the ranks of middle-income countries, an example for the continent.

The Ghanaian model is not perfect, but what is best about it has spread. The Rawlings government began the process of returning Ghana to multi-party democracy in the elections of 1992. Successes include Botswana, too, where a succession of post-independence leaders laid the foundation for a vibrant, market economy, and Mauritius, an island that opened itself to migrants and has ranked at the top of Africa's prosperity index for decades.

But these were exceptions until recently. In 1990 there were only three electoral democracies in the whole of SSA. By 1995 there were 18. Today Renaissance counts 30 democracies across the continent. According to Freedom House there are now nine African states that rank as 'completely free,' and there are 24 that are in transition to complete freedom. What began as a lone counter-trend has in the space of two decades become the dominant trend. By the year 2050 there will be 50 strong African democracies: being anything else is going to look very strange indeed.

Yet investors still express caution when it comes to Africa. It is a caution born of ingrained attitudes formed over decades – but Renaissance is convinced that the time to revise those attitudes is overdue.

What are these inhibitions when it comes to investing in the oldest continent? Let us review some of the things we have learned from the foregoing chapters, and tally the score.

First, says our investor, it scares me. Africa is a continent marked by disease, hunger and early death, and always will be. Right?

No, wrong.

⊿   On almost every metric of quality of life and human health, Africa is on a marked upward trend: several African countries now rank higher than East Asian peers on the overall UN Human Development Index. Over a five year period ending between 2008 and 2010, World Bank data show that 16 out of 20 African countries saw significant improvements in Under-5 mortality rates, in some cases very sharp improvements. Ten countries improved more than 5% each year, with Kenya, Senegal and Rwanda improving 8-10% annually and cumulatively by over a third in just five years. Maternal mortality has dropped sharply, and life expectancy (which was reduced by the HIV and AIDS epidemic) bottomed shortly after the year 2000 and is now in strong recovery in all but a handful of countries in the region. New HIV infections peaked as long ago as 1997, and the prevalence of HIV is also decreasing (although thanks to the use of effective therapies, prevalence will not fall as far as infection rates). Access to water and improved sanitation is on a sharply rising track everywhere in the region. Just one example: while only 30% of rural Nigerians had access to adequate clean water supplies in 1990, today that figure is 43%, and rising fast.

But Africa is an educational desert. It will never generate the skills to support an advanced economy. Right?

No, wrong, dead wrong.

⊿   At the moment of de-colonisation Africa was educationally bereft: that much is true. Colonial education had concentrated on creating a tiny elite, and most often educating it abroad. Independent Africa often continued that approach, building universities but not primary or secondary schools. In 1960 only 3% of school-aged children entered secondary schools. Even by 1975 only 61% were enrolling in primary education, and a mere 13% in secondary education. Today the richest countries have 88% secondary enrolment, and the poorest are not far behind – Renaissance estimates that by 2020 the minimum regional secondary enrolment rate will be over 50%, but may well be a lot closer to 90%. Already SSA's primary enrolment rate of 93% is equivalent to that of India little more than a decade ago. It is still true that SSA does not have as many educators as it should. It is also true that it is catching up so fast that education is set to be one of the boom areas of a booming economy.

But what about Africa's endless corruption and bureaucratic interference in business? There is no way crooked Africa is ever going to be a friend to the investor. Right?

Sorry – wrong again.

↘   Corruption is a function of many things, including the quality of leadership and of institutions. Africa has had its fair share of it, just as most countries have in the past. Above all, corruption correlates with per capita income. When there is not enough to go around, rules will always be bent and bribes will always be paid. As Africa gets richer, corruption diminishes. That explains why three of the four African countries have made it into the Top 50 of Transparency International's global ranking of the honesty of countries – Botswana (32nd place), Cape Verde (41st) and Mauritius (46th) with Rwanda in 49th place despite low per capita income. The first three are among Africa's richest countries, and as more countries reach this wealth level, they, too, will see corruption decline. As for bureaucracy, that is easy enough to measure through the World Bank's Doing Business Survey. Already two African countries are ranked in the top 40 in terms of ease of doing business – Mauritius and South Africa – and in the top 50% globally they are joined by Rwanda, Tunisia, Botswana, Ghana, Namibia and Zambia. One statistic that the investor would be wise to digest is this: one of the world's quickest countries when it comes to processing construction permits is now Nigeria. And the world's best reformer of the business climate in 2010, according the World Bank? Answer: Rwanda.

But wait a minute – official Africa is broke. It has foreign debts it can never pay, domestic liabilities it can never discharge, so business cannot grow. Right?

No, wrong, quite wrong.

↘ If you are looking for highly indebted governments struggling to maintain services, then you have come to the wrong place. While many developed-world economies have government debt at 100% of GDP or above, Africa has been busy reducing its sovereign debt ratios. Total official debt in SSA fell from 70% of GDP in 2000 to 32% in 2009. That is not all Africa's own work – debt cancellation by creditors helped – but only when domestic policy was greatly improved. What is all Africa's work is the fall in budget deficits. SSA as a whole ran a budget surplus for five years from 2004. That turned negative again in 2009 as governments sought to counteract the effects of the global financial crisis, but the improvement track since then has been sharp, thanks in part to better fiscal policy, and in part to better tax receipts in a growing economy. Since recording a regional budget deficit of just over 5% of GDP in 2009, SSA has improved each year since and 2011 saw close to a 1% deficit. That gap will close further.

And if that is not enough, let us take our investor on a tour of some of the most important hard indicators of Africa's current and potential performance.

First, the big picture. Africa is now a stable, low-inflation, fast-growth region, the second-fastest-growing region in the global economy, on course to become the fastest. SSA underperformed the global growth trend in the last two decades of the 20th century, growing at a little over 2% compared with global growth of a little over 3%. In the first decade of the new millennium, that underperformance has turned into marked outperformance. The region grew at almost 6%, compared with global growth of 3.6%.

That is good, but it will get better. Global growth in the foreseeable future is going to be weighed down by stalled developed economies and slower BRICs. But Africa will barely feel that gravitational pull. The reasons for that are many: relatively low exposure to developed export markets, the cycle of mineral discoveries and exploitation, and the leap-frog effect of new technologies that are already revolutionising the way Africa does business (and who would have expected that one of the fastest urban mobile broadband systems in the world would be rolled out in Luanda, Angola, ahead of London and New York?). Urbanisation will be a core component of the growth acceleration, and rising GDP will further boost the improvements in governance and lessen corruption, which in turn will foster additional investments.

But one factor probably trumps all others, and that factor is demography.

Most of the world is growing richer and older – and the two things are connected. As individuals grow richer, they have fewer children, in part because they have less need of old-age support from subsequent generations, in part because they have better expectations of their children's survival. They also live longer, because they can afford to. The population as a whole ages. But such patterns of ageing are also associated with lower GDP growth and stressed public finances, as the ever-increasing ranks of the retired have to be supported by an ever-diminishing working-age population.

This is happening in Europe, in the Americas, and most acutely in Japan. It is beginning to happen in China (India is somewhat better off). The only continent that will see its young workforce grow in the next 30 years is Africa, where the number of 15–24 year-olds will continue to rise at least until 2040. There will be up to 15 working-age people for every pensioner in SSA as late as 2030, and there will still be 10 by 2050. Compare that favourable dependency ratio to what Japan has to look forward to: 2.6 workers for every pensioner now, and less than two by 2020. Even China will have only five workers per pensioner by the end of this decade. Young people are the fundamental resource of economic growth – and for the next half century, Africa will be the best place to find them.

This is not to say that our region faces no problems of its own. It does, and they are serious.

SSA does not have enough educational institutions or teachers to staff them. It does not have enough healthcare facilities of the right sort, or enough qualified health workers – a challenge that is exacerbated by the fact that cash-strapped developed economies look to Africa for many of their health workers, draining the African talent pool, and they are likely to continue doing so.

Africa also faces some of the problems that the rest of the world is grappling with, but it faces them in a particularly acute form. One of these is climate change. For decades the southern fringes of the Sahara have been encroaching on the more fertile lands to the south, driving conflicts between pastoral and nomadic peoples, helping to provoke ethnic strife in West Africa and civil war in Sudan. And as this great Sahelian divide is often a divide between Islam to the north and Christianity to the south, the addition of radical Islamism to the mix has sharpened the conflict. Yet as the case of Sudan shows, even the most deeply embedded conflicts can be resolved, when there is a common good of economic growth as the prize.

Charles Robertson

From an investment point of view, one of Africa's greatest challenges is its infrastructural deficit. There are not enough roads (Africa must build 10 times its 10,000 km of main roads before a real trans-continental highway becomes a reality), there are not enough ports, and there is not enough power generation ($40 billion a year of investment is estimated to be the bill just to redress the regional power shortfall). A different mindset is needed, too – Africa has a history of regarding infrastructure as a resource to be consumed. But that mindset can be changed, and is changing. It is the shift from a donation mindset, when infrastructure was the gift of the outside world, to an investment mindset. As that shift occurs, those figures for the infrastructure bill become a measure of opportunity as much as of cost.

And that is characteristic of Africa. What was challenge has become opportunity. It was always inevitable that the forces that have transformed the economies of East Asia and Eastern Europe would be felt in Africa. It is Africa's luck that the transformation is beginning at a moment when the fundamentals of political maturity, technological transfer and demographic spring-loading are all set perfectly for an unprecedented period of strong, stable growth.

It only remains for our investor to grasp this reality, and ride the fundamentals to the horizon. Africa waits no more; Africa's time is now.

Index

Note: f following a page number denotes a figure or table. This is only used where there is no textual discussion of the topic on the same page.